Introduction to Philosophy for Young People

Douglas McManaman

Second Edition

DPM Publishing
Aurora, Ontario

First published 2012
Second edition published 2015

DPM also publishes its books in a variety of electronic formats.

Library and Archives Canada Cataloguing in Publication

McManaman, Douglas
Introduction to Philosophy for Young People
Aurora, Ontario: DPM Publishing. 2015

Cover by Jennifer Johnson, 2015.

To Professor Floyd Centore, who taught me how to think and how to teach.

Contents

This is a book for beginning philosophy students or for the general public. It began in the early 90s as summary notes for my philosophy students, which I would later edit and expand. Eventually they became chapters for the "textbook" that I decided to write for them; for there were a host of great books I could have chosen for them to read, but they were all slightly beyond their ability to appreciate at that point, about three or four steps up from where they were standing, and so my goal was to provide them with the two or three steps they needed to comfortably graduate into reading some of the great books that have been available for them for decades now, many of which I have listed at the end under *Suggested Reading*.

Now imagine walking in on a group of people who are having what looks to be a very intense discussion. You begin to listen and you try to figure out what it is they are talking about, but you find it very difficult. So, you ask one of them: "What in the world are you all talking about?" If you are to make any sense out of the discussion, one of them is going to have to take you back to the first question or claim that initiated the discussion and then summarize each response, showing you how this point led to that question, which in turn led to this other more complicated problem, etc. After a while, you begin to make sense out of the conversation, because you begin to see the present moment of this symposium within the context of the entire movement of the discussion, from beginning to end.

The problem with the typical university philosophy course today is that it very often ignores the fact that the history of philosophy is one very long conversation and that in order to make any sense out of it, one has to go back to the beginning and trace its movement. One has to actually enter into the discussion by asking the very same questions that preoccupied the great thinkers of the past. Instead, young students are handed a copy of Descartes' *Meditations*, or a piece of writing by John Stewart Mill and Friedrich Nietzsche, and very soon afterwards students have the impression that philosophical knowledge is radically inconclusive and that it is just a haphazard collection of a variety of diverse and conflicting points of view. At that point, many of my students, who were inspired to study philosophy at the university level, simply go on to choose another major.

In keeping with the nature of this book as an introduction to philosophy, I have chosen not to spend a great deal of time on footnotes. Where I have relied heavily on a particular thinker's idea(s), I have included a reference, the complete details of which are found at the end in *Suggested Reading*.

This book is designed to provide young people with a foundation that will allow them to become familiar with some of the most basic concepts that one finds within the tradition of Catholic philosophy in particular, thus enabling them to navigate slowly through the murky waters of our post-modern culture without sinking.

Douglas P. McManaman

Douglas McManaman studied Philosophy at St. Jerome's College in Waterloo, and Theology at the University of Montreal. He is a regular columnist for the *Canadian Messenger of the Sacred Heart* and writes regularly for *Catholic Insight Magazine, Lifeissues.net,* and the *Catholic Educator's Resource Center.* He has been interviewed twice on EWTN Radio, *The Good Fight* with Barbara McGuigan. He is a Permanent Deacon for the Archdiocese of Toronto, the current chaplain of the Catholic Teachers Guild, and he has been teaching Religion and Philosophy to senior high school students for over 25 years. He is currently teaching at Father Michael McGivney Catholic Academy in Markham, Ontario, Canada. He is the past president of the Canadian Fellowship of Catholic Scholars.

The introduction to any discipline is a thing fraught with difficulty. At one and the same time, the author must balance the demands of his discipline with the capacity of his audience, desiring always to do justice to the material and to engage his readers and both with a certain style that is intelligent, readable and indicative of the passion of its author. Sometimes these difficulties are mitigated by the nature of the material: some disciplines are easier to present than others, and among those that are more difficult, again, some often receive more help than others through an appeal to factors that are incidental to the material itself (perhaps the material will be useful to one's career or in one's aspirations thereto; perhaps the culture smiles benignly upon the discipline, encouraging the neophyte to buckle down and learn and even master it, and so on). But when you consider that the work before you introduces that most ancient discipline of philosophy, a discipline that is not only most difficult to engage at any level, but is considered by many to be arcane, practically useless, and wholly subjective, generating nothing other than opinion, the odds for success seem very low.

For the past 14 years, I have taught many and diverse courses in philosophy at the undergraduate level at a liberal-arts institution in the United States. While I enjoy teaching this wide variety of courses, I consider the Introduction to Philosophy to be not only the most challenging of them all but also the most important. The challenge is clear from what has been said previously (add to this the fact that the course is taken in a student's first year at college and is a course required of all who attend our institution, and it becomes very clear that I have "my job cut out for me," as the saying goes). The importance of the course lies in the fact that were it not for this one course of philosophy, taught with an eye firmly fixed upon the very best the Catholic intellectual tradition has to offer, the scientism and materialism that so commonly afflicts the minds (and characters) of so many people today would very likely remain unchallenged, resulting, at the very least, in their dismissal of the artistic, literary and philosophical realms as important avenues whereby they might come to understand themselves and the world, a dismissal that reduces all learning, let alone life itself, to the quantifiable and the manipulable. In this climate, wisdom, goodness, beauty, truth, human nature, and justice (to name but a few of the so-called "intangibles" that have occupied the minds and hearts of our brightest and best these past 2500 years), fade from their former robust glory into pale thin specters that seemingly haunt only the most orthodox of churches, as the eternal realities are increasingly seen as products of sheer will rather than those to which we must conform our minds and hearts if we are truly to be happy and blessed.

This *Introduction to Philosophy for Young People* that you have begun to read is a valuable contribution to the preservation and promotion of these eternal realities, presenting them solidly from the perspective of the Catholic intellectual tradition, one of the few traditions left to us today that is willing and able to critique effectively the spirit of this age. Doug McManaman takes his years of experience in teaching philosophy to the young at the secondary school level (not to mention his constant contributions in writing to many and diverse newspapers, magazines and to his own web site) and has distilled these into the book before you, one that is much needed both from the perspective detailed above and, frankly speaking, because there are so very few books of this type available that represent the tradition from which he (and I) hail to the intelligent young reader. It is clear, well-written and intelligently presented, never condescending, and always desirous to invite that sort of discussion and debate that will, at the very least, put forward, in no uncertain terms, the reasonable positions that form the backbone of philosophy as practiced within the Catholic intellectual tradition, something that then allows the reader to understand that reason itself may indeed be capable of grasping the things that escape the empirical method of science, and that perhaps the doctrines of the Catholic faith do indeed have a certain reasonability to them and are not all of them reducible to faith alone.

Stephen J. Loughlin
Associate Professor of Philosophy
Chair of the Philosophy and Theology Department
DeSales University
Center Valley, Pennsylvania

Chapter 1: What in the World is Philosophy?

What in the world is philosophy? The word itself comes from the two Greek words: *philia* and *sophia*. *Philia* is the Greek word for 'love' (a bond of friendship), while *sophia* is Greek for 'wisdom'. Philosophy is literally the "love of wisdom". But what does it mean to love, pursue, and possess wisdom?

To understand this better, consider that most of us know through experience that not everyone who is knowledgeable is wise. Some people have a great deal of learning, but very little wisdom. Clearly there is a difference between knowledge and wisdom. What exactly is the difference between the two?

Let us begin with knowledge of the scientific kind, since most of us are more familiar with it; for even kids can possess it. The word "science" comes from the Latin verb *scire*, which means "to know". Thus, science has to do with possessing a certain kind of knowledge. Now some people are under the impression that science is about knowing facts. But science is much more than that; for everyone knows certain basic facts, such as "leaves are green", or "the sky is blue", or that "people get cancer", etc., but that does not make them scientists. A person has science, however, when he knows *the reason for* the fact, such as why leaves are green, or the reason for cancer, etc. Science is about *reasoned facts*. In other words, one has science when one knows *the cause* of the fact.

Now that which manifests a desire to possess "science" is the act of questioning. The very word 'question' comes from the Latin *querere*, which means to quest, to journey, or to search. To question is to go out on a quest in search of something, namely the cause of a fact, or the reason for it. That is why science is fundamentally *a knowledge of things through their proper causes.*

Wisdom is a kind of science, and so it too is a knowledge of things through causes. But, more precisely, wisdom is a knowledge of the highest causes; it is the intellectual virtue by which a person judges (or sees things) in light of the highest or first causes. That is why we sometimes find wisdom in older people, for they have had the years of experience to "see the larger picture", so to speak. They have encountered many kinds of people throughout their lives, they have been deceived before, lied to, have been pleasantly or unpleasantly surprised by things they weren't aware of, they've made mistakes, have had time to reflect upon their mistakes and the mistakes of their friends, associates, and family, and they have come to learn how to distinguish the genuine friend from the false friend, they know something about what marriage really is as opposed to what they thought it was when they first married, they understand what love really is and what it is not, they understand that they knew very little when they thought they knew a lot, and so they know something about human limitations, which they didn't quite appreciate when they were younger, etc. And so they understand something about human nature and human frailty, and they are able to give us advice about the kind of people we ought to be wary of, whom we can trust, what to expect in the future, etc.

Such people are wise as a result of experience, honest reflection, and the ability to reason. Not everyone over 50, however, is wise because not everyone over 50 is honest, reflective, or rational. Moreover, one has no need of a microscope in order to be wise; but one cannot do biology, for example, without a microscope. And so philosophy, which is the love of wisdom, is not dependent upon technology—some of the most brilliant philosophers in history lived well before the invention of the first telescope, etc. The reason is that philosophy is the pursuit of first or ultimate causes, and first causes cannot be investigated through the senses; they must be arrived at through reason alone. Philosophy is the study of the ultimate nature of things; empiriological (or empiriometric) science, unlike philosophy, seeks the proximate causes of things, not their ultimate causes.

A few simple examples may help to clarify these points. Consider the growth of living things. The biologist would like to know why things grow, that is, the cause of growth. Why do cells multiply? How does cell division work? When he understands the cause of cell division, he can be said to possess science. But if he claims to know the cause of cell division, he must be able to demonstrate it. He can only do so definitively through empirical means (i.e., some sort of experiment, or via the use of something that enhances the sense of sight, such as a microscope).

But sometimes people ask questions about causes of a different sort. Cells that are not alive would not divide, and if they divide, they are alive. So, what is it that makes the cell living in the first place? That question bears upon a first cause. Moreover, a cell is not living unless it first exists, and a thing need not be alive in order to exist (i.e., carbon atoms exist, but they are not alive). Thus, what is the cause of a thing's very existence? That question too bears upon a first or ultimate cause. Now every part of the living cell is alive, which is why we are not going to find the cause of its life within some part of the cell. One cannot say, for instance, that the cause of its life is the DNA, for the DNA is alive in so far as it is a part of the living cell. One only has to ask what it is that causes the DNA to be living DNA? If it is a part of the cell, the cause will be the same as the cause of the whole cell's life. Furthermore, existence is not a part of the cell; for the whole cell exists. The cause of the cell's existence is not going to be something that you will be able to see under a microscope. In other words, first causes cannot be investigated via the senses. And so we have no choice but to reason our way to first or ultimate causes.

Philosophical knowledge is the knowledge of things through their first causes. Experimental science (investigative) is not a search for first causes, but rather proximate or secondary causes. The cause of the blue in your eyes is a secondary cause, for you cannot have blue eyes unless you first have an eye which is alive, and you cannot have a living eye unless you as a whole are alive. The first cause is that which accounts for your being alive, the secondary cause accounts for the blue in your eyes, or the brown in your hair, etc. A few more examples may clarify this further.

Biology is the study of living organisms (botany, zoology, physiology, neurology, histology, etc.). The question: "What is the cause of cancer?" is a question that only a biologist can answer. Philosophy, on the other hand, does not investigate plant life, or the physiology of an insect, etc. Rather, philosophy would seek an answer to the question: "What does it mean to be a living thing as opposed to a non-living thing?" The philosopher is not concerned with the nervous system of a rabbit or the DNA of a frog. To study these is to study the secondary causes of a frog or rabbit. Rather, philosophy would like to know what it means to be an animal, or what it means to be a species as opposed to an individual of a species, etc. All the investigating in the world is not going to tell us what it means to be a species as opposed to an individual of the species. One has to reason to the answer.

Similarly, the chemist studies the composition, properties and structure of substances (organic chemistry, inorganic chemistry, biochemistry). And so the chemist wants to know how a metal reacts with a gas, or why iron rusts. But the philosopher seeks to understand what it means to be a substance. He asks: "What makes a substance to be what it is?" Or, "What is the difference between substance and attribute?" A chemist does not ask such questions. He takes substance for granted, as a carpenter takes a hammer for granted; the carpenter (scientist) uses the hammer to build houses, but it is the tool maker (philosopher) who studies the hammer.

Physics studies matter and energy and their interactions. The philosopher studies the ultimate constitution of matter, and so he will seek an answer to the question: "What is matter?" and "What is time?" "What is place?" and "What is motion?" Psychology studies human behaviour, but the philosophy of human nature studies what it means to be man: "Is there an essential difference between man and brute?" The lawyer studies existing laws and how they apply in particular circumstances, but the philosophy of law studies the ultimate principles of law: "What does it mean to be a law?" or, "Are there natural laws?" Political philosophy asks: "Is anarchy reasonable or disordered?" Moral philosophy asks: "What constitutes a just law?" and "What is justice?" Moreover, the mathematician studies numbers and their relations, but the philosopher asks: "What is number?" "What is quantity?" "What is a relation?" "Is mathematical infinity real?" "What is infinity?" Such questions cannot be answered using mathematics.

Science investigates specific modes of being in the physical universe, such as living being, chemical being, mobile being, human being, etc. But metaphysics (the highest branch of philosophy) studies not specific modes of being such as living, chemical, or physical, but simply *being insofar as it is being*. Metaphysics would like to know what it means to be and what the properties of being as being are. And so philosophers ask: "Does non-being exist?" "Why is there anything rather than nothing?" and "Is a thing good to the degree that it has being?" and "What is the cause of all being?" Metaphysics will concern itself with the question of God's existence in so far as He can be known through the natural light of human reason.

Science investigates the various aspects of the material universe, but philosophy seeks to know the answer to the question: "What is science?", and "What does it mean to know?" as well as "What does it mean to know scientifically?" Epistemology is that branch of philosophy that seeks to understand how it is we come to know and what exactly is the content of consciousness.

And so, returning to our example of the wise person who understands something about human nature, virtue, love, marriage, relationships, things that matter as opposed to things that do not, etc., what he understands, to a certain degree at least, is the ultimate nature of either the human person, or marriage, or friendship, etc. As a result of experience, reflection and reasoning, he knows something about the nature of love, for example, that it is more than a feeling, or something about the nature of happiness, that is has an essential connection to virtue, or something about the nature of genuine friendship, for example, that true friendship is founded not so much on utility or pleasure as on good character, and that people of bad character have no real friends and are incapable of being a friend, etc.

Wisdom (philosophy) begins on the level of ordinary experience and ascends upward by means of human reason in order to take in "the whole picture" from a bird's eye point of view, a point of view that is beyond the realm of ordinary experience. Thus, in philosophy, sensation is at the service of reason. Experimental science, on the other hand, begins on the level of ordinary experience and descends by means of empirical investigation in order to take in not so much the whole as the parts of the whole that are beyond the realm of ordinary experience. Thus, in the investigative sciences, reason is at the service of sensation.

Concluding Thoughts

What if a person were to deny that ultimate causes are really distinct from what is referred to above as proximate causes? For example, what if someone were to assert that the only genuine knowledge we have is that which is, in the end, resolved in sensation (the investigative sciences) and that if a claim cannot be resolved or verified in sensation or experiment (the scientific method), it is not genuine knowledge.

One can say this, but to be consistent, the one who makes this assertion will have to demonstrate the truth of it through the scientific method, that is, he will have to resolve his conclusion in the realm of sensation. But he will not be able to do so. How does one show, through visible and tangible evidence, that the only valid knowledge we have is scientific knowledge? The assertion is not a scientific conclusion at all, but an assumption.

Moreover, science takes place on the basis of many principles that science itself cannot establish. For example, science presupposes the intelligibility of things. The world is meaningful and can be studied and known, yet science cannot explain why or account for its intelligibility. Also, there is no science of particulars, only universals. In other words, anatomy does not study this particular cadaver (which belonged to John

Smith, who just died) in order to know this cadaver, but in order to know all cadavers of that species. But science cannot account for this universality, does not concern itself with it, but accepts the fact as part and parcel of what science is. Similarly, mathematics depends upon "one" as the principle of number, but it cannot account for unity or oneness, or explain what it is.

What about those who deny truth altogether, and who maintain that all assertions of truth are merely subjective (from the subject himself), and thus conclude that there is no truth, only individual perspectives and that what is true for you may not be true for me?

Indeed, there are many today who maintain this. But the denial of truth is self-refuting. If there is absolutely no truth, then the very statement "there is no truth" must be false (because there is no truth). If the statement "there is no truth" is false, then there is truth, and it is possible to know the truth. So denying truth only serves to prove that there is truth.

But take note at this point that we did not resolve this question about truth through sense investigation; our method was not investigative as is the scientific method. The problem was resolved through reason; our method was philosophical in the strict sense of the word. Take that as an example of the fundamental difference between philosophy and empiriometric science.

Chapter 2: Some Points on Knowledge and Opinion

Most people today have one foot in subjectivism, which is the doctrine that all knowledge is purely subjective, that is, nothing more than one's opinion, and that objective knowledge is not possible. They may not be total subjectivists, but they seem to be when it comes to philosophical or moral questions. Many people are under the false impression that science is about knowledge, whereas philosophy is about opinions. But this, again, is an impossible position.

Opinion, as Plato pointed out, is neither ignorance nor knowledge, but something midway between the two. To know something as true is to know it as it is. Thus, knowledge bears upon *what is*, that is, its object is being. To hold an opinion is to make a judgment that might or might not correspond to what really is. Thus, opinion is a judgment that is possibly true, thus possibly false. To be ignorant about something is to possess no knowledge of it. Thus, ignorance bears upon nothing at all.

Knowledge, however, is characterized by necessity. It is not my opinion that I am, nor is it my opinion that in any right angled triangle, the area of the square whose side is the hypotenuse is equal to the sum of the areas of the squares whose sides are the two sides that meet at the right angle (Pythagorean theorem). It is not my opinion that the conclusion John is mortal is true because *All men are mortal* and *John is a man*. I know these conclusions are true, for they carry the force of necessity. But if I were to interview you for ten minutes and conclude that you would make a good nurse, that conclusion would be no more than an opinion. My judgment could be mistaken. Thus, opinion is less certain, whereas knowledge is certain.

A little reflection will also show that not every opinion is as valid as any other opinion. Your mother's opinion, contrary to mine, might be that you would not make a good nurse. Whose opinion is better? The answer is: the opinion with more data to support it. Your mother knows you better than I do, has seen how you handle yourself in stressful situations. She might know that you faint every time you see blood and can't stand hospitals, etc. Our opinions are not equally valid. Moreover, the one who makes the claim that "every opinion is just as valid as any other opinion" does not really believe that its contradictory is a valid opinion, namely, that "some opinions have less validity than other opinions"; but he should if he really holds that "every opinion is just as valid as any other opinion".

Furthermore, if everything is a matter of opinion, as many people like to believe today, then knowledge is impossible. And if knowledge is impossible, it is impossible to understand what an opinion is, or even to know that everything is a matter of opinion. For we only know what an opinion is against the background of knowing what "knowledge" is; we know that opinion is uncertain, possibly mistaken, possibly not, but if we could not know anything for certain (since everything is a matter of opinion), we wouldn't know what an opinion really is in the first place. And so it is simply not true that everything is a matter of opinion, nor is it true that every opinion is just as valid as any other.

Chapter 3: Thoughts on Certitude, Necessity, and Self-Refuting Claims

Certitude arises when we apprehend the necessity of something, that such and such *cannot not be*. For example, if there is a triangle in this box, then I am certain that it has three sides—it cannot not have three sides, that is, it is necessarily three-sided. I am not certain, however, of its color or size. It might be red, or it might be blue, and it might be small, or it might be big, it might be made of steel, or paper, etc. A triangle need not be red, 6 inches each side, and made of wood, but it necessarily is three sided.

In other words, human beings are able to apprehend necessary connections between things (i.e., there is a necessary connection between a triangle and the property "three sided"). Whenever we do not apprehend the necessary connection between one thing and another (i.e., the idea of Christmas 2050 and the weather condition "cold temperature and 10 cm of snow"), we lack certitude; thus, it is possible that it will snow on Christmas 2050, but there is also a possibility that it will be mild and green.

Knowledge carries the force of necessity, opinion lacks the force of necessity, thus it can only settle for possibility (may or may not be so). And so we can see that the statement "It is necessarily the case that everything is a matter of opinion" is contradictory. Translating that claim, we have the following: "It is necessarily the case that we cannot apprehend necessities, only possibilities." Other contradictory claims are "It is impossible to possess certitude (translation: 'I am certain that we cannot be certain of anything'), as well as "Knowledge is impossible" (translation: 'I know that I cannot know anything'). Consider again the following: "The only valid knowledge worthy of the name is that which is derived from and verified through empirical investigation". This is self-refuting because the claim was not derived from, nor can it be verified through, empirical investigation—what does one do in a lab to test such a claim? Or, consider Christopher Hitchens' now famous line which he asserted in the context of a debate on the existence of God: "That which can be asserted without evidence can be dismissed without evidence." That very claim, however, is asserted without any evidence; therefore, it can be dismissed. He refused to dismiss it, however.

A favorite of mine, a variation on an idea of Lord Kelvin, was handed to me by an atheist friend who despises philosophy but loves mathematics: "Without the predictive precision of mathematics, any claim to truth is illusory. If you cannot express your knowledge in mathematical form, you may know something; you may have the beginnings of knowledge, but your knowledge is inevitably of a rudimentary and incomplete form." Nicely said, but what he claims to know here must be illusory, for it was not, nor can it be, expressed in mathematical form. If he is serious about the claim, then he ought to regard his claim as rudimentary and incomplete. Needless to say, he does not, but regards it as entirely true.

Another self-refuting proposition is the well-known dictum: "Follow your heart, not your head". It is self-refuting because the counsel that one ought to follow the heart, not the head, is a counsel of the head, not the heart. It is the intellect (head) that understands that "one ought not to follow one's understanding, but one's heart". Thus, no matter what one chooses to do, one is following one's head (the important question is whether your head is providing a wise directive).

Chapter 4: First Self-Evident Principles of Speculative Reason

Philosophy is the study of the ultimate natures of things. It is the study of first causes and principles. Philosophy is not investigative, that is, its conclusions are not resolved on the level of sensation. Rather, philosophy begins with ordinary experience, but from that point it ascends to principles that can only be discovered through reason alone; and finally, it reasons on the basis of these principles.

Let us explore some of these first principles of speculative reason; we can be absolutely certain of the truth of these principles, for they are known whenever we know anything at all, and to deny them leads to absurdities; for one has to use them—thus regarding them as true—in order to deny them. But this is contradictory.

Now, we have a natural aversion to contradictions. Any claim that is shown to be contradictory is immediately seen to be false, such as the following claim used in the previous chapter: "It is impossible to possess certitude", which when carefully translated runs: "I am certain that we cannot be certain of anything". We know that self-refuting claims are necessarily false because we know, intuitively and even pre-consciously, that contradictories cannot be true at one and the same time. This principle or starting point of all speculative knowledge (knowledge sought for its own sake) is called **the principle of non-contradiction**, which runs: "Nothing can both be and not be at the same time and in the same respect." The logical formulation of this principle runs: "Nothing can be both true and not true at the same time and in the same respect."

To deny the principle of non-contradiction leads to an absurd state of affairs; for one has to use the principle in order to deny it. Consider the following: If I claim that the principle of non-contradiction is false, then I am claiming that it is not true that "nothing can both be and not be at the same time and in the same respect". Hence, I am claiming that something can both be and not be at the same time and in the same respect. If that is the case, then I cannot assert that the principle of non-contradiction is false; I could not put forth my claim as something definitively true. Rather, I'd have to assert that what I am claiming is both true and not true at the same time and in the same respect. In other words, I would have to hold that affirming the principle of non-contradiction is just as true as denying it. Thus, my denying it is pointless; it is entirely meaningless.

Furthermore, if the principle of non-contradiction were not true, then I could assign an F to all the best students, and an A to all the worst students, and those marks would mean whatever I want them to mean. A pass would mean a fail, and vice versa. An insult would be a compliment, and a compliment would be an insult; a blessing would be a curse, and a curse would be a blessing; but if a curse is a blessing and that very blessing is a curse at the same time, then no meaningful course of action in response to such a curse can be determined—indignation can be no more reasonably expected than complacency. In other words, without the principle of non-contradiction, communication would be utterly impossible, and thus so too would science.

The principle of identity has a different formulation, but it is really the same principle: "Each being is what it is". For example, a carrot is a carrot, not a watermelon; a dog is a dog, not a cat; etc. Without the principle of identity, one could not know anything at all. For example, if it is not true that each thing is what it is, then it follows that each being is what it is not, which is absurd. It would mean that no being has any intelligible determination whatsoever. In other words, nothing exists determinately; and if nothing exists determinately, including myself, then nothing is known. In other words, knowledge is impossible; for it would mean that 'is' and 'is not' are the same (nothing is being, and being is nothing). In other words, one could not distinguish or "mark off" one thing from another.

Note that if one denies the principle of identity, one denies the principle of non-contradiction, and vice versa. If it is not true that "each thing is what it is", then each thing is what it is not; but that, of course, is contradictory.

From the above principle (non-contradiction), another principle necessarily follows, namely, **the principle of causality:** for every effect, there is a cause. In other words, from nothing comes nothing. Another way of expressing this same principle is to say that nothing moves itself from potentiality to actuality except by something already in actuality. A more popular way has been to say that a thing cannot give what it does not have.

The principle of causality is otherwise known as **the principle of sufficient reason**, which runs thus: Everything which is, to the extent to which it is, possesses a sufficient reason for its being so that it is capable of explaining itself to the intellect. In other words, whatever is, has that whereby it is.

For example, whatever is (i.e., this broken window), has that whereby it is (i.e., a sufficient reason for its being a broken window). Now, it has its sufficient reason either in itself or outside itself. If the sufficient reason for its being broken is within it, then simply knowing that this window is broken is enough to know the sufficient reason for its being broken. And if that were so, I would not ask the question: "Why is this window broken?" The reason would be contained in itself.

But that is clearly not the case. If we come home one day to find a window broken, we immediately enquire of the reason. This means that "broken window" does not contain within itself the reason for its being a broken window. The sufficient reason is outside of it. "Broken window" depends upon this outside factor in order to be a broken window. And so, we inquire, and we discover that kids were playing baseball nearby, someone hit a home run, the ball hit the window, etc.

As an example of the sufficient reason that is contained within a thing, consider the following: I am not in awe that any one of my students asks questions. Now, if a sunflower were to ask me a philosophical question, I'd be in awe and would wonder how that is possible. But I know that my student has a rational nature, and so he has the power and desire to know, thus he asks questions. His rational nature is the sufficient reason for the very fact that he asked a question. A sunflower does not possess a rational nature, and so the nature of a flower is insufficient to account for a philosophical question. In knowing my student, I know the sufficient reason for his question or questions.

Now, how can we be certain that the principle of causality (sufficient reason) is absolutely and necessarily true? How can I be certain that "from nothing comes nothing" or that "a thing cannot give what it does not have"? The certainty is derived from the principle of non-contradiction. If something comes from nothing, then nothing is something. But if nothing is something and something is nothing, then contradictories can be true at one and the same time. Thus, to fail is to pass, to lie is to tell the truth, to eat is to starve, and vice versa, etc.

If something could move itself from potentiality to actuality, for example, if a stone which is at rest (but potentially in motion), could move itself from potential motion to actual motion on its own, then it would give to itself what it does not have. It does not have motion, yet it gives itself motion as a whole (as opposed to one part moving another part, as living things move), then something comes from nothing. But this once again violates non-contradiction. To deny the principle of causality is to assert that a thing can simultaneously 'have' and 'not have' a specific perfection at the same time and in the very same respect. If a pool ball could move itself from rest to motion, then it could impart to itself what it lacks. It would both have and not have the very same motion. But the truth of the matter is that the pool ball receives a perfection that it lacks, namely motion, from an actually moving ball, which in turn received its motion from another actually moving ball, etc.

The effect cannot be greater than the cause

The principle of causality is often formulated thus: The effect cannot be greater than the cause. This is necessarily true because a cause can only give what it has, not what it does not have. If the effect can be greater than the cause, then the cause can give what it does not have. This would mean that from nothing comes something. If I have only 10 dollars, I cannot give you 100 dollars. If you end up with 100 dollars, 90 dollars of that money is unaccounted for. I can account for the 10 dollars, but not for the remaining 90 dollars.

The reason we naturally seek to know the causes of things is that we immediately know, consciously or unconsciously, that for every effect there is a cause that accounts for the effect. Or, to put it another way, we immediately know that there is a sufficient reason that something is so, such that it is capable of explaining itself to the intellect, thus sufficiently satisfying the intellect, which then stops searching for the reason or cause.

This principle is naturally known (pre-consciously or consciously), it is grasped through intuition (an immediate apprehension by the intellect), and it is self-evident. It cannot be demonstrated through reason because reason needs the principle of causality to demonstrate anything. If I give you reasons that prove something or other, I say something like this is true on account of such and such, or, this is true because such and such. For example, Robert asks questions because Robert is rational. But Robert is rational because 1) all men are rational, and 2) Robert is a man. Twice we use "because" in order to account for the fact that Robert asks questions. In other words, we are employing the principle of causality, and this is evident in the use of "because" (the cause being…). One cannot prove a principle by using it, for that is the fallacy of "begging the question" (assuming the point we are trying to prove). And so, the principle of causality (sufficient reason) is self-evidently true and is employed whenever we try to prove anything at all. And so if the principle of causality were not true, we could not prove anything at all. Most importantly, if one denies the principle of causality and provides "reasons for" denying it, then one is using it to deny it.

Chapter 5: A Note on Holding Truth in Common

You will often hear people say things like: "What is true for you may not be true for me". Recently I overheard a teacher say to another teacher that each one of us constructs our own reality and that your reality has nothing in common with mine. He concluded that there is no single truth that we hold in common. Just as beauty is said to be in the eye of the beholder, so too is truth. This is called Subjectivism.

But it is not possible to maintain this position consistently, and just a bit of reflection will show why this is the case. All you have to do is ask the subjectivist (i.e., the one who holds that there is no common or universal truth) the reasons for which he asserts that there is no universal truth, only individual perspectives equally valid or "true". He will either sit there, silent, with a smile on his face, or he will begin providing you with the reasons for his position. The problem is that when he begins providing you with "the reasons" for his position, he begins sharing "truths" with you, "truths" that he clearly believes you hold in common with him—otherwise he wouldn't attempt to communicate with you, for he'd see the futility of it immediately.

In other words, he begins to establish premises that he holds to be true for you as well as for himself. Now the only reason any of us establish premises is to eventually draw a conclusion. For example, if we lay down the premise that "All men are equal" as well as the premise that "John and Trevor are both men", we can conclude that "John and Trevor are equal". The conclusion "John and Trevor are equal" is a single and universal truth only on condition that our premises are true and our reasoning is valid.

And so the instant the subjectivist begins to offer any kind of rational basis for his position, he reveals then and there that he indeed holds for the existence of a body of truths that human beings can and do hold in common.

Note the irrationality and self-refuting nature of the subjectivist's entire reasoning process. He begins to provide reasons for holding that there is no common truth and in doing so he establishes premises that he regards as valid for both of you, in order to eventually deny the existence of a single common truth—except perhaps the truth that "there is no common truth". If his conclusion is correct, then the premises he used to establish it are false. But if his premises are false, then he cannot validly establish that there is no common truth. The situation can be compared to a person who gets into a boat, rows out into the water and announces to those on the shore that boats do not exist.

Moreover, it is obvious to everyone that there are many truths we hold in common that even subjectivists cannot deny. For example, it is true that we have ideas in common; it is true that we can communicate those ideas; it is true that we can disagree; it is true that truth is worth knowing and worth trying to communicate; it is true that I can know something other than myself; it is true that you can know something other than yourself, otherwise I wouldn't bother trying to communicate with you, and if I affirm that I could be wrong about something, then I affirm that it is true that I can be mistaken; and if it is true that I can be mistaken, then I also imply that it is true that I am not the measure of what is true, and that there is something outside of me that is the measure of what is true, and that I ought to conform to that measure. In other words, I acknowledge that reality is not at all my own construct.

Also, to be able to see or understand that there is no common or universal truth implies the intellectual ability to grasp what is common and what is not common. In other words, it requires the ability to grasp universals, for I cannot deny what I cannot grasp; and so, if the subjectivist can grasp universals—because he clearly denies them—, then it follows that he grasps universal truths.

Also, to be able to understand that there is no common or universal truth also implies the ability to" step outside myself" so to speak. In other words, I am able to know something other than myself. The subjectivist at least believes that he can see into your reality, enough to "know" that you and he do not hold any truth in common. He also presupposes that you can do the same, for he is telling you that there is no common truth and thus he expects you to grasp this. But if he is completely locked inside himself, if he has no contact with that which is outside of him, then he cannot affirm or deny that there are truths that we all hold in common.

But the subjectivist would not go this far. He believes that he can know something outside of himself, and if he attempts to communicate to others what he thinks he has discovered, he seems to believe that others have the same ability, otherwise they couldn't begin to understand him. For if I communicate something to you, I imply that I at least believe that we have some abilities in common. For we are able to *commun*icate, that is, enter into communion or a common arena, so to speak. We have a lot in common, which is why we are able to communicate, and which is why the subjectivist tries to communicate what he regards as important to know (namely, that there is no common or universal truth). And yet it is true that we have "common ground" on which to communicate; we have this common ability to "exit ourselves" and know something other than ourselves. The subjectivist can know something about you, and he seems to believe that what he knows about you is that you and he cannot hold truth in common. If he knows that, then what he knows about you is not merely an opinion, but something true—and true for both of you.

No matter how we come at this problem, denying universal truth is entirely self-refuting.

Chapter 6: Some Points on Chance, the Relative, and Change

It is important to keep in mind that there is quite a bit you know, but which you are not aware that you know. In other words, a great deal of your knowledge is pre-conscious. Much of this pre-conscious knowledge is intuition, which is an immediate apprehension of the truth of something, such as the intuition of the first self-evident principles (the principle of non-contradiction, the principle of identity, the principle of causality, etc.). But in addition, you have a great deal of "reasoned" knowledge that also takes place on a pre-conscious level. And so, at times you will have a sense about something, for example, that a claim is false, but you just can't put your finger on it or articulate it properly. That does not necessarily mean you don't really "know"; what it might mean is that you are not yet able to move your pre-conscious knowledge to the status of a fully conscious understanding. In other words, you can't explain what you seem to know. But all that is required for you to do so is a bit of time, reflection, and sound reasoning. Often people don't have the time but wish they did, or they can't be bothered, or their reasoning is impeded by some kind of emotional factor (i.e., fear that something is true that I don't want to be true, etc.).

Thinking about "Chance"

Consider the claim that "Everything in the universe happens by chance". In order to test the claim, let's begin by reflecting on what it is we mean by 'chance'. When something happens by chance, we are often moved to wonder: "What were the chances of that happening?" That's a natural reaction, because chance is an aberration, a kind of disorder. I receive a call from the President of the United States, but his call was the result of chance; he intended to call the President of France, but misdialed one number on the area code and another number, and so my phone rang. That was a genuine chance event. What are the chances that my phone number would be different from that of the President of France by only two numbers, and that the President of the United States would misdial those two numbers at the exact time when I was at home watching TV?

But I can also ask: "What are the chances that my friend will call me today?" Clearly, I have a much greater chance of receiving a call from my friend than from the President. Were my friend to call me, we would not conclude that his call was a chance happening. His call is not a disorder, an aberration or irregularity (from the Latin *regulus*, or rule). On the contrary, as a rule my friend calls me; the President of the United States does not.

A chance happening occurs as a result of an *intersection of two lines of action that are not chance*, but purposeful or intentional. For example, I am asked to walk to the store to buy milk, and Jane has to use the library in order to do her research project. She puts on her shoes, packs her books, grabs a snack, walks north to the library, while I put on my shoes, grab my wallet, put on my jacket, and proceed east towards the milk store. We just happen to run into each other. Our meeting was a chance happening. It is not something that belongs to the series of acts ordered towards the purchase of milk, nor the series of acts ordered towards using the library to do research. It is "incidental" and unpredictable. Now, walking home with a plastic bag is not a chance event, for it is not incidental to purchasing milk, because it regularly happens (as a rule, it is the norm) that when we buy something, the clerk typically puts it all in a plastic bag—it is part of a series of events ordered towards an end, namely, enabling the buyer to conveniently leave the store with his goods. Moreover, it is not incidental (chance) that I picked up my wallet before going to the store, because that is a necessary step in the series of acts ordered towards buying milk. But crossing paths with Jane is incidental (chance), as is getting rained on, or getting mugged because I just happened to be in the store when it was being robbed, or slipping on a banana peel and breaking my wrist on the way home, etc.

The very idea of chance can only be understood against the backdrop of that which is not chance, but purposeful or intentional (acting for an end). It follows that if everything were a chance happening, then nothing would occur by chance; for no act would be purposeful, that is, there would be no series of acts ordered to an end. Thus, chance would be utterly indiscernible.

Orange trees act for a determinate end, they grow and bear oranges, apple trees grow to maturity and bear apples, bees produce honey, chickens lay eggs, and fire flies radiate light, etc. These are regular patterns, ordered acts, lawful behavior, and that is why they are meaningful. If everything occurred by chance, then everything would occur without order or regularity: apple trees would produce acorns one year, apples the next month, honey the next, and bees would meow, dogs would sting, but the next minute they might fly, etc. But even that would not be entirely true, because in order for a dog to fly, it would have to have wings, and its act of flying would involve a series of acts ordered towards flapping those wings and flying, but that is an example of order and purpose. In the end, if everything was a chance occurrence, the universe would be absurd and unintelligible. Knowledge would simply be impossible.

Thinking about "the Relative"

Consider the claim: "Everything is relative. Nothing is absolute". This claim is usually associated with the claim that there is no absolute truth, especially in the area of morality. But let's consider the claim on its own terms.

Firstly, what it means to be relative? If something is relative, it can only be understood "in relation to" something else. The left side of a stone depends upon, or can be understood only in relation to, the observer. So, left and right are indeed relative; there is no absolute left side. I cannot ask someone to meet me on the left side of the school, for that depends on a point of reference (i.e., left side when looking at the school from the north side, or left side when looking at the school from the south side, etc.).

"Tall" is a relative term, not absolute. A person is tall in relation to the observer—or some other point of reference, i.e., the person standing next to him. If the observer is shorter, the person will appear taller, but if the observer is 7 feet tall, the person may not be tall at all, but short. Hence, to understand something relative depends on understanding X, but if X is relative, then understanding it (X) depends on understanding Y. If Y is relative, then understanding Y depends on an understanding of something outside of it (W), etc.

But not everything can be relative in that series of dependents. There must be an absolute first that is not relative. Why? The reason is that if there is no absolute first, then there is an indefinite series of relatives (infinite series). If your understanding of R depended upon knowing an infinite series of factors, you would never understand R; your understanding of R would depend upon understanding an indefinite (without end) number of factors or causes, and so your understanding would remain indefinite; you would never achieve a "definite" understanding, for an infinity cannot be crossed or completed. Hence, if you know anything that is relative, it means that something in your knowledge is not relative, but absolute.

Some Implications of the Principle of Causality

If we think about what we have discovered up to this point using reason alone, we can arrive at a rather interesting conclusion. We saw that an infinite series of relatives is impossible. This means that my understanding of something truly relative (R) depends upon an understanding of something else that exists in relation to R. But my understanding of R cannot depend on an indefinite series of relatives, otherwise I would never achieve a definite understanding of R (such as Robert is tall). But I do understand that "Robert is tall". Therefore, not everything is relative; something in my understanding is absolute (we need not concern ourselves with what exactly that is at this point).

Thus, an infinite series (or regress) of causes is impossible. Now a cause is a principle (a starting point or source) upon which something proceeds with dependence (the movement of the keys under my fingers proceeds with dependence upon my fingers). Now to get a better handle on how an infinite series of dependents or causes is insufficient to the intellect, consider a chandelier that is held up by a single series of links. Imagine that we are at an angle such that when we look up at it, we cannot see the top. We know, however, that if the chandelier is actually suspended, it follows that there is a finite number of chain links, however long it turns out to be.

The suggestion that there might be an infinite number of chain links is repugnant to the intellect; for it leaves the mind unsatisfied. In other words, the explanation is insufficient to the intellect. Each link in the chain is dependent upon the link above it; in other words, the sufficient reason for the first link holding up the chandelier is the link directly above it, and the sufficient reason or cause of that link holding up the first link is found in the third link above it, etc. Each link on its own is insufficient to account for the suspension of the chandelier; the sufficient reason for each link doing what it does is outside it (each other link). If the series of links stretched on to infinity, there would be no sufficient reason for the suspension of the chandelier—in other words, we'd have an infinite number of insufficient reasons for the suspension of the chandelier. The chandelier would not be actually or definitively suspended, but would be forever "waiting" to be suspended, or what amounts to the same thing, indefinitely unsuspended.

And so, for every series of causes, there is a first cause that is uncaused, or a first mover that is unmoved. Or, we can put it this way: each link in the chain is a dependent cause (dependent upon the link above it); the first cause is an absolutely independent cause.

It is important not to try to imagine this in the concrete, but to keep the principle on an abstracted level, just as in doing math, we abstract number from the concrete (1, 2, 3, from three apples) in order to free ourselves to discover more than would otherwise be possible. Now, that there is a first uncaused cause behind every motion or change is true with regard to any change or motion whatsoever, i.e., locomotion, change in quality (i.e., color, habit, shape, etc.), quantity (growth), etc.

Moreover, if the effect cannot be greater than the cause, then the first uncaused cause cannot be less than the effect or the sum of the total combination of effects, for that would imply that something comes from nothing. Now, consider the motions found in the world. Those motions are intelligible, such as the development of a flower, the birth of a calf, a shooting star, the fall of a leaf, the budding of a leaf, etc. The motions are also experienced as beautiful and good. In other words, we experience the world as intelligible (knowable), good (desirable), and beautiful (harmonious and radiant). Thus, the first uncaused cause must possess intelligence, goodness, and beauty to an eminent degree; otherwise the effect would be given perfections that are lacking in the first cause. This first uncaused cause is what we mean by "God".

Now this argument is rather sketchy at this point and will gradually become filled out, that is, thicker and richer. Nevertheless, it is still a sound argument and, we would argue, accounts for the fact that man has always possessed a natural sense or knowledge of God, however confused and general it might be.

Thinking about Change

Finally, consider the claim that everything is in a pure state of "becoming". Nothing is permanent, absolutely everything changes.

With just a bit of reflection, we can see that this too is impossible. For in order for change to be intelligible, there must be *something* that changes, that is, something that undergoes the change. Robert changes, that is, he goes from being 180 pounds to 200 pounds. His weight changed, but the subject of the change, the subject that endured throughout the change, is Robert. Unless there is an enduring subject that does not change, we could not make sense out of change. Again, change depends upon an unchanging subject in order to be understood. If everything about the thing changed, such that there is no enduring "thing", there would be no "it" that changed; there would be nothing for the mind to grab onto or grasp, and so one could not describe the change. Pure becoming is thus unintelligible.

The contention that everything is in a pure state of change implies that nothing has an enduring identity. But recall the principle of identity: "Each being is what it is". If everything were in a pure state of change, then it would follow that "Each being is not what it is". Each being would lack a stable identity. One could not even talk about "each being". And so, if a thing lacked a stable identity, knowledge would be impossible; for we only know "beings" or "things". It is only when we know an enduring thing that we can grasp the way or ways in which it undergoes change. For example, it is grass that grows; it is a human being who graduates; it is a carbon atom that moves; it is light that travels, etc.

Chapter 7: A Brief Introduction to Logic

Logic is a very important branch of philosophy. In fact, logic is the basic tool of all science; for logic is the study of how to reason validly. Not everyone who reasons does so validly. Some people draw conclusions that simply do not follow from the given premises. In logic, this is called a *non-sequitur*. It is very important that we become familiar with the most common logical fallacies so as not to fall victim to the deceptive reasoning of modern sophists.

Let us jump right into a study of syllogisms. A syllogism is an argument. It involves the deduction of a conclusion from two premises. The following is an example of a categorical syllogism:

All those on a high fat diet are at risk for colon cancer.
John is on a high fat diet.
Therefore, John is at risk for colon cancer.

Or, a standard and simpler example

All men are mortal
John is a man
Therefore, John is mortal.

Any argument that you might have with somebody is -- if it is a genuine argument -- reducible to a syllogism. Let us begin with the categorical syllogism. This is an argument made up of categorical propositions, such as the two examples above. The categorical proposition is a complete sentence, with one subject and one predicate that is either true or false. For example,

All giraffes are animals

The **subject** of a proposition is *that about which something is said*. For example, in the proposition above, "giraffes" is the subject; for something is being said about giraffes, namely, that they are animals.

The **predicate** of a proposition is *that which is said about something*. For example, what is being said about giraffes (the subject)? What is being said is that they are animals. Thus, "animals" is the predicate of the above.

The copula joins or separates the subject and the predicate. In our categorical proposition above, "is" joins 'giraffes' and 'animals', thus "is" is the copula. The copula that separates the subject and the predicate will be 'is not', as in *some men are not Italian.*

Standard Propositional Codes

Logicians have devised an easy way to identify categorical statements. These simple codes were derived from two Latin words: *affirmo* (I affirm) and *nego* (I deny). There are only four possible forms of a categorical proposition, two are affirmative statements, and two are negative statements. For example, one can say:

All dogs are vicious

or,

Some dogs are vicious

or,

Some dogs are not vicious

or,

No dogs are vicious

Logicians simply took the first two vowels of *affirmo* (I affirm), the A and the I, as well as the first two vowels of *nego*, the E and the O, and employed them as codes for these kinds of statements. Hence, we speak of A statements, I statements, O statements, and E statements.

The A statement is called the universal affirmative, and it takes the form: All S (subject) is P (predicate), for example: All giraffes are animals. The I statement is called the particular affirmative, and it takes the form: Some S is P, for example, Some men are Italian. The O statement takes the form: Some S is not P, for example, Some women are not French. Finally, the E statement, which takes the form: No S is P, for example, No fish is a marathon runner.

A: All S is P
I: Some S is P
O: Some S is not P
E: No S is P

Major, Minor, and Middle Terms

There are only three terms in a syllogism: the major term, the minor term, and the middle term. The major term is the predicate of the conclusion, the minor term is the subject of the conclusion, and the middle term is never in the conclusion but appears twice in the premises. For example:

All men are mortal
John is a man
Therefore, John is mortal.

In the syllogism above, the major term is mortal, the minor term is John, and the middle term is man. The premise that contains the major term is the major premise, and the premise containing the minor term is called the minor premise. Thus, All men are mortal is the major premise; John is a man is the minor premise.

A cause is a principle from which something proceeds with dependence. Thus, the middle term is **the cause** of the conclusion. Without a middle term, there is no conclusion.

Thus, we know something about the nature of man, namely that man is mortal. So,

John is a [man; all men] are mortal. Therefore, we can deduce that John is mortal. Note the middle term in the middle, causing the conclusion.

Distribution

Distribution is a very important concept in logic. We speak of terms (such as the major, minor, or middle terms) as being either distributed or undistributed. To distribute something is to spread it out, and so a distributed term is completely 'spread out'. In other words, a distributed term covers 100% of the things referred to by the term. An undistributed term is not spread out, in other words, it is a term that covers less than 100% of the things referred to by the term. For example, in the categorical proposition: All men are mortal, 'man' is distributed, because the statement indicates that all men (100%) are mortal.

In the statement: No men have wings, 'man' is also distributed, because the statement indicates that all men (100%) are lacking wings.

Consider the proposition: Some men are fast runners. In this case, the term 'man' is undistributed, because the statement indicates that only some men are fast runners, not all men. In other words, less than 100% of men are fast runners. In the proposition: Some men are not good cooks, 'man' is undistributed for the same reason.

Predicates can also be distributed or undistributed. Consider again the proposition: No men have wings. 'Wings' is distributed, because if no men have wings, then 100% of winged creatures are not men.

Consider the proposition: All men are animals. The predicate 'animals' is undistributed, because it is not the case that 100% of animals are men. Rather, only some animals are men, while some are horses, dogs, cats, etc. In the proposition: Some men are fast runners, the predicate 'fast runners' is undistributed for the same reason. It is not the case that 100% of fast runners are men. Some are men, but other fast runners include cheetahs, deer, cougars, etc.

Finally, consider the proposition: Some men are not American. The predicate 'American' is distributed. The reason is the following. Imagine we have a group of five men in the room who are not American, and these are the men we refer to when we assert that some men are not American. It is true that 100% of Americans are not these men. Thus,

A: All **S** is P
I: Some S is P
O: Some S is not **P**
E: No **S** is **P**

The Rules of Logic

There are certain basic rules of logic that need to be observed. If any one of these rules are violated, then our reasoning is invalid. This means that the conclusion cannot be deduced from the given premises. In other words, the conclusion lacks the force of necessity.

1) **The middle term must be distributed at least once**

For example, consider the following syllogism:

All <u>men</u> are mortal (A statement)
<u>John</u> is a man (A statement)
Therefore, <u>John</u> is mortal (A statement)

Notice that the middle term 'man' is distributed at least once. Note also that we treat a singular as a Universal Affirmative (A) statement. For example, 100% of John is a man. But consider the following argument:

All Conservatives favor privatization. (A statement)
All members of the CBA favor privatization. (A statement)

Therefore, all members of the CBA are Conservatives. (A statement)

The conclusion simply does not necessarily follow from the given premises (*non-sequitur*). The problem with this reasoning is that the middle term is, in both, cases undistributed. To make this clearer, we will bracket the middle term and underline all distributed terms. Notice that each categorical proposition is an A statement, and in an A statement, the subject is always distributed, while the predicate is always undistributed. Hence,

All <u>Conservatives</u> [favor privatization]. (A statement)
All <u>members of the CBA</u> [favor privatization]. (A statement)
Therefore, <u>all members of the CBA</u> are Conservatives. (A statement)

Notice that the middle term remains undistributed in both premises. Hence, it is invalid.

Do not be misled by the fact that the above statements do not appear to follow the simpler form: All S is P. The copula is hidden. For example, the proposition: All Conservatives favor privatization is really the same as: All Conservatives are people who favor privatization.

2) **Any term which is distributed in the conclusion, must also be distributed in the premises**

All social workers know about the difficulties of life on the street.
No abstract philosopher is a social worker.
Therefore, no abstract philosopher knows about the difficulties of life on the street.

The conclusion of this argument does not necessarily follow from the given premises. The problem is that there is a distributed term in the conclusion, but that same term is not distributed in the premise in which it first appears. Consider the syllogism with the distributed terms underlined:

All <u>social workers</u> know about the difficulties of life on the street. (A statement)
No <u>abstract philosopher</u> is a <u>social worker</u>. (E statement)
Therefore, no <u>abstract philosopher</u> <u>knows about the difficulties of life on the street</u>. (E statement)

The predicate of the conclusion "knows about the difficulties of life on the street" is distributed, but it is undistributed in the major premise, because it is the predicate of an A statement.

Consider the first premise: All social workers know about the difficulties of life on the street (All social workers are people who know about the difficulties of life on the street). The predicate "know...street" is undistributed. This means that it is not the case that 100% of those who know about the difficulties of life on the street are social workers, but only some of them are social workers (less than 100%). And so, one cannot conclude that because no abstract philosopher is a social worker, no abstract philosopher knows about the difficulties of life on the street. There might very well be an abstract philosopher who has spent a number of years on the street.

3) From two negative premises, no conclusion can be drawn

No student of this school is Irish (from Ireland).
No Filipino is Irish (from Ireland).
Therefore, No Filipino is a student of this school.

The conclusion, once again, does not follow from the premises. One simply cannot draw any conclusion from the two given premises. Consider the following:

No oak trees bear fruit

No maple trees bear fruit
Therefore, no maple trees are oaks

Even though we know through experience that no maple trees are oak trees, it is not true that we can deduce that no maples are oaks because neither one bears fruit.

4) **If a premise is negative, the conclusion must be negative**

No student from this school is musically gifted.
Some of the musically gifted are neurotic.
Therefore, some neurotics are students from this school.

This, of course, is an invalid syllogism. The conclusion is completely unwarranted. Notice that the conclusion is affirmative (I statement). But the major premise is negative (E statement). But if a premise is negative, the conclusion must be negative. For it is not necessarily the case that some neurotics are from this school, for this school might very well be neurotic free.

5) **A syllogism must have only three terms.**

All who consume a lot of sugar are at risk for diabetes.
All sugar sweetens the flavor of food.
Therefore, ...

No conclusion can be drawn from these two premises; for there are four terms: "sugar consumers", "people who are at risk for diabetes", "sugar" and "that which sweetens the flavor of food".

Before moving on to the Conditional Syllogism, try to determine the validity of the following categorical syllogisms (Check your answers at the back of the eBook):

Logic Exercises

Indicate a) whether the following arguments are valid or invalid by checking the appropriate square. Also, if the syllogism is invalid indicate which rule of logic was violated.

To make this easier, use the following steps:

Step 1: Circle the middle term.
Step 2: Determine what kind of statement (i.e., A, I, E, or O) is the first premise. Then do the same for the second premise. Finally, determine what kind of statement is the conclusion.
Step 3: Highlight all the distributed terms using a colored highlighter.
Step 4: Check to see if the middle term is distributed at least once. If it is not, no need to proceed further, the syllogism is invalid.
Step 5: If there are any distributed terms in the conclusion, check to see if those very terms are distributed in the premises.
Step 6: Check the rest of the rules. If no rules are violated, the syllogism is valid.

Exercises on the Categorical Syllogism

1.
All C is P.
J is P.
Ergo, J is C.
Valid [ ] Invalid [ ]
Reason for Invalidity:

2.
Some Kobo readers are philosophers.
Sean is a philosopher.
Ergo, Sean is a Kobo reader.
Valid [ ] Invalid [ ]
Reason:

3.
No man is perfect
Some men are presidents.
Ergo, some presidents are not perfect.
Valid [ ] Invalid [ ]
Reason:

4.
All matter obeys probability equations
All waves obey probability equations
Ergo, all matter is waves.
Valid [ ] Invalid [ ]
Reason:

5.
All human action is conditioned by circumstances.
All human action involves morality.
Ergo, all that involves morality is conditioned by circumstances
(moral relativism).
Valid [ ] Invalid [ ]
Reason:

6.
All that is good is pleasant.
All eating is pleasant.
Ergo, all eating is good.
Valid [ ] Invalid [ ]
Reason

7.
All patriots are voters.
Some citizens are not voters.
Ergo, some citizens are not patriots.
Valid [ ] Invalid [ ]
Reason:

8.
All those who cause poverty exploit the poor.
All those who exploit the poor are rich.
Therefore, the rich are (or being rich is) the causes of poverty.
Valid [ ] Invalid [ ]
Reason:

9.
All A are B
Some C are not B.
Ergo, some C are not A.
Valid [ ] Invalid [ ]
Reason:

10.
All a priori categories are conditions for the possibility of knowing anything.
Some a posteriori imperatives of an a-cosmic ethics are not conditions for the possibility of knowing anything.
Ergo, some a posteriori imperatives of an a-cosmic ethics are not a priori categories.
Valid [ ] Invalid [ ]
Reason:

11.
All socialists favor higher taxes.
Some Liberals favor higher taxes.
Ergo, some Liberals are Socialists.
Valid [ ] Invalid [ ]
Reason:

12.
All educated people have worked hard.
Some students are not educated.
Ergo, some students have not worked hard.
Valid [ ] Invalid [ ]
Reason:

13.
Mathematicians know what mathematics is.
No philosopher is a mathematician.
Ergo, no philosopher knows what mathematics is.
Valid [ ] Invalid [ ]
Reason:

14.
All scientific knowledge is a work of reason.
All scientific knowledge is true.
Ergo, all that is true is a work of reason.
Valid [ ] Invalid [ ]
Reason:

15.
All married people know about marriage problems.
No priests are married people.
Ergo, no priests know about marriage problems.
Valid [ ] Invalid [ ]
Reason:

16.
All C are B
All T are B
Ergo, all T are C
Valid [ ] Invalid [ ]
Reason:

17.
Nothing easy is worthwhile.
Nothing good is easy.
Ergo, nothing good is worthwhile.
Valid [ ] Invalid [ ]
Reason:

18.
All contraceptives acts are for avoiding pregnancy.
All use of NFP is for avoiding pregnancy.
Ergo, All use of NFP is contraceptive.
Valid [ ] Invalid [ ]
Reason:

19.
All Germans despise Judaism.
All of the people reading this text are German.
Ergo, all of the people reading this text despise Judaism.
Valid [ ] Invalid [ ]
Reason:

20.
All parts of a living organism are inside the body.
The fetus is inside the (mother's) body.
Therefore, the fetus is a part of the living organism (mother's body)
Valid [ ] Invalid [ ]
Reason:

The Conditional (Hypothetical) Syllogism

There is another type of syllogism besides the categorical, namely, the conditional syllogism, and it takes the following form:

If p, then q
p
q

For example:

If Johnnie eats cake every day, then he is placing himself at risk for diabetes.
Johnnie eats cake every day.
Therefore, Johnnie is placing himself at risk for diabetes.

The major premise in this kind of syllogism is a conditional proposition: "If Johnnie eats cake every day, then he is placing himself at risk for diabetes". There are two parts to the conditional proposition. Notice that one clause begins with "if", the other with "then". The "if" clause is called the antecedent, the "then" clause is called the consequent.

In a true conditional proposition, the major premise provides a condition upon which the consequent depends for its truth. For example, the truth of whether Johnnie is placing himself at risk for diabetes depends upon whether or not he chooses to eat cake every day.

The minor premise is the second proposition in the syllogism. It will do one of four possible things. It will either affirm the antecedent, or affirm the consequent, or it will deny the antecedent, or deny the consequent. Consider the following:

Affirming the Antecedent

If Johnnie eats cake every day, then he is placing himself at risk for diabetes.

Johnnie eats cake every day. (Affirming the Antecedent)
Therefore, Johnnie is placing himself at risk for diabetes.

Affirming the Consequent

If Johnnie eats cake every day, then he is placing himself at risk for diabetes.
Johnnie is placing himself at risk for diabetes. (Affirming the Consequent)
Therefore, Johnnie eats cake every day.

Denying the Antecedent

If Johnnie eats cake every day, then he is placing himself at risk for diabetes.
Johnnie does not eat cake every day. (Denying the Antecedent)
Therefore, Johnnie is not placing himself at risk for diabetes.

Denying the Consequent

If Johnnie eats cake every day, then he is placing himself at risk for diabetes.
Johnnie is not placing himself at risk for diabetes. (Denying the Consequent)
Therefore, Johnnie is not eating cake every day.

Two of the above syllogisms are valid, while two are invalid. The syllogism that affirms the antecedent is obviously valid. But is it valid to affirm the consequent and conclude by affirming the antecedent? For example, given that "If Johnnie eats cake every day, then he is placing himself at risk for diabetes", can we conclude that Johnnie eats cake every day **because** he is placing himself at risk for diabetes? The answer is, no. If Johnnie is placing himself at risk for diabetes, he might be eating cake, but he might not be. He might hate cake, but love soda pop instead.

Consider the next example, denying the antecedent. Can we conclude that Johnnie is not placing himself at risk for diabetes **because** he is not eating cake every day? The answer, once again, is no. He might be drinking ten cans of soda pop instead, which places him at risk for diabetes. But can we conclude that Johnnie is not eating cake every day **because** he is not placing himself at risk for diabetes? Indeed, we can. If he is not placing himself at risk for diabetes, then it follows that he is not eating cake.

Hence, affirming the antecedent (AA) and denying the consequent (DC) are valid forms of reasoning. However, affirming the consequent (AC) and denying the antecedent (DA) are invalid forms of reasoning.

An easy way to remember this is the following.

Affirming the Consequent = AC = Acne (invalid)
Denying the Antecedent = DA = Dumb Animal = (invalid)
Denying the Consequent = DC = Washington DC = (valid: a nice city to visit).
Affirming the Antecedent = AA = Alcoholics Anonymous = (valid: a good twelve step program)

Try the following exercises on the Conditional syllogisms. You can check your answers at the back of the book.

Exercises on the Conditional Syllogism

1.

If one chooses vice over virtue, one will suffer in life.
One is suffering in life.
Ergo, one has chosen vice over virtue.
Valid [ ] Invalid [ ]
Reason:

2.

If government is for the common good, it is not for the good
of only the few.
Government is for the common good.
Ergo, government is not for the good of only the few.
Valid [ ] Invalid [ ]
Reason:

3.

If life exists on Mars, then there is water on Mars.
There is water on Mars.
Ergo, life exists on Mars.
Valid [ ] Invalid [ ]
Reason:

4.

If life involves quantity, it is physical.
Life does not involve quantity.
Ergo, life is not physical.
Valid [ ] Invalid [ ]
Reason:

5.

If atoms are ultimate particles, they are indivisible.
Atoms are not indivisible.
Ergo, they are not ultimate.
Valid [ ] Invalid [ ]
Reason:

6.
If the premises of this argument are true, then the conclusion of this argument is true (i.e., the argument is valid).
The conclusion of this argument is true.
Ergo, the premises of this argument are true.
Valid [ ] Invalid [ ]
Reason:

7.
If the premises of this argument are true, then the conclusion of this argument is true (i.e., the argument is valid).
The premises of this argument are not true.
Ergo, the conclusion of this argument is not true.
Valid [ ] Invalid [ ]
Reason:

8.
If you learn to type fast when you are young, you will be grateful later on.
You are learning to type fast when you are young.
Ergo, you will be grateful later on.
[ ] Valid [ ] Invalid
Reason:

9.
If you breath in mold or mildew, you will get a cold.
You have a cold.
Ergo, you breathed in mold or mildew.
[ ] Valid [ ] Invalid
Reason:

10.
If you pray, God will draw close to you.
God did not draw close to you.
Ergo, you did not pray.
[ ] Valid [ ] Invalid
Reason:

11.

If you eat right, you will be healthy.
I don't eat right
Ergo, you are not healthy.
[ ] Valid [ ] Invalid
Reason:

12.

If you learn to think, life will be much easier for you.
Life is not much easier for me.
Ergo, you didn't learn to think.
[ ] Valid [ ] Invalid
Reason:

13.

Eat lots of vegetables and fruit, and you reduce your risk of cancer.
I eat lots of veggies and fruit.
Ergo, I have reduced my risk of cancer.
[ ] Valid [ ] Invalid
Reason:

14.

If Robert has moral scruples against drinking, then Robert never drinks.
Robert never drinks.
Ergo, Robert has moral scruples against drinking.
Valid [ ] Invalid [ ]
Reason:

15.

If the defendant is willing to testify, then he is innocent.
The defendant is not willing to testify.
Ergo, the defendant is not innocent.
Valid [ ] Invalid [ ]
Reason:

Chapter 8: Inductive Arguments (Inferences)

Most of our day to day reasoning, not to mention the scientific method, is inductive. Deduction, as we have seen, is a mode of reasoning that begins with a universal proposition and proceeds to the particular: i.e., all men are rational; Some living things are men; therefore, some living things are rational. The major premise in this example is a universal affirmative, the minor premise is a particular affirmative, and the conclusion is a particular affirmative.

Inductive arguments, on the other hand, begin with the particular (with the evidence) and move towards a universal conclusion. It is only inductive arguments that provide grounds for accepting, on the basis of reason, new information. In other words, if we were limited to accepting only that which could be established by deductive means, we would never go beyond that which we already have available in the premises of an argument, because *all the information in the conclusion is contained in the premises*. For example, some living things are rational is included in the premises 1) all men are rational and 2) some living things are men.

To repeat, a large amount of work in the natural and social sciences is inductive in character. This means that conclusions are often made on the basis of observations *in a number of cases*, and then they are generalized to cover as yet unobserved cases. Let us examine three kinds of inductive arguments: 1) induction by enumeration, 2) the statistical syllogism, and 3) modified induction by enumeration.

Induction by Enumeration

Consider the following argument, which is an instance of induction by enumeration:

Since 90% of the eggs sampled from Bill's chicken farm have been grade A, 90% of all the eggs on that farm are grade A.

46

90% of sampled E are A
Therefore, 90% of all E are A

The evidence before us is a sample of eggs, and on the basis of that evidence we infer that the reason that 90% of that sample are grade A is that 90% of all the eggs on Bill's farm are grade A. Consider too the following example of induction by enumeration:

81% of all Canadians favor the Prime Minister's position on an increase in the federal tax on gasoline. We know this because a recent poll showed that 81% of Canadians polled favored his position.

81% of polled A are F
Therefore, 81% of all A are F

Both arguments are a generalization based on a sample.

The fundamental difference between induction and deduction is that if the premises are true in an inductive argument, the conclusion is *probably true*, though it might be false. The reason for this possibility is that the conclusion contains information that is *not contained in the premise*. In our first example, the conclusion is about all the eggs on Bill's farm, while the premise only gives us information about those eggs that were sampled. Because of this, it follows that the degree to which our conclusion is probably true depends on two important factors: 1) the **size** of the sample, and 2) whether or not the sample is **representative**.

In order for a sample to be properly representative, the parts of the sample must be taken from a widely distributed source. Consider an urn full of marbles; I deposit 80 red marbles in it, and 60 yellow marbles on top of the red, and 30 black marbles on top of the yellow without mixing them all up. The marbles are not properly distributed, and so anyone who reaches in and takes one marble, then another, and another, etc., will end up with an unrepresentative sample. He may conclude that 90% of the marbles in the urn are black. If the pollster sampled from one city only, or one section of a city (i.e., Little Italy), the degree to which the conclusion is probably true would be low; for his sample is unrepresentative. In other words, the conclusion is inductively invalid.

Consider two more examples of induction by enumeration:

Breanne received an 'A' in every course she has so far taken; therefore, she will get an 'A' in all her remaining courses.

100% of past M have been A
Therefore, 100 percent of future M will be A

In this example, all the courses that Breanne has taken so far are a subset of all the courses she will take. This particular argument predicts future occurrences on the basis of past occurrences. Once again, the conclusion is probably true, but it may be false.

Consider the following:

None of the IB students interviewed thought that final exams were very well scheduled. Hence, no IB student thinks that final exams are very well scheduled.

0% of interviewed S are I (impressed)
Therefore, 0% of all S are I

Like the previous example, this argument draws a conclusion that is a generalization about all the members of a particular class based on a sample of the class. In fact, this is the general feature of all examples of induction by enumeration.

We can generalize the above argument forms as follows:

Y% of observed A are B
Therefore, Y% of all A are B (where Y is equal to or greater than 0 and equal to or less than 100)

The Statistical Argument

An inductive argument can also be statistical. In this case, we begin with information about *all members of a class*, and we draw a conclusion about a particular member of that class. Once again, the conclusion is only probable, not necessary. Consider the following:

80% of the pigs on this farm are healthy. Since Fred is a pig on this farm, Fred is healthy.

80% of all P are H
F is P
Therefore, F is H

Consider too the following:

Most of the remarks made by Brenda are insulting. The next remark made will be insulting because Brenda will make the remark.

More than half of all R is I
N is R
Therefore, N is I

The following example appears to be different, but on closer inspection, it has basically the same form:

60,000 of the tickets in the drum were purchased by people from Markham, 15,000 of the tickets were purchased by people from Newmarket, and 5000 of the tickets were purchased by people from Aurora. The winning ticket will be drawn from the drum. Hence, the winning ticket was purchased by someone from Markham.

75% of all T are M
D is T
Therefore, D is M

In a good inductive argument in the form of a statistical syllogism, more than 50% of the class in question must have the property in question. The generalized form of this argument is as follows:

Y% of all A are B (where Y is greater than 50 and less than 100)
X is A
Therefore, X is B

Modified Induction by Enumeration

In the two argument forms above, we made inferences about all the members of a class based on the results of sampling some of the members of the class (induction by enumeration), and we made inferences about a particular member of a class given information about all the members of a class (statistical syllogism). Now we shall examine an argument form which enables us to make inferences about a particular member of a class given the results of sampling some of the members of the class. These arguments are instances of modified induction by enumeration. For example:

87% of IB students polled were dissatisfied with the scheduling of final exams. Since Shikha is an IB student, she is dissatisfied with the scheduling of final exams.

87% of polled IBS are D
S is IBS
Therefore, S is D

To understand why this is a good inductive argument, consider the following:

[Induction by enumeration]
87% of polled IBS are D
Therefore 87% of all IBS are D

Assuming that the sample was large enough and
representative, the above is an example of a valid induction by
enumeration. Now, consider the following argument:

[Statistical syllogism]
87% of all IBS are D (the conclusion of the above argument)
S is IBS
Therefore, S is D

This is a standard statistical syllogism, and it is valid
because over 50% of the members of a class are dissatisfied.
We know this because that is our conclusion taken from a valid
induction by enumeration.

Consider the following invalid modified induction by
enumeration:

10% of the students polled favored the principal's proposal.
Banushan is a student, and therefore Banushan favors the
principal's proposal.

The form of this argument is:

10% of observed S are F
B is S
Therefore, B is F

The relevant parts of this argument are the following:

10% of observed S are F
Therefore 10% of all S are F

10% of all S are F
B is S
Therefore, B is F.

Although the first argument satisfies all the conditions
required for a good induction by enumeration, the second
argument is not an acceptable instance of a statistical syllogism;

for the percentage of students that are in favor is not greater than 50%. Hence, the above example of modified induction by enumeration is unacceptable.

The general argument form of modified induction by enumeration is the following:

Y% of observed A are B (where Y is greater than 50% and less than or equal to 100)
X is A
Therefore, X is B

Summary

Induction by Enumeration
Y% of observed A are B
Therefore, Y% of all A are B (where Y is equal to or greater than 0 and equal to or less than 100)

Statistical Syllogism
Y% of all A are B (where Y is greater than 50 and less than 100)
X is A
Therefore, X is B

Modified Induction by Enumeration
Y% of observed A are B
X is A
Therefore, X is B (where Y is greater than 50% and less than or equal to 100)

The Logic of Induction (Circle the correct answer)

1.
85% of polled grade 9s thinks that Rohan should be elected President of the Student Council. Therefore, 85% of the students at McGivney think that Rohan should be elected President of the Student Council.

Valid Inductive Argument.   Invalid Inductive Argument.

2.
80% of the citizens of this country think abortion is wrong. Since Billy is a citizen of this country, Billy thinks abortion is wrong.

There is an 80% probability that this statement is true.
There is a 20% chance that this statement is true.

3.
35% of the remarks made by Steve are insulting. The next remark made will be insulting because Steve will make the remark.

It is improbable that this statement is true.
It is highly probable that this statement is true.

4.
600 of the tickets in the drum were purchased by grade 12s, 90 of the tickets were purchased by grade 11s, 60 tickets were purchased by grade 10s, and 50 of the tickets were purchased by the grade 9s. The winning ticket will be drawn from the drum. Hence, the winning ticket was purchased by a grade 12 student.

The conclusion is probably true.
The conclusion is probably false.
No probable conclusion can be drawn.

5.

75% of polled students at McGivney think that we need to change the uniform.
Therefore, 75% of all the students at McGivney think that we need to change the uniform.

[The students polled were the IB students in grade 9 (pre-IB), 10 (pre-IB), 11 and 12 IB].

Valid Inductive Argument.
Invalid Inductive Argument.

6.

75% of polled parents think that we need to change the uniform. Therefore, 75% of all the parents think that we need to change the uniform.

[The parents polled were selected from 50 grade 9 students (randomly chosen), 50 grade 10 students (randomly chosen), 50 grade 11 students (randomly chosen), and 50 grade 12 students (randomly chosen)]

Valid Inductive Argument.
Invalid Inductive Argument.

7.

87% of polled Catholics from Holland are in favor of IVF.
Mr. McManaman is a Catholic.
Therefore, Mr. McManaman is in favor of IVF.

This is a good statistical syllogism.
This is an invalid modified induction by enumeration.
It is a good statistical syllogism in that it has a high probability of being true, even though it is actually false that he favors IVF.

8. "I spent my last two weeks of August last year in Rome, and although Italians drive fast, I didn't see one accident. I am now convinced that because people drive so fast in Italy, they are naturally more aware, more alert, more on the watch for pedestrians. In Canada, people drive more slowly, so they are not as aware, hence the reason I've witnessed many accidents within the past 5 years."

What kind of argument is the above?

Deductive (categorical syllogism)
Statistical argument
Hypothetical argument
Induction by enumeration.

9. "I've been dating this guy for 3 months now, he's really charming, he's nice to me, and whenever we get together, we have a great time. Only two or three times did I have my doubts about his character. All the other times were great. That's why I've consented to marrying him—all future times with him will be great as well. The wedding is next week."

The conclusion in the above is a form of:

Deduction
A statistical argument
Induction by enumeration
Modified Induction by enumeration

10. "Betty, Jason, and Carole had the highest overall average, in the nation, upon graduation from high school. They all went to St. Mary's High School. Therefore, St. Mary's High School is the best high school in the nation."

This is necessarily true.
This is an invalid induction by enumeration.
Given the evidence, it is highly probable.
This is a good statistical argument.

Chapter 9: The Round-Trip Fallacy

The following is a valid statistical argument:

87% of oranges in this box are grade A.
This orange is from this box.
Therefore, this orange is grade A.

The truth of the conclusion has high probability. A subtly defective statistical argument, however, is the following:

87% of oranges in this box are grade A.
This orange is grade A.
Therefore, this orange came from this box.

This has been called the Round-trip fallacy. The terms in the major premise have been flipped, as it were. The major premise is "87% of the oranges in this box are grade A", but the lazy mind reads it as "87% of Grade A oranges are in this box". The results of this subtle fallacy are invalid conclusions that can have serious repercussions. For example, let's assume statistics show that 99% of terrorists are Muslim. Consider the following statistical argument:

99% of all terrorists are Muslim.
John is a Muslim.
Therefore, John is a terrorist. (i.e., a good probability that this is true)

Or,

Most of the criminals on First 48 are black.
Zuri is black.
Therefore, Zuri is a criminal. (i.e., a good probability that this is true).

As Statistician Nassim Taleb points out, the confusion is very trivial, but it is a crucial mistake. "Unless we concentrate very hard, we are likely to unwittingly simplify the problem because our minds routinely do so without our knowing it"

Consider the terrorist example above; the major premise is: "99% of all terrorists are Muslims". A lazy mind reads it as "99% of all Muslims are terrorists". A proper statistical argument using the correct major and minor premise is the following:

99% of all terrorists are Muslim.
John is a terrorist.
Therefore, John is a Muslim.

The truth of the conclusion has a high degree of probability, but it is still *underdetermined*, that is, uncertain, so there is a possibility that John is a non-Muslim terrorist (i.e., Jewish, Latino, Chechnian, etc.). The erroneous version, however, is seriously mistaken; for there are about 2 billion Muslims in a world of about 7 billion. Thus, about 30% of the world's population is Muslim. If there are about 10,000 terrorists in the world, 99% of whom—we assume—are Muslims, then 9,900 terrorists are Muslim, out of the 2 billion Muslims in the world. That gives us .00000495; or 0.000495 %. Thus, it is very unlikely (very low probability) that a Muslim in your neighborhood is a terrorist. Consider, however, the practical implications of such a trivial logical error.

Let us return to our original example:

87% of oranges in this box are grade A.
This orange is grade A.
Therefore, this orange came from this box.

There is an even lower probability that this grade A orange is from this box, considering how many grade A oranges there are in the world compared to how many oranges are in this box.

Another variation on this fallacy is to equate *absence of evidence* with *evidence of absence*. In other words, absence of evidence is **not** evidence of absence. For example, little or no evidence of violence is **not** evidence that this person is not violent.

If he's not a violent man, then we will not see significant evidence (to be specified).
We have not seen specified evidence.
Therefore, there he is not a violent man (i.e., there nothing wrong, nothing to worry about, all is well).

This is an instance of affirming the consequent, which is logically invalid. Hence, the conclusion is unwarranted.

The following are examples of popular confusions of absence of evidence with evidence of absence. Each one is, of course, a non-sequitur.

1) Little or no evidence of narcissism is evidence that a person is not a narcissist.

This is false; for this person is careful, he is devious and underhanded, so he leaves no evidence of his narcissism.

2) No evidence of a disease is evidence that a person does not have a disease (i.e., no evidence of cancer is evidence that a person does not have cancer).

This is false; a person may very well have cancer that no test has yet been able to detect.

3) No evidence of a terrorist threat is evidence that there is no terrorist threat.

Again, this is false; little or no evidence of a terrorist threat is not the same as evidence that there is no terrorist threat (or no significant terrorist threat). The terrorists might be careful, blending nicely into the daily life of the society they wish to eventually terrorize.

4) No evidence that this person is innocent is evidence that he/she is not innocent (guilty).

False. This person might have been at the wrong place at the wrong time; he/she was alone when the murder took place and just happened to be seen near the place where the body was recovered on the very day that the pathologist determined that it was dumped there. Thus, there is no evidence of his/her innocence; but that does not mean there is evidence that the person is not innocent.

5) No evidence that this person is the killer is evidence that he is not the killer.

False. He is a cunning and careful criminal, so there is no evidence that he killed his victim.

6) No evidence of understanding is evidence of a lack of understanding.

Again, this is not necessarily true; for some students with a serious learning disability (output disability) show little or no evidence of grasping concepts—at least by means of traditional measures—, but they may very well understand a great deal of what is taught. Of course, there would have to be some evidence, some way of knowing that he has learned something, but the evidence is typically unconventional, such as the teacher has their attention the entire time, or their questions reveal a profound grasp of the concepts.

7) No evidence of interest (yawning, head down, etc.) is evidence of a lack of interest.

Some students who appear to be bored and uninterested in class talk of little else when they are outside of class, i.e., at home. Or, they might desperately want to be there but are suffering from a sudden onset of an illness, or sleep deprivation, etc.

Chapter 10: An Introduction to Universals

Recall the principle of identity, which runs: "Each being is what it is". As was said earlier, it is a first self-evident principle that is presupposed whenever anyone knows anything at all. Moreover, one cannot deny it without using it. In fact, without it, one cannot argue anything at all; for in order to draw a conclusion, one must start with premises, such as "All men desire to know" or "Truth is something worth pursuing". But at the very root of these premises is the principle that each being is what it is, for example, a man is not just anything at all, but a man, a knower, etc., or, truth is not just anything at all, but something determinate, namely, something desirable.

Now consider the "what" in the principle of identity. The first thing the intellect tends to whenever it is confronted with an object of knowledge is the "what" of the thing. The first question a person asks is: "What is it?" Some may say it is a bird, others may say it is a plane, but after a time one might even suggest it is Superman. Whatever the answers, they bear upon the "what" of the thing.

Now when a person asks *what* a thing is, he is not asking about its quantity. For example, if one were to ask: "What is that over there?" and someone were to say "it is 50 pounds, very tall, 2 feet wide", the intellect would remain unsatisfied, because the answer bears upon quantity, and quantity does not tell us "what" a thing is. A human being, a dog, and a small bear might all weigh pretty much the same, but weight tells us nothing about "what" they are specifically.

Quantity bears upon "how much a thing is", not "what a thing is". "What" is a matter of quality, not quantity. When we ask about "what" a thing is, we are asking about its kind, its type, its nature.

Plato of Athens (427-347 BC), who is one of the greatest thinkers in intellectual history, was, thanks to Socrates, preoccupied with the "what" of things and their relationship to particular things themselves. Socrates, his greatest inspiration, would inquire of the essential form of a particular virtue, such as piety, or courage, etc., and he implied that when we come to know the essence of courage, or piety, etc., then we will be in a position to consider any particular action and determine whether or not it is truly courageous, or pious, etc.

Plato took this insight outside the limits of ethics and saw that everything that is intelligible has an "essential form". The word 'idea' comes from the Greek word *eidos*, which in the writings of Plato means 'form'. Things, such as a group of rectangles, have a common idea or form. The Greek word *physis*, from which is derived the word 'physics', means nature, as in "the nature of things". When we ask "what" a thing is, we are inquiring of its nature. We speak of a man as someone who has a human nature. Plato also employed the Greek word *genos*, from which is derived the word 'genus', which means 'kind' or 'type'. When we ask 'what' a thing is, we are asking: "What kind of thing is it?" In our case, we are a human kind of thing. Finally, Plato speaks of *ousia*, which means 'essence' or 'being'. When we ask "what" a thing is, we are asking about its essence, that is, what it is essentially.

All these words point to the same thing; they all refer to that essential quality that renders things intelligible. To say "each being is what it is" is to say that each being is its nature. You are human, your cat is feline, your dog is canine, and the cow down the street is bovine.

Imagine an equilateral, isosceles, and scalene triangle. We can discern that all these figures have something in common; they are all triangles. They have the same basic *eidos*, for they are the same essentially. Each of these figures participates in the form "triangularity". One is equilateral, one is isosceles, another is an obtuse triangle, but they all have that same basic form designated by the word 'triangularity'.

Let us imagine an equilateral triangle whose sides measure 5 cm. This means that a 5-centimeter side belongs to that particular triangle in your imagination, but not to the very essence of triangle, otherwise all triangles would have to have 5-centimeter sides, and any triangle that does not, is not a triangle essentially.

Nor does a triangle have to be drawn in pencil, or chalk, nor does it have to have a particular color. The idea of a triangle contains no color, no lead, no metal, has no particular place and no particular size. And if we were to erase a triangle on a chalkboard, we'd have one less triangle in the world, but "triangularity" would remain entirely unchanged. Moreover, there are not two "triangularities", only one. But there are many triangles.

Thus, it is impossible to draw an image of "triangularity"; thus, it is impossible to imagine "triangularity". All one can do is imagine a particular triangle. Thus, all we can hope to draw is a particular triangle. But the essence of triangle, its basic *eidos*, is not something that, in itself, one can illustrate or imagine. It has no size, no particular shape, no color, no matter, no visibility, etc.

So what is this mysterious *eidos*? Everything we just said about triangularity applies also to humanity, circularity, equality, animality, particularity, quantity, goodness, otherness, canine, bovine, feline, calculus, biology, chemistry, meaning, strength, weakness, regularity, movement, etc. Essences are not particular, they are universal, they are not plural, they are one; they are not subject to change, they are unchanging; they are not subject to quantity, they have no quantity; they are not subject to place, so they are nowhere.

But according to Plato, the essence or *ousia* of a thing is its very being. What makes a desk *to be* a desk? Is it the wood? According to Plato, the answer is no, for a desk can be made out of any matter and it would still be a desk. It is the form that makes a desk to be a desk. It is the form that makes a chair to be a chair, not its matter, or its location, or its color, etc.

Things to Wonder About

We are certainly a long way from solving the problem of universals, that is, coming to understand their existential status or what they really are in themselves. Nevertheless, the more one thinks about them, the more one realizes how fascinating and mysterious reality is.

For example, most of us think that if something is real, it means we can see it and touch it. But Plato's insights would seem to challenge this. What makes the chair real, that is, what makes it to really be a chair, is something that cannot be seen, touched, felt, picked up, handled, thrown, etc. It isn't the wood or the steel that makes it to be a chair, but its form.

Moreover, it isn't your black hair, dark skin, long legs, strong arms, etc., that makes you to be a human. You can lose your hair, your legs, your arms, and you'd still be "what" you are, namely human. But without "humanness" or "humanity" (whatever that is), you wouldn't be human at all. And yet we cannot see and touch humanity, nor can we imagine it. What we have in our imaginations is a particular human, but not the universal form or essence of humanness/humanity. What is this essential quality without which you would not be what you are?

Furthermore, it should be clear at this point that there is a real difference between intelligence and sensation. The intellect desires to know "what" a thing is, first and foremost. But the "what" of things, their nature, is not something that the senses (even the internal sense of imagination) can apprehend. The senses, as well as imagination, bears upon particulars only, for example, particular humans, particular triangles, particular rabbits, etc. But the intellect apprehends what it means to be a human, a triangle, a rabbit, etc. The intellect apprehends essences (which are universal), while the imagination internally perceives particulars.

Consider too that there is no science of particulars. The word "science" comes from the Latin *scire*, which means 'to know'. Since the object of knowledge is the *physis*, science is about coming to know the natures (*physis*) of things. In other words, science is about universals, not particulars. There are no animal scientists; not one veterinarian who is a non-human animal; for brute animals cannot grasp the natures of things. An animal is a living sentient creature, and sensation bears upon particulars, but intelligence is the ability to apprehend essences.

Consider how racism has some relationship to the problem of universals. In philosophical terms, racism is the confusion between what belongs to the essence of a thing and what is outside the essence. Does 'white' belong to the essence of "human"? No more than 'white' belongs to the essence of a triangle, or a square. Universal forms, essences, etc., have no color. But the racist mistakenly thinks that a particular color belongs to the essence of man, such that anyone not of that color is not a man, but something essentially different.

Note too how it is self-refuting to deny that intelligence is the ability to apprehend the essences of things (universals) by reducing universals, for instance, to linguistic constructs. A person who argues against what has been said up to this point insists that what we assert lacks the force of necessity and that our grasp of what intelligence is, is inaccurate. In other words, our conclusion regarding intelligence is not warranted by the given premises. But this only shows that he regards intelligence in the same way we do, namely, as the ability to understand the natures of things. For he demands that our conclusion have the force of necessity; for he understands that science bears upon universals, for he demands that what we assert about intelligence be universal, and not just true in particular cases. But whatever he asserts about intelligence against our view will inevitably have a universal character.

For example, imagine someone asserting the following: "Intelligence is not about apprehending the natures of things. Rather, intelligence is effectively perceiving, interpreting and responding to the environment. It is the ability to survive and meet desired goals and objectives."

Now we would argue that this is incorrect; for even brute animals have the ability to survive, but we would not say that they are intelligent. Nevertheless, we need not even go there. All we need to do is call attention to what was asserted about intelligence in general; notice that there are a number of universal concepts in the assertion, namely, perception, interpretation, response, environment, ability, survival, desire, goal, and the concept of an objective. Clearly, our opponent apprehends universal concepts and has strung them together in order to express what he thinks intelligence is essentially, that is, universally. He is only able to do this because he is intelligent and can grasp the natures of things, including the nature of certain behaviours and activities.

Chapter 11: An Introduction to Definitions

The object of the first act of the intellect is the "what" of things, that is, the essence or nature of things. That is why the intellect tends to define things. A definition expresses the essence of a thing, which is why a good definition will contain only that which belongs to a thing's essence. For example, blond hair does not belong to the definition of man, because blond hair is a non-essential trait of a human person. If it were not, then anyone without blond hair would not be a man. Rationality, on the other hand, is found in the definition of man, because man is essentially a rational creature.

Note 'fin' in the word 'definition'. The word *finis* is Latin for 'end', 'term' 'limit' or 'boundary'. To define is to determine the meaning of a thing, to determine the intelligible limits or boundaries of a thing. In other words, a thing with a nature is a determinate, limited thing that is intelligible and definable. This means that one can establish what a thing is essentially, allowing us to distinguish that from the many non-essential aspects of the thing.

A definition is composed to two parts: a genus and a specific difference. Together they give us the species, that is, what the thing is specifically.

The genus tells us what a thing is generally and indeterminately. More accurately, the genus is that which is predicated essentially of several things that differ in species. For example, when it comes to things like birds, dogs, cows, horses, chickens, etc., we can ask: what is it that can be predicated essentially of the all? Certainly not that they all fly, or they all run fast, or that they are all gray, etc. Rather, they are all essentially animals, that is, various species of animals. And so "animal" is the genus of the definition of man, horse, chicken, etc.

The specific difference is that which reduces the genus to a species, making one species different from another within a genus.

For example, consider the definition of man: rational animal. This definition tells us what man is generally, namely, an animal. But so too is a horse, cow, bird, etc. How does man differ specifically from these latter? The answer is: rational. Man is essentially a rational animal. Hence, whatever is not rational is not a man. And since "animal" is included in the definition of man, and since an animal is a living sentient creature, whatever is not sentient is not a man. And so an angel, who is intelligent but not sentient, is not a man.

Consider the following definitions. We have bracketed the genus and underlined the specific difference.

Animal: [Living] <u>sentient</u> [creature]
Triangle: A [plane figure] with <u>three sides</u>.
Temperance: The [virtue] that <u>moderates the pleasures of touch</u>.
Fortitude: The [virtue] that <u>moderates fear and daring</u>.
Virtue: A [habit] that <u>makes its possessor good.</u>
Polygon: A [plane figure] <u>made up of several line segments that are joined together</u>.

The Three Acts of the Intellect

At this point it should be evident that intelligence is essentially different from sensation. The intellect can define things because it can apprehend what things are essentially. The senses do not grasp the "what" of things, but only their sensible properties. Hearing, for example, does not grasp the nature of sensation, nor does seeing grasp the conditions for perceiving color, or the nature of light, electromagnetic radiation, etc. What we see are particular colors and what we hear are particular sounds.

But a definition is more than the simple apprehension of a thing's nature. It is complex. And so there is more to intelligence than the simple apprehension of essences. The first act is that by which the intellect grasps the essence of a thing, that is, what a thing is, and this is called *simple apprehension*. It is through simple apprehension that the intellect conceives ideas or concepts, which are universal ideas (*eidos*) within the mind, for example, apple in general, or quantity, or man, triangle, intelligence, number, beauty, vegetable, animal, etc.

The second act of the intellect is not simple, but complex and thus depends upon simple apprehension. This act is called *judgment*, which is either a composition or division. For example, Polly is a bird, or a bird is an egg-laying vertebrate with wings. Here we have the concepts 'bird', 'egg' 'laying', 'egg-laying' 'vertebrate' and 'wings' and we are composing them, that is, bringing them together in the judgment that a bird is an egg-laying vertebrate with wings. A judgment might also be a division, such as: A bird is not rational. Here we are dividing bird from rational.

The third act of the intellect is called *reasoning*, which is the act of drawing a conclusion from two judgments, such as:

All birds have wings.
Jimmy is a bird.
Therefore, Jimmy has wings.

Concluding Thoughts

If there were no difference between intelligence and sensation, one would not be able to apprehend universal natures. If one could not understand universal natures, one could not make universal statements, such as universal affirmative or universal negative propositions. And if one could not make universal statements, one could not reason, that is, one would not be able to draw rational conclusions. In other words, science would be impossible.

Allow me to call attention to some of the principles of post-modernism. For Friedrich Nietzsche, knowledge is impossible because all is in a pure state of change. In other words, there are no stable natures that render things intelligible. Reality is nothing but an unintelligible network of pure becoming. Hence, all science is a fiction, including logic, which is a construct, founded upon the illusion of being, that is, the illusion of permanency. There are no things, no intelligible essences, and no self-evident first principles, such as the principle of identity, non-contradiction, etc. And so the rules of logic are purely arbitrary, all of them lacking the force of necessity. And yet if one reads Nietzsche carefully, one is struck by his logical consistency as he reasons from the premises he establishes to conclusions having the force of necessity. In other words, he uses logic in order to deny it, employs universal propositions containing universal concepts in order to deny the possibility of universal ideas, and draws conclusions that deny the very possibility of determinate knowledge at all.

Chapter 12: Some Informal Fallacies

It is important to become familiar with some of the basic logical fallacies that people frequently commit. The more familiar you are with these, the more you will discover how specious are the arguments that many people today employ, including teachers, journalists and politicians.

The first is the **fallacy of accident**. This fallacy involves confusing what is accidental (outside the essence) with what is essential.

He's a capitalist. Therefore, he loves money and thinks the poor are lazy.
He's from the Middle East. Therefore, he's dangerous.
Penguins are birds. Therefore, penguins fly.

This fallacy is also called the fallacy of composition, or the fallacy of part and whole, for it occurs when a person attributes to the part what belongs only to the whole; for example, when a person concludes that since America is such a prosperous nation, all of its citizens must be well off. In other words, what belongs only to a whole is predicated of the parts. The fallacy also occurs when one attributes to the whole what belongs only to the part. Reductionism is an instance of this fallacy; for example, an atom is mostly empty space. Hence, this table is mostly empty space and thus solidity is an illusion.

The **fallacy of ignoring the question** (or ignoring the issue) consists in proving something other than the point to be established. Essentially, it consists in evading the original issue. Consider the following argument from Bertrand Russell:

There is an incredible amount of empty space in the universe. The distance from the sun to the nearest star is about 4.2 light years, or 25 followed by 12 noughts miles...And as to mass: the sun weighs about 2 followed by 27 noughts tons, the Milky Way weights about 160,000 times as much as the sun and is one of a collection of

galaxies of which, as I said before, about 30 million are known. It is not very easy to retain a belief in one's own cosmic importance in view of such overwhelming statistics.

His figures show that our universe is immense, but they show nothing about the importance or dignity of the human person, which does not consist in physical dimensions, otherwise the heaviest among us would necessarily be the greatest. Russell proves something other than the point he wishes to establish.

On a discussion forum dealing with the issue of mercy killing, a person, John, argues that euthanasia is not murder. Bill argues it is:

John: Even the bible does not state that abortion and euthanasia are acts of murder. It states simply: "Thou shalt not kill". That mercy killing is murder is your inference. It is your precept.
Bill: John, my dictionary defines murder as the 'premeditated killing of one human being by another'.
John: Bill, your dictionary has nothing to do with this.

For it is true that Bill's dictionary has nothing to do with the topic of the forum; Bill's dictionary has nothing to do with much of anything, such as the economy, my life or your life, with nutrition or the national debt. Bill's dictionary has nothing to do with anything except the space that it occupies in Bill's house. But it does not follow that the proper definition of words has nothing to do with a sound argument.

Another example of ignoring the question is taken from an interview with Charles Curren, a Catholic moral theologian who dissents from the Church's teaching on a number of moral issues. Before actually reading the Encyclical *Humanae Vitae* (the Church document condemning the use of contraceptive birth control), he published an attack on the document as soon as he heard that it was out. One reporter asked him: **"Shouldn't you read the document first, before**

**you come out publicly against it?"   To which Curren
replied: "There's no virtue in delay".**

Indeed, there is no virtue in delay. Virtue is a disposition,
a good habit, and 'delay' is an unexpected lapse of time, or
lateness. Virtue and delay have nothing to do with one
another. But the question was: "Shouldn't you read the
document first, before you come out publicly against it?"

Or, consider Pierre Elliot Trudeau's classic statement that
duped a generation of Canadians

"There's no place for the state in the bedrooms of the nation."

The issue is not whether there is a place for the state in the
bedrooms of the nation, but whether the state should make
laws governing sexual behaviour which bears upon character,
and which in turn plays a part in determining the character of
the state as a whole; for law makes a statement which instructs
and shapes the characters of the people who obey the law. In
order to bolster his position that people should be allowed to
do what they want when it comes to sexual matters, Trudeau
asserts that there is no place for the state in the bedrooms of
the nation, evoking images of police or public officials entering
into a person's bedroom in order to take note of what is going
on.

Another popular fallacy is called **ad hominem** (to the
man), which involves the criticism of some person's position
or belief by criticizing the person rather than the position itself.
For instance:

**"Einstein couldn't have been right about Relativity, for just
look at the way he combs his hair."**
**"Father Damian couldn't be a good and holy priest, for just
look at his belly."**
**"He doesn't know what he's talking about. Just listen to his
stuttering."**
"I'm not going to vote for him; I can't stand the way he looks."

The **fallacy of the double standard** involves applying a principle or standard differently and without a rational basis to two different persons or groups. For example, some liberals have argued that although former President Bill Clinton (a Democrat) committed adultery and lied about it under oath, he is nevertheless a good president, for "his private life has nothing to do with his public life." But when these same people discover the slightest moral flaw in the history of a Republican candidate, the latter is immediately be dismissed as unworthy of political office.

The fallacy of misplaced authority (*ad verecundiam*, from the Latin *verecundia*, or "shame") consists of appealing to the testimony of an authority on an issue that is outside his or her proper field of expertise.

"My doctor assured me that Fords are the best cars. Therefore, I'm going to buy a Ford. After all, he is a doctor, and you're just a lowly mechanic."

Often a person will appeal to an authority in order to shame an opponent in debate: "Who are you to argue against his point of view. He's got a Ph.D. What do you have?" Sometimes the debate is about a philosophical issue, although it appears to be about science (i.e., whether the universe came from nothing), and so we often hear the argument to the effect that "He doesn't have a degree in science, so he has no business spouting off about things he knows nothing about."

I once watched a televised symposium involving the year's Nobel Laureates in Chemistry, Physics, and Medicine, Literature, etc. The point was to have them shed light on world issues and offer political solutions to the world's problems. This was clearly an instance of the fallacy of misplaced authority; for their responses were no more enlightened than the average high school student—with the exception of the Nobel Prize winner for Literature, I might add.

The fallacy of **ad populum** (appeal to the people) occurs when a speaker attempts to get some group to agree to a particular position by appealing solely to their bigotry, biases, and prejudices or, in some cases, merely to their desire to hear what they already believe. As an example, consider the election year when Canadian politicians appealed to the people's fears about Medicare and began to accuse the Conservative Party (then Alliance Party of Canada) of advocating a two tiered heath care system. They were appealing to the fears and prejudices of Canadian, but they were not engaged in rational argument.

The **fallacy of false cause** (*post hoc ergo propter hoc*) consists in assuming that when one event precedes another, it is the cause of the succeeding event. Consider the following:

"On the road I travel to the mall in Wheaton, Md., two white men severely beat two black women Tuesday. One was doused with lighter fluid, and her attacker tried to set her afire. Both men cursed the women for being black. I couldn't help but shudder: That could have been me. This heinous act happened only hours after Pat Buchanan voters gave him 30 percent of the vote in the Maryland GOP presidential primary." — USA Today columnist and former "Inquiry" page editor Barbara Reynolds, March 6, 1992."

The **fallacy of begging the question** involves assuming the point that needs to be proven; one ends up arguing in a vicious circle. For example, to show that abortion is a basic right and thus should be enshrined in law, a person argues:

All rights should be enshrined in law.
Abortion is a basic human right.
Therefore, abortion should be enshrined in law.

The problem is that the person must show that abortion is a basic human right; he merely assumes the point that he needs to establish. Consider the following argument for Same-Sex Marriage legislation, which again assumes the point that needs to be proven:

"The rights of individuals should be protected. If you allow the government to take away their freedom of expression, then you

will be allowing government to dictate to other minorities what they can or cannot believe in. Whether we are talking about moral values or a certain lifestyle, government is still infringing on people's rights as citizens of a free society, which is what this country is built on."

Or consider this classic example of the fallacy of begging the question by novelist John Irving (My Movie Business), put forth as an argument for the right to abort an unwanted child.

"If you expect people to be responsible for their children, then you have to give them the right to choose whether or not to have children".

Everyone expects people to be responsible for their children, but it does not follow (non-sequitur) that we must therefore give people the right to kill their offspring; but that is precisely what pro-choice advocates need to show. His argument is identical in form to the following: "If you expect people to be responsible for their fellow citizens, you have to give them the right to choose whether or not to pay income tax." Or, "If you expect teachers to be responsible for their students, you have to give them the right to choose whether or not to teach those students."

The **fallacy of equivocation** occurs when some word or expression is used with more than one meaning in an argument. For instance, consider the following:

Addicts, who have serious emotional problems, tend to think in black and white terms, that is, they tend to be absolutists.
John argues that there are absolute moral precepts.
Therefore, John has serious emotional problems.

It is unreasonable to be inflexible.
Bill will not compromise (is inflexible) on abortion.
Therefore, Bill is unreasonable.

The **fallacy of false analogy** occurs when a person argues a position merely by drawing an analogy, without a justification for the analogy (thus, it is a form of begging the question). For example, comparing the issue of Same-Sex Marriage with Interracial Marriage in order to argue for its legalization is an instance of the fallacy of false analogy; for homosexual activity is a behaviour, belonging to a race is not.

Consider the following that was argued on a discussion forum on the issue of abortion:

The reality is that there is a gradual transition from germ cell to human being. Is a set of plans a building? Most people would say no, not until there are foundations, walls, windows, a roof, etc., something resembling a functional building. A zygote is really nothing but a set of plans. It has a set of instructions, but nothing else. It will become a genuine human only after a lot of materials are delivered and assembled properly.

The analogy employed above is false. A living organism is not at all like an artifact, such as a computer or a building. An organism is a unified and living whole that has an internal principle of movement. An artifact is the sum of its parts, a multiplicity of substances—not one substance—and its principle of movement is not internal, but external, namely the builders.

Chapter 13: An Introduction to the Idea of Happiness

Most people tend to associate happiness with feeling good, that is, with a life that offers a variety of pleasures and comforts. Some tend to associate happiness with being able to do whatever they want to do, still others associate it with achieving everything they have set out to achieve in life. But ask yourself whether it is possible to have many and frequent pleasures in life, yet remain unhappy. And is it possible to have few pleasures in life, yet be happy? Moreover, is it possible to be able to do whatever you want, yet still be unhappy? Finally, is it possible to achieve everything you have set out to achieve in life, yet remain profoundly unhappy?

The answers to these questions almost never vary among young people, for they consistently answer in the affirmative. But if it is possible to have many and frequent pleasures in life yet remain unhappy, then it logically follows that happiness is not necessarily having many and frequent pleasures. And if it is possible to achieve everything you have set out to achieve in life yet remain unhappy, then it is clear that happiness is not necessarily achieving everything you have set out to achieve. And if it is possible to be able to do whatever you want in life yet remain unhappy, then happiness is not necessarily doing what you want to do.

This last point is intriguing, for it is so counterintuitive: Happiness is not necessarily doing what you want to do. How is that possible? Could happiness possibly consist in doing what you don't want to do? Indeed. It would seem very possible for a person to take himself down a road at the end of which he will fail to find what he originally thought would be there, ready to greet him, namely, happiness. In other words, it is very possible to mislead ourselves. In short, one can very well be one's own worst enemy.

And so, what could be more important than to set out on a quest for the answer to the question about what exactly constitutes human happiness? Out of all the ends we may pursue, what end is alone worthy of desire? And what could be more important than to examine the choices we are currently making in order to determine whether or not we have made that end our own, namely the end which alone is worthy of desire?

That is what Socrates was all about. He was aware that human persons make choices for the sake of some end, which in turn is pursued for the sake of some other end, which in turn is pursued for the sake of some further end, etc. For example, why did you choose to dress in these cloths this morning? You might answer: In order to get ready for school. Why are you choosing to go to school? You might reply: In order to get into university. Why are you choosing to go to university? In order to receive an education. Why are you choosing an education? In order to become employed. Why do you want employment? In order to make money. Why do you want to make money? In order to buy a house. Why do you want to buy a house? In order to raise my family.

What is the end, however, that is sought not as a means to some other end, but for its own sake? In other words, what is the ultimate end? We will know the answer to that question when we can no longer answer the question "why" any further. For example, why do you want to raise a family? At this point, you might say, because I just want to. But why? The answer is: for its own sake. In other words, that is the end I seek for its own sake, and I believe that achieving this end will make me happy.

And so at this point, the question is whether or not that end really will make you happy. Is it possible to achieve all that, namely, a university education, employment, financial stability, a house in the suburbs, a wife/husband and family, and yet be unhappy? The facts tell us that indeed, it is possible.

Socrates was aware that happiness is universally pursued by everyone as the ultimate end, desired not for the sake of some other end, but for its own sake. But what is the content of that end? What are the choices that we ought to make in order to achieve happiness? Socrates divided humanity into three groups on the basis of what each group regarded as the ultimate end that promises happiness. The first group is in the

majority. Those in this group make choices that are directed
ultimately towards pleasure as the chief good.

But not everyone pursues pleasure as their chief end; some
are willing to sacrifice pleasures for the sake of what they
regard as the chief end, namely, honors, fame, or social status.

Then there are those people who pursue neither honors,
nor social status, nor a life devoted to pleasure. Rather, they
have made wisdom or knowledge their chief end. These latter
are in the minority, and of course, Socrates belongs to this
group.

Socrates does not mean to suggest that any kind of
knowledge is the ultimate end that alone brings happiness. One
might be very learned, but that does not mean such a one will
necessarily be happy. Rather, Socrates refers to a certain kind
of knowledge, namely, practical knowledge, that is, wisdom,
which is moral knowledge. Diogenes tells us that Socrates used
to say: "there was one only good, namely, knowledge; and one
only evil, namely ignorance." For Socrates, knowledge is the
only good because if one knows the good, one will choose the
good, and if one chooses the good, one becomes good. Hence,
to say that happiness is knowledge is, for Socrates, to say that
happiness is goodness. That is why Socrates says that
knowledge is virtue. Hence, happiness is virtue, which means
that happiness is the perfection of the soul. To perfect the soul
is to make it as good as possible. In his Apology, Plato depicts
Socrates thus:

Men of Athens, I honor and love you; but I shall obey
God rather than you, and while I have life and strength I shall
never cease from the practice and teaching of philosophy,
exhorting anyone whom I meet after my manner, and
convincing him, saying: O my friend, why do you who are a
citizen of the great and mighty and wise city of Athens, care so
much about laying up the greatest amount of money and
honor and reputation, and so little about wisdom and truth and
the greatest improvement of the soul, which you never regard
or heed at all? Are you not ashamed of this? And if the person
with whom I am arguing says: Yes, but I do care; I do not

depart or let him go at once; I interrogate and examine and cross-examine him, and if I think that he has no virtue, but only says that he has, I reproach him with undervaluing the greater, and overvaluing the less. And this I should say to everyone whom I meet, young and old, citizen and alien, but especially to the citizens, inasmuch as they are my brethren. For this is the command of God, as I would have you know; and I believe that to this day no greater good has ever happened in the state than my service to the God. For I do nothing but go about persuading you all, old and young alike, not to take thought for your persons and your properties, but first and chiefly to care about the greatest improvement of the soul. I tell you that virtue is not given by money, but that from virtue come money and every other good of man, public as well as private. This is my teaching, and if this is the doctrine which corrupts the youth, my influence is ruinous indeed. But if anyone says that this is not my teaching, he is speaking an untruth. (Translated by Benjamin Jowett)

For Socrates, the starting point of the life of virtue is to "know thyself". For Socrates, this means that a person must realize that the soul is the true self, not the body. Those who pursue pleasure mistakenly believe that the body is the true self. And since "the unexamined life is not worth living", the next step is to examine the choices that we make in order to determine whether those choices are rooted in the judgment of the soul, or merely the desire for property, pleasure, or honors. Finally, one must be able to govern oneself, for this is true freedom, not the false notion that sees freedom as nothing more than doing whatever you want to do. Genuine freedom is inextricably linked to knowledge, and so the more knowledge a person has, the freer he is. Hence, freedom is knowing what one ought to want as well as having the ability to direct oneself to that end. Without knowledge, one is simply a slave to one's passions as well as social custom.

Chapter 14: Introduction to the Idea of the Soul

Socrates spoke of the soul as the true self. But is this true? And is there really a soul? How can we be sure that happiness is the perfection of the soul if we are not sure whether or not the soul actually exists?

These are important questions, but Socrates does not answer them. Rather, it is Plato who first attempts to prove the existence of the soul through reason. And the best place to begin reasoning to the existence of the soul is to consider what it means to be a living thing. How do we know that something is alive or not? And would we consider a computer, for example, to be a living thing?

If we want to determine whether or not something is alive, we usually do something that we anticipate will cause a certain kind of reaction. We might poke someone to see if he moves, or we might listen for a heartbeat or feel for a pulse, or check for breathing. The reason we do these things is that we understand that life has something to do with movement. But even non-living things move, like planes, trains, and automobiles. The difference, however, is that a plane, for example, does not move on its own. The football, baseball, and billiard ball do not move on their own, but as a result of being moved by something outside themselves. Hence, the principle (source) of motion of a non-living thing is extrinsic to the moving thing. But a living thing moves itself (self-ambulation). Hence, the principle of motion of a living thing is intrinsic.

Living things have an intrinsic principle of motion. But what exactly is this intrinsic principle? Consider what living material things have in common with non-living material things? The answer is, evidently, matter. A chemist might tell us that our bodies are 65% Oxygen, 18% Carbon, 10% Hydrogen, 3% Nitrogen, etc. But is a thing alive by virtue of its matter? Clearly not, for if a thing is alive by virtue of its matter, then all material things would be living. But this is clearly not the case. Matter is inert; and so a thing is alive by virtue of a principle that is non-matter, or immaterial. For Plato, this is the soul. He writes:

> ...self-motion is precisely the essence and definition of soul. Body that has an external source of motion is soulless, but a body moved from within is alive or besouled, which implies that the nature of soul is what we have said. (Phaedrus, 245e-246a)

The Greek word for soul is psyche, which is often translated as "mind". Recall that the object of the intellect is the essence of things. Concepts, as they exist in the mind, are universal, thus they are not material. But a material thing cannot be the receiver of an immaterial form; rather, a material thing, like a blob of puddy, receives a material form or imprint. The form, as it is received by matter, is individuated and is subject to change. But the mind receives forms or conceives ideas that are one, unchanging and universal. Thus, the mind is immaterial.

But there are not two immaterial principles within man, for he is not two things, but one thing. The soul of man is thus an intellectual soul, capable of apprehending the natures of things. As Plato says: "The soul resembles the eternal Ideas, which are the proper object of all its attentions" (Phaedrus, 247d).

Now Plato understood the relationship between soul and body dualistically. In other words, he regarded man as two substances (body and soul). The body, for Plato, is the prison of the soul: "Every seeker after wisdom knows that up to the time when philosophy takes over his soul is a helpless prisoner, chained hand and foot inside the body, forced to view reality not directly but only through the prison bars, and wallowing in utter ignorance" (Phaedo, 82e).

The problem, however, is that we do not experience ourselves as two substances, but one. How, then, can we talk about body and soul without implying that they are two "things"? Plato was not able to resolve that question, but Aristotle had more success, for he seemed to be more interested in the philosophy of human nature than was Plato,

for he seems to have taken matter more seriously than did
Plato.

Chapter 15: An Introduction to Aristotle's Ten Categories of Being

We speak of "things" in the world: my cat is a thing, birds are living things, so too are plants, etc., but what does it mean to be a "thing"? Is my finger a thing? And if it is a thing, then is the surface of my finger a thing? Is my foot a thing and my leg a separate thing? Is color a thing? Is the quantity of a thing itself a thing? Chemists study the properties and structures of substances, but what is a substance? And is a substance distinct from its properties? If so, in what ways are they distinct?

Beings that exist outside the mind exist not primarily as numbers (as Pythagoras thought), or atoms (as Democritus thought), or essences (as Plato thought), but as entities or things. In other words, beings exist primarily as substances, according to Aristotle. Substance is the primary way that beings exist, thus it is the primary mode of being.

But there are secondary modes of being that *exist in* substance. They do not exist independently, but dependently, that is, their mode of being is to exist in something more primary, such as substance. For example, there is no such thing as red, or 50 pounds. There are only red things, or 50 pound things. Nor is there such a thing as equality. Rather, there are things that are equal, either in size, or in quality, etc. These secondary modes of being are called accidents, from the Latin *ac-cidere*, to fall on or inhere in. A substance, on the contrary, does not exist in anything, but exists *per se*, that is, in itself (independently).

1. Substance (primary mode of being): water, gold, a tree, a dog, or a human being, etc.

2. Accidents (secondary modes of being that "exist in" substance):

1.   Quantity: having parts outside of parts, divided into continuous and discrete.

2.   Quality: a) affective qualities (color, taste, etc.), b) habit and disposition (wisdom, malleable, etc.) c) shape or figure (i.e., round), d) abilities and debilities (fly, walk).

3.   The Relative (Relation): for example, father and son, equal, in front, beside, etc.

4.   Action: walking, running, thinking, etc.

5.   Passion (to undergo): being attacked, mugged, or rained on, etc.

6.   Where (place): for example, in this place here.

7.   Posture: sitting, standing, upside down.

8.   When (time): for example, now.

9.   State or Environment: the state of being clothed, for example.

The substance is that in which the accidents inhere; it is the substratum of the accidental modes of being. Accidents actuate the substance in a secondary. The first accidental mode of being quantifies a substance, gives it extension into parts. But quantity is a distinct mode of being than substance; to inquire of a substance is not necessarily to inquire of its quantity. Moreover, quantity can change while the substance endures. A human being, for instance, was at one time smaller than your hand. He increased in quantity and is now six feet, five inches, and weighing three hundred pounds. Although his quantity changed, he (the substance) remained the same substance. If substance were to be identified with quantity, then a change in quantity would amount to a change in substance.

Similarly, to inquire of a thing's quality is not necessarily to inquire of its quantity. Quality is a distinct mode of being than quantity and substance, and so on with all the other remaining accidents.

Corresponding to the two modes of being (substance and accident) are two types of changes: substantial and accidental. An example of an accidental change is a change in quantity (a substance becomes larger), or a change in quality (a substance changes from being bitter to being sweet). In these cases, it is the substance that remains the same throughout the change, that is, the substance is the subject that underlies the change.

A substantial change is a change in substance, for example, the change from wood to ash, living organism to rotting corpse, or hydrogen and oxygen to water, or sodium and chlorine to salt, or sperm and ovum to embryo, etc.

A Thought Experiment

In order to come to a deeper appreciation of what it is we are talking about when we speak of substance, try this thought experiment. Imagine a living substance, such as a small green cedar shrub. We touch it and feel the smooth leaves that are bright green. The color and texture of the shrub belong to the category of affective qualities, which is an accident. It is because the shrub is colored that we can see it and behold its extension, its various parts, branches, leaves, etc. Over time, this shrub will grow, that is, it will become larger. It may even change color slightly, going from a bright green to a darker green. But the substance is the same over time; it is the same shrub that we planted initially. Now, accidents depend upon substance in order exist—I cannot show you "green", only a green shrub; I cannot show you "heavy", only a heavy shrub, etc. Without substance, there are no accidents; but substance exists in itself, *per se*, not in another. Substance is thus independent. Indeed, substance depends upon the accidents (i.e., effective qualities) in order to be sensed, but it does not depend on the accidents in order to exist.

In our thought experiment, we are going to call on God's assistance. Let us ask God to take away all the affective qualities of the shrub. He does so. As a result, we cannot perceive the substance with its extension. But, logically speaking, does the substance still exist? If accidents depend on substance, not vice versa, then the answer is in the affirmative. Now we ask God to take away the quantity so that the substance has no parts. Does the substance still exist, logically speaking? The answer is once again in the affirmative.

This, of course, is only a thought experiment, not something that can be done in the realm of the real. But after the accidents have been removed, what then is left? The answer is: the substance; the actual shrub, which is now potentially quantified and potentially qualified, not actually so.

Thus, ordinary material reality, that is, ordinary material substance, is far more mysterious than we might have been led to believe. Material substance always exists as quantified and qualified, in relation to other substances, occupying place and existing in time, etc., but considered in itself (without considering accidents, even though substance does not exist without accidents), substance is other than its accidents.

It was this insight that allowed Aquinas, for example, to show that what Catholics choose to believe about the Eucharist (namely, that it is really the substance of Christ's body and blood, not merely a symbol) is not contrary to reason, that is, not a violation of the principle of non-contradiction, because substance is really distinct from its accidents, and so if God chooses to work the miracle, He can change the substance of bread into the substance of Christ's body, leaving the accidents of the bread to remain, so that it looks like bread, tastes like bread, feels like bread, etc., and so too with the substance of wine. That, of course, does not prove that the Eucharist really is Christ, but it shows that to believe such a thing (transubstantiation) is not irrational.

Chapter 16: Aristotle's Four Causes

In order to account for change, Aristotle understood that one cause was not enough. There are four causes that go into a complete or sufficient explanation of change. For example, consider the simple change of a sculptor who changes marble from a cube to a statue of a dove. The marble is not enough to account for the change, for the matter by itself does not completely explain the new product. One requires further causes. There are four in total. These are:

The **agent** cause - that by which there is coming to be.
The **formal** cause - that for the sake of which there is coming to be.
The **material** cause - that from which there is coming to be.
The **final** cause - that for the sake of which there is coming to be.

In the change from marble cube to marble dove, the agent cause, or that by which there is a change, is the sculptor himself. He is the agent who moves the marble from being potentially a dove to being actually a marble dove.

But in order to carry out the change, the agent cause (the sculptor) requires something further, namely that for the sake of which he will act. He requires a form that the marble at this point does not have, namely the form of a dove. Without a form, there is no reason to act, that is, there is nothing for the sake of which to move. "Dove" is the formal cause, or that for the sake of which the change takes place.

Considered in themselves, however, forms do not change. "Triangle" or "cube" does not change except in as much as such forms exist in matter. In other words, only marble cubes or wooden triangles or metal rectangles can undergo change. Try destroying "triangularity" or "circularity". We cannot, unless they exist in matter. Then and only then can we destroy them, such as burn a wooden triangle in a fire, or melt a square sign made of metal. And so the sculptor cannot move to sculpt a dove unless he has before him some matter, or that from which there is coming to be—in this case, the marble.

Finally, the agent cause acts for a purpose, that is, an end. The final cause (purpose or end) is defined as that for the sake of which there is coming to be. Notice, however, that this definition coincides with that of the formal cause. That is why Aristotle points out that the final cause is twofold. There is a) the end of the **generation** and b) the end of the **generated**. The end of the generation or change is the fully formed dove in the marble; for that is when the agent stops working; thus, the end of the generation coincides with the formal cause. The end of the generated, however, is the ultimate end or purpose of his action. In other words, what is the ultimate reason why is he making a dove? We'll say he is making it as an anniversary gift to his parents. "Anniversary gift" is the end of the generated, the purpose or end of his action.

Notice also that the final cause is the cause of all the other causes. It is "anniversary gift" that moves the sculptor to be an agent cause. A sculpture that lasts a day is not all that wonderful, so instead of using a type of matter that will not last, such as chocolate, he uses one that will last a long time as well as one that is pleasing to look at. And so we can see how the final cause plays a fundamental role in determining the material cause. The final cause also plays a role in determining the form. If his parents like doves and his goal is to please them with an anniversary gift, a marble dove is a nice idea, as opposed to a cobra snake or a skull.

Chapter 17: Aristotle's Hylomorphic Doctrine

To come to an understanding of accidental change using the four causes is relatively easy, but to understand Aristotle's explanation of substantial change (chemical change) is extremely difficult. In fact, I would argue that Aristotle's hylomorphic doctrine (his doctrine of matter and form) is the most difficult of all philosophical ideas to grasp, but I am convinced that it is highly relevant and accurately explains substantial change—although I would argue that it takes years to begin to fully appreciate it, for old habits are difficult to replace. The only way to understand this doctrine, however, is through analogy.

An analogy is a ratio of one thing to another, a comparison of two things that are the same in one respect, though different in other respects. For example, 3 is to 6 as 20 is to 40, or fall is to leaves as winter is to snow. 20 and 40 are different numbers than 3 and 6, but there is similarity of proportion between them; so too, there is a proportion between fall/leaves and winter/snow. If a person has never seen winter and snow before, we could provide some understanding through an analogy using what he already knows: "As fall is to leaves, so too is winter to snow". Although he is still unable to form a picture of winter and snow in his imagination, he comes to some understanding as a result of that analogy.

This brings me to an important point that must be made before we go any further. There is a region that we are about to explore, but it is one where the imagination has no access. The intellect, however, has access, it can penetrate this veil, like light, but the imagination is a power that is too large to fit through the pores of this veil, so to speak. In other words, the intellect alone can grasp the ultimate principles that constitute material substance; the imagination cannot. That can be a very uncomfortable experience at first, because we are so used to "picturing" things, so much so that if we cannot form a picture of what it is we are trying to understand, we tend not to believe we have properly understood it. But that is not the case at all in philosophy. There are certain principles that are inaccessible to the imagination, but not the intellect.

To come to a correct understanding of matter, let us begin, as Aristotle does, by employing an analogy from the realm of art. Consider the bronze block that is sculpted by Auguste Rodin into *The Thinker*. Recall the doctrine of the four causes: a) agent cause, b) formal cause, c) material cause, and d) final cause. Two of these causes are intrinsic, while two are extrinsic. The two intrinsic causes are the material and formal cause (matter and form are in the sculpture). The two extrinsic causes are the agent and final cause (the agent is outside the sculpture, and the ultimate purpose for making it is also outside the sculpture, i.e., presenting it as a gift to someone). At this point, we will focus solely on the two intrinsic principles (material and formal cause) in order to come to an understanding of the two intrinsic principles of a substance, namely **prime matter** and **substantial form**.

Let it be said at the beginning that even though we treat bronze as if it is one substance, it is in fact an alloy of three metals (zinc, copper, and tin, in various percentages). For purposes of demonstration, Aristotle calls this matter (that an artist would use) **secondary matter** – what the modern science textbook usually refers to as matter, namely that which has mass and extension. The artist approaches the secondary matter, which has the shape (accidental form) of a cube. But the artist has another form in mind, namely the figure of *The Thinker*. He wishes to impose that form on the secondary matter. The matter (bronze), which is actually a cube, is in potentiality to a new form, namely *The Thinker*. It is not actually *The Thinker* yet, only potentially.

The artist, who is the agent cause, begins his work and after a period of time we have *The Thinker*. The matter has taken on or acquired a new form. It is no longer actually a cube, rather it is actually *The Thinker*. Still, it is potentially another sculpture—the artist may come along and chisel away at it, giving the matter the form of a banana, or a tree stump, etc.

Secondary matter (in this case, the bronze) is not what Aristotle means ultimately by matter. The reason is that for Aristotle, matter is pure potentiality. But the secondary matter, the bronze, is actually bronze. All secondary matter is actually some "thing" or substance. Pure matter is not actually anything, as I will try to explain. In the meantime, consider the relationship between the bronze and the various accidental forms that it (the bronze) is open to receiving. The bronze (material cause) is that which remains the same throughout the change, that is, it is the **subject** of the change. What does not endure is the form (in this case, the accidental form cube). But it is the bronze that **has** the form, that is, it is the bronze that is the subject of the form, and thus the subject of the entire change. It is always the material cause that endures as the subject throughout a change.

Moreover, the bronze is actually a cube by virtue of the form (cube) it possesses, but the bronze cube is potentially *The Thinker* not by virtue of the cube (the form), but by virtue of the bronze. It is because the cube exists in the bronze, which is the secondary matter, that it (the bronze cube) is potentially *The Thinker*. The secondary matter (the bronze) is the source of the thing's potentiality to be another sculpture. Hence, matter is openness to form. The form determines the work of art to be what it is, but it is the matter that **is determined by** the form. Once again, however, change is only possible because the form exists in matter. No one can change the form of cube to something else until that form exists in some sort of secondary matter, such as bronze, gold, or clay, etc. Matter, then, is the potential principle, and the potential principle is the subject of the form. On the other hand, form is the principle of actuality, that is, the determining principle that gives matter its intelligible structure.

Now let's move into that region where the imagination has no place, into to the realm of substance and substantial change. A substantial change is an absolute change, that is, a change of the entire substance itself. In other words, it is the secondary matter that changes to a completely different substance. Examples of substantial change include the change from wood to ash, bread to living human tissue, iron to rust, etc. Consider the change from iron to rust: Fe changes to Fe2 O3 (Hematite). Iron is a substance. It has certain accidents, such as quantity, quality, place, relativity, etc. As an example of quality, iron is malleable, that is, you can twist it and turn it without breaking it, it can be hammered into sheets, it is ductile, that is, it can be strewn out into wire, and it conducts an electric current.

As secondary matter, iron exists in potentiality to certain accidental forms, such as wire, or the hood of a car, etc. It is the iron that will endure throughout all these accidental changes. But what happens when the iron itself changes? What underlies the change in that case? In other words, what is the underlying matter of a substantial change? What is the subject of the change from iron to rust? In this case, it is not a change of accidental form, such as the shape of the iron; it is the entire substance that is being transformed. The word "transform" is important here, because it indicates precisely what is happening when change occurs. In an accidental change, it is the composite of secondary matter and accidental form that changes, but the secondary matter endures. Similarly, in a substantial change, it is the composite of prime matter and substantial form that changes, while primary matter endures.

What is Prime Matter?

Prime matter is the ultimate matter of a material substance. Considered in itself, it is nothing other than potentiality. Prime matter receives its intelligible determination from the substantial form, and the composite of the two is the substance. The substantial form is the intelligible structure of the substance, or as in the case of iron, it is the "ironness". Now, ironness is just a word, but it expresses *the intelligible structure* that we apprehend when we know what iron is. The substance iron is itself a composite of prime matter (pure potentiality) and substantial form (the intelligible density or intelligible nature of iron). The substance is a unity of potency and act, or prime matter and substantial form.

These two principles, potency and act, are not "things" that one can picture in the imagination. They are real principles that can only be understood by means of analogy. The whole substance iron is actually something, but potentially something else. It is actually something, namely iron, by virtue of the substantial form, but it is potentially something else (i.e., rust) by virtue of the prime matter. Or, to put it another way, prime matter is precisely that potentiality of the whole substance to be something else entirely.

How are the two principles related to one another? As bronze (secondary matter) is to the accidental form *The Thinker*, prime matter is to the substantial form "ironness". As the accidental form *The Thinker* determines the bronze to be the sculpture that it is, the substantial form "ironness" determines prime matter to be what it is (the substance iron). As secondary matter underlies and is the subject of an accidental change, prime matter underlies and is the subject of substantial change. And just as a bronze statue is potentially something else by virtue of the bronze, a substance is mutable by virtue of its prime matter; for mutability is nothing but the potentiality to be something else. If a substance is potentially something else, for example, if wood is potentially ash, then wood has a potential principle. That potential principle of a substance is what we mean by prime matter.

But, though one can see and touch bronze, or wood, or soap stone, and actually observe the change over time, one cannot see and touch prime matter. And just as one does not find secondary matter without it possessing some sort of accidental form, i.e., planks, or board, or splinters, etc., so too prime matter cannot exist without a substantial form of one kind or another. What exists in the world primarily are substances, which are potency/act unities, that is, composites of prime matter and substantial form. If prime matter, which is pure potentiality, could exist without a substantial form, which is the principle of actuality, then prime matter would not be actually anything; for a substance is actually something determinate and intelligible by virtue of the substantial form. Hence, it is not possible to know prime matter directly.

A Closer Look at Substantial Form

To come to know a substance is to come to know *what* it is. Hence, a substance has a "whatness". That is, a substance is always a certain kind of thing. That is why we can ask the question: what is it? In other words, it has form, or idea (*eidos*), a certain intelligible nature (*physis*). According to Aristotle, the substantial form is in the substance, not in some separated World of Forms, as we saw in Plato. The substantial form is that principle that determines the substance to be what it is. This is not something that one can imagine or form a picture of, rather it is intelligible. Just as one cannot picture beauty, for beauty is an intelligible idea, not something sensible, so too the substantial form is not something sensible, but is the intelligible content of a substance (i.e., bovine, feline, humanness, ironness, treeness, goldness, etc.). Hence, substantial form is not located in any place, rather, it is the total quantified and qualified substance that occupies place. The substantial form is not located in any part of the substance, rather, every part of the substance shares in the whole form. For example, every part of my body is human. Also, only an already constituted substance has parts, i.e., sub-atomic parts, molecules, etc. But the substantial form is not a part alongside other parts. It is a principle, not a part. It is the intelligible principle of the substance. The substantial form is prior to quantity, for it is the formal principle of the whole substance itself. The substance, for example, gold, carbon, hydrogen, or water, has a certain nature (*physis*), it is a certain kind of thing (*genos*), it has an essence that I can come to know by studying its behavior or how it acts or reacts. The substantial form is a real principle of a substance, the principle of actuality, the formal principle, or the formal cause of the substance.

A Closer Look at Prime Matter

Keep in mind that substance is not the same as quantity, which is the first accident of a material substance. Nor is substance the same as quality. Quantity and quality, as well as every other accident, can change while the substance remains the same thing. Because iron has the accident of quantity, it has extension, that is, parts outside of parts that can be measured. The substance, though, is not itself the quantity. The substance considered in itself is prior to its quantity. So too is the substantial form; for the quantity of a substance, such as a living thing, may increase or decrease, but the living thing remains the same kind of thing (it is essentially the same thing).

And because the substance has accidental qualities, you and I can now perceive it, for it has color, solidity, smell, luster, it is smooth, one can twist it, etc. These qualities can change, however, while the substance remains the same. A tree can change color, water can change to ice, a plant can begin to smell nice, etc. Hence, quality is a distinct mode of being from substance. Affective qualities enable us to see and perceive a substance. But the qualities inhere in the substance, and so they depend upon the substance just like quantity depends upon and inheres in the substance (there is no large in itself; only large things).

Consider too that one cannot picture the substance in itself. One can only picture the substance when it has sense qualities as well as the other accidents. The substance does not exist separately from the accidents; nevertheless, the substance is distinct from its accidents.

But what is it in the substance that has the substantial form (ironness, or goldness, or feline, etc.)? The answer is that it is always matter that has form. It belongs to matter "to have", "to receive", to be actualized by, to be determined by an act, a form (an intelligible configuration). In our example above, the iron is not primary matter, for iron is a material substance. But it is prime matter that has the substantial form "ironness", and the unity of the two principles constitutes the substance, which in itself is not something that one can see and touch (one can only see and touch a quantified, qualified substance). The source or principle that renders a new substantial form possible (thus a new substance) is prime matter.

The substance gold is nothing other than prime matter *golding*, that is, having the substantial form of gold. The substance iron is nothing other than prime matter *ironing*. Without prime matter, the substantial form of gold would be unchanging, because forms in themselves do not change. But the substance gold is mutable. Iron, too, changes to rust. The mutability of substances is nothing other than their potentiality to absolute change. This radical potentiality is what prime matter is.

Can one see prime matter? No, one can only see a qualified/quantified substance. Can one measure prime matter? No, one can only measure what is quantified. Can one see substantial form? No, one can only see a qualified/quantified substance. Can one measure substantial form? Again, the answer is no, one can only measure a quantified substance. How do I know a substantial form is there if I can't see it? If there was no substantial form, one could not know *what* the substance is that one is trying to measure. Where is the substantial form located in a substance? It is not located anywhere. What has location is the whole quantified/qualified substance, or the internal parts of a substance, like the heart or liver. Location is place, an accident of an already constituted material substance. If the form is nowhere, could it be everywhere in the substance? Yes, the whole substance is gold, every part is gold. The form is found in every part, just as the substantial form of man is found in every part of man.

Why Reductionistic Materialism is Insufficient as an Explanation of Matter

Those with good minds for science tend to think in a reductionist framework, because the scientific method is essentially reductionist—one comes to know the whole by studying its parts. Consequently, these people quite naturally tend to think that it is the parts that determine a thing to be what it is. For example, some will speak about DNA as if it is the DNA that determines man to be what he is. But "parts" belong to the accident of quantity, and accidents do not determine a substance to be the kind of thing it is, for the accidents can change while the substance remains the same.

Consider quantity, for a moment, which is the extension of the substance into parts outside of parts; one part is not another part, which is not another part, which is not another part, etc. For example, your arm is not your leg, this cell is not that cell, etc. But the substantial form exists whole and entire in every part. For example, your finger is not partially human, but completely human; your toe is not partially human, etc. Hence, the form is not the parts. You have one form (you are one kind of thing), but many parts.

Hence, atoms don't make things to be what they are; neither do cells, nor DNA, etc. Rather, the substantial form determines you to be what you are. Also, parts do not unify themselves any more than the parts of an army unify themselves. Rather, they are unified by a unifying principle. A unifying principle is not many - that would be a contradiction; a unifying principle is one, but the parts are many. The unifying principle of a living organism is the substantial form, for wherever we find unity, we find form. Now the substantial form of an organism cannot be many, otherwise a thing would "actually" be many things, which is a contradiction.

Let's look at this in more detail. Quantity is the first accident of a material substance. Quantity is not itself the substance, otherwise a change in quantity would amount to a change in substance. Considered in itself, the substance is not extended. It is capable of extension, but the substance becomes actually extended only through the accident of quantity. Prime matter is not that which has mass and extension; rather, that which has mass and extension is an already constituted substance (a matter/form unity). That which has mass and extension is an intelligible thing or substance, which itself is a potency/act unity. This thing or substance considered in itself, prior to its accidents, is not something that the empiriological sciences can explain or even investigate directly. This is the first point that all mechanistic explanations fail to realize. The mechanistic approach takes quantified material substance for granted and attempts to explain the material world on that level alone. This makes for good science, but bad philosophy.

To get a better handle on this, consider that quantity is divided into continuous quantity (extension) and discrete quantity. Everything in the sensible world has size or extension. Any sensible object is spread out in the three dimensions of length, breadth, and thickness. As was said, the substantial form (nature) of the substance is found whole and entire in every part of a thing's extension (i.e., every part of a man's body is human, and every part of the iron is equally metal). Its extension, on the other hand, is not found whole and entire in each part. Rather, one part is not found in another, but outside the other. Every part of the human body will possess the same substantial nature as any other part, but not the same extension. The parts really coincide in nature substantially; but they do not coincide in their extension, for each part really lies outside the others. Hence, the substance is not the parts, nor the totality of parts that constitute the thing's extension or quantity. The substance has parts, but is not the sum of its parts.

Parts are divided into heterogeneous (i.e., bone, marrow, muscle, nerves) or homogeneous (as in iron or gold). Now it is not the bone, the muscle, nerves etc., that make up the human substance. These parts are already human parts; that is, they are parts of a human thing (person). The parts receive their nature, their intelligible structure from the form of the substance, not vice versa. And so, it is not the DNA that makes up the substance. The DNA is part of a human cell, and it is already human DNA. It is the whole substance that determines the parts to be what they are.

The habit that inclines us to conceive of this the other way around (i.e., parts determining the whole substance) simply comes from the world of artifacts. We build things, for instance, as children we built things with blocks, Lego, and later on we build bookshelves, furniture, etc. But when it comes to constructing anything artificially, the parts that will determine the thing we are building pre-exist the whole. We have the Lego pieces in front of us, then we proceed to add part outside of part, increasing the quantity of parts, eventually building a wall, a floor, a roof, etc., until the whole comes into being. The whole is the result of bringing together the pre-existing parts, thus the whole is a conglomeration of parts.

The artifact, however, is not really one entity, that is, it is not substantially one. It is not a thing in itself, or a substance. Rather, it is accidentally one; the parts that make up the whole are themselves distinct substances. In other words, artifacts do not have a substantial nature that is whole and entire in every part. My computer screen is glass, while the back of my computer is metal, etc.

The problem with atomism is that it treats what is radically and substantially one as if it was accidentally one and merely the sum of its parts. But a dog, for example, is radically one, that is, it is one substance with one nature, found entire in every part of the dog. The paw is not partially canine, while the tail is partially canine, etc. Rather, every part is wholly canine, and every part is part of the whole dog. The substantial form of the dog is the principle that determines the whole dog to be what it is, namely a living sentient canine substance. Its DNA is responsible for the inheritable traits of the dog, but DNA is not prior to the whole, rather, the whole is prior—the parts depend upon the whole as accidents depend upon substance. The parts of a natural substance are consequent upon the whole, that is, parts *of the* whole. And so it is the whole that determines the parts.

Moreover, reductionism begs the question. Consider the attempt to explain the whole by appealing to its material parts. The material parts, however, need explaining. If the matter is explained by appealing to its parts, how are the parts to be explained? If one continues to appeal to something outside the thing one is trying to explain, one will never end up explaining that which one is trying to explain. Eventually one will have to come up against one thing that exists in itself—we should keep in mind that for reductionists, the cat is not a thing in itself, ultimate constituent parts (atoms?) are what exist primarily. But that ultimate part itself needs explaining. How do we explain its intelligibility and its mutability? If we appeal to its parts, as if the atom, for example, were nothing but the sum of its parts and not a thing in itself, then we are left having to explain these parts. If we maintain that there is an actual infinity of constituents, then there is nothing that exists in itself. In the end, everything is simply a potential something, but not an actual anything. The result is that everything is outside of itself, as a painting is something outside of its matter. And just as a painting has no intrinsic intelligibility, but has only what we recognize, similarly, the universe will have no intrinsic intelligibility or meaning.

Chapter 18: A Historical Note on Reductionistic Materialism

Reductionistic materialism began back in the Pre-Socratic era (ca. early 5th century BCE), and it was resurrected again in the modern world thanks to Rene Descartes. It began with Parmenides, the first metaphysician -- metaphysics is the study of being and its properties, as opposed to physics (*physis*), which is the study of nature. Parmenides argued that the world as we see it is an illusion; multiplicity is an illusion, as well as change and time. He argued that what all things have in common is "being" ('is' is the most fundamental thing we can say about all things). If all things have being in common, what is to distinguish one being from another? It will have to be something outside of what things have in common; for we distinguish one thing from another not on the basis of what the two have in common, but on the basis of what two things do not have in common. Now, since all things have being in common, what distinguishes one being from another will be something outside of being. But outside of being is "non-being"; and non-being is "nothing". Hence, nothing distinguishes one being from another. Thus being is one, and multiplicity is an illusion of sensation.

He also argued that change is impossible, because to change is to "come into being" and to "go out of being" (from 'is' to 'is not'). But outside of being is "non-being" or nothing, and it is impossible to go into nothing, for there is nothing to go into. It is also impossible to come into being, because that implies that what came into being was outside of being, but outside of being is "non-being" or nothing. And since time is grounded in change, time is likewise an illusion.

If this sounds strange, then you probably know how many of the early Greek philosophers felt in the face of this. But they were unable to refute Parmenides; his argument seemed irrefutable. The sentiment was that "if you can't beat 'em, join 'em"; so they went half way. Empedocles and Democritus were both convinced that change was not an illusion and that it can be explained. So what Empedocles did was simple. He saw that Parmenides argued convincingly that being is one, unchanging, material, spherical (for a reason that is difficult to explain), and indivisible. To preserve common sense (the reality of change), Empedocles reversed a few things and argued that being is therefore matter, and matter is spherical, and it is unchanging and indivisible. Being now becomes the particle of matter (a small sphere of indivisible matter). And according to Empedocles, there are four types of particles, namely the elements: air, earth, fire and water (Empedocles would readily accept that there are in fact 118 of them and that fire, earth and water are not elements). So, for Empedocles, change is now explainable; these particles of matter conglomerate and form wholes (i.e., what we call cats, dogs, people, trees, etc.). The particles do not change. Why? Because Parmenides reasoned that being does not change. But the "wholes" do change. The whole is nothing other than the sum of its parts. So everything is merely a conglomeration of the particles of elements. We see this today in the ordinary chemistry book that depicts man as 65% Oxygen, 10% Hydrogen, 18% Carbon, 3% Nitrogen, etc.

Democritus comes along and notes that Empedocles does not explain the differences in the elements themselves. How does one account for the fact that one element is different than another? Democritus argues as well that wholes come to be and pass away and that the constituent parts do not, but he goes back to the Pythagoreans, who argued that number was the substance of things. Everything is reducible to number, and number is ultimately the geometric point. The line is made up of points, and the surface is made up of lines, etc. Even numbers produce oblong figures, odd numbers produce square figures, etc.

The elements are really arrangements of number. Fire is a composite of whole numbers (which form triangles), earth is a composite of square numbers, etc. Democritus was drawn to this, but he too was unable to refute Parmenides. So he joined the two together, endowing the numbers of Pythagoras with the properties of Parmenides' being. So, at the basis of reality we have these discrete quantities that are indivisible, unchanging, impenetrable, have shape and position in empty space. And so reality is made up of being and non-being. Non-being is the void, or empty space, and being is the "indivisible", or in Greek "atomai", or atoms. The atom is the indivisible particle that is a pure quantity. What distinguishes one atom from another (i.e., air from fire) is quantity and shape (like Pythagoras, quantity is the basis of reality). The only properties an atom has are size, shape, impenetrability and position in space. The atoms of one element are alike in size and shape. The rest of the world is merely a conglomeration of atoms, which move through empty space and cluster and mechanically link up with one another by accident. So, the whole changes, but not the parts.

So, the whole is nothing other than the sum of its parts. Being is the atom, not your dog, or cat, or you, or the oak tree in the backyard (these are merely the results of unguided processes that occur on the atomic level). Being is on the level of the particle, or the atom. This is the reductionistic habitus.

What Aristotle shows is that it isn't the atom that is the primary mode of being, but substance. We live in a world of substances. The atom is the smallest part of an element. The atom is really a substance. But so too are you, and your dog, and the apple tree, a molecule of water, etc. A substance, he will argue, is a whole that is not determined by its parts. Rather, it is the whole that determines the parts. The whole is more than the sum of its parts. Substances are potency and act unities. Things have form, or intelligible structure, or substantial quality, which is very different than the non-substantial qualities, such as color, taste, texture, smell, figure, etc. These non-substantial qualities can change while the substance endures or remains the same. Matter for Aristotle, as you are now aware, is potentiality. He will argue for an ultimate matter, which isn't an atom, but pure potentiality.

Now quantity, he will argue, is the first "accident" of a material substance. Accident is a non-substantial mode of being, such as where, when, posture, quality, action, passivity, relation, etc. These can change, while the substance remains the same. Substances exist in place, for example, and they change place, but they remain the same substance (walking to the store and back). A substance can change in quality, or posture, but endure through the change. Water freezes, but it is still water. These are non-substantial changes. A substance can change in quantity, and yet remain the same substance. If substance and quantity were identical, then a quantitative change would amount to a substantial change. To gain 100 pounds would be to become a different substance. But quantity gives us more of the same thing. Furthermore, the "whatness" of a substance is not its quantity. Rather, the "whatness" is its nature, its substantial form. When we ask the question "what is it?" we are asking about its essential quality, not its accidental quantity.

But to explain substantial change is much more difficult. Aristotle argues that substantial change is not merely the rearranging of atoms on the atomic level. This is because the substance or entity is not merely a multiplicity of atoms, but a real being that is really one and indivisible. Change is a "transformation". Note the word "trans" and "form"; change is a change in form, and not an absolute coming into being and going out of being, as Parmenides thought. The substance is a substantial form existing in what he calls first matter (or pure potentiality). A substantial change involves a change in substantial form. Matter, which has intelligible form, acquires another intelligible form.

A substance, according to this Aristotelian perspective, is far more mysterious than most people tend to think. If substance is distinct from quantity and sense qualities, then how do we come to know substance itself? David Hume (1711-1776) played with this and ended up denying substance. He argued that things are just conglomerations of sense impressions, a position contrary to common sense, but consistent with his strict empiricism. But for Aristotle, substance is intelligible, and so it is the intellect that grasps substance, while the senses grasp the sensible properties of things. So, if we were to define matter as that which has mass and extension, as our science books typically do, then it would follow that substance is more immaterial than material.

We define matter that way today (mass and extension) thanks to Rene Descartes (1596-1650). He was a mathematical physicist and philosopher who tried to establish an absolutely certain philosophy that everyone would agree with, as they agree mathematics. This led to his famous "method of doubt". Descartes arbitrarily established the principle that we should be able to apprehend one thing clearly and distinctly apart from another to be assured that the two are really different and that the one can be created without the other. He then begins to ask what it is that we perceive clearly and distinctly as an indispensable attribute of material things, so that all other attributes, properties, and qualities are seen to presuppose it and depend upon it. For Desacrtes, this is extension. He assumes that the principal attribute constitutes the nature of the thing. So, matter is essentially quantity, for Descartes.

Aristotle would not have allowed this. Nevertheless, this identification of material substance with extension gave rise to modern atomism (Hobbes, Gassendi, etc.), and thus modern reductionism.

Reductionism produced great things for science, but it could not explain "things", or change, as Aristotle demonstrated. Reductionism makes for good science, but it is bad philosophy. For one thing, it led to that branch of psychology known as "Behaviourism", which ends up denying our ability to make free and self-determined choices, among other things.

But reductionism is rooted in false premises (Pythagoras' number and Parmenides' notion of being and change, as well as Descartes identification of substance with extension). Change, as Aristotle shows, is the fulfillment of what exists potentially insofar as it exists potentially. It is not, as Parmenides argued, coming into being and going into non-being. Nor is it merely the rearrangement of atoms in space. It is the realization of potency to act, that is, potential being to actual being.

Consider the following insight by mathematician Rudy Rucker:

> "A human body changes most of its atoms every few years. Daily one eats and inhales billions of new atoms, daily one excretes, sheds, and breathes out billions of old ones. Physically, my present body has almost nothing in common with the body I had twenty years ago. Since I feel that I am still the same person, it must be that "I" am something other than the collection of atoms making up my body. "I" am not so much my atoms as I am the PATTERN in which my atoms are arranged. Some of the atom patterns in my brain code up certain memories; it is continuity of these memories that gives me my sense of personal identity."

If Aristotle were to comment on this, he'd say yes, the "I" is the substance that I am, which is not the same as the parts (quantity gives us "parts outside of parts"), or atoms. That "PATTERN" Rucker refers to is what Aristotle would call the substantial form that determines the substance to be what it is. The parts are what they are by virtue of that form. In other words, your parts are human parts, your DNA is human DNA, human cells, human tissue, etc., because the substantial form is the form of the whole, including the parts of the whole. Or, let's put it this way: one part is outside of another part, and so one cannot say that this part exists whole and entire in every part. But we can say that the form "human" exists in every part, since every part is human. Parts do not determine the whole (substance), as they do in the world of artifacts (i.e., the computer, the automobile, the television, etc.). The whole determines the parts. And so one can say that you are not human because you have human DNA, rather, you have human DNA because you are human. A man is not alive because his organs are alive, rather his organs are alive because he is alive (the whole determines the parts).

On the subatomic level, differences in quantities can and often do lead to differences in quality, such as substantial quality, or substantial form. As we move towards the subatomic level, this becomes more and more the case, and I think there is a reason for this.

Contrary to the reductionist mind frame, "being" is not the atom. It is the macroscopic level that is more real than the atomic or subatomic level. The reductionist tends to see the subatomic level as the primary level, the most real and the ultimate locus of causality. But as we move towards that subatomic level, we are moving towards a level that is poorer in property and more open to determination. For example, the electron is more open to determination (potential) than the atom, the atom more open to further determination than the molecule, the molecule more open or more potential than a flower, etc. Allow me to draw an analogy. Consider the following:

A book is made up of parts, the parts are made up of chapters, the chapters are made up of paragraphs, the paragraphs are made up of sentences, the sentences are made up of phrases and words, and the words are made up of letters. When a novelist writes the book, he begins by writing a letter, such as the letter "t". When we read the book, we begin with the first letter of the first word. The novel comes to be at the end of the writing process, and our understanding of it is relatively complete at the end of the reading process.

But it is the whole that comes first absolutely (the whole is prior not in terms of time, but in the order of dependence). A letter of the alphabet, i.e., "c", is more open to determination (has more potentiality, or less actual meaning) than is a word, i.e., "cool", and a word is more open to determination than a phrase, such as "cool glass of water", but a phrase is more open, has more potentiality, than the full sentence: "After a jog on a hot day, you should be sure to replenish yourself with a cool glass of water". A full sentence, however, is more open to determination than is a paragraph. We do not think one letter at a time, nor do we think one word at a time. We think of an entire idea, and then we think of the best way to express that idea, searching as we do for the proper matter (the right words).

To be less open to determination is to have more meaning. A letter is very poor in property and has far less intelligibility (meaning) than a word. The letter "e" means much less than the word "love" or "truth". When the letter "e" becomes part of the word "love", it becomes part of a larger whole, with far more meaning than the letters "e" "l" "v" "o" taken separately. We can do a lot more with the letter "e" than we can do with the word "love", precisely because "e" has greater indeterminacy, that is, less intelligibility and thus less meaning. "Love" has greater intelligibility, that is, more definition than the letter "e".

If I were to ask a group of students to write any meaningful word using the letter "e", they'd have no difficulty. Ask them to write anything using the word "love", and they would have to think a little harder. Ask them to write something that incorporates the phrase "love is blind", and they'd have to think even harder, but they could do it. But ask them to write an entire paragraph that incorporates the sentence: "A certain kind of love is blind, for it is passion that has a tendency to blind the intellect, and so the kind of love that blinds is an emotion, not an act of the will", and they'd spend much more time thinking about how to incorporate it into a larger idea. They'd need to think of a much larger meaning (idea), one that exceeds the limited intelligibility of the part; for the meaning of that sentence exceeds that meaning contained in the phrase "love is blind". "Love is blind" is open to further determination, but it does not and cannot determine itself to that larger end, an end that gives full expression to the idea contained in the full sentence above. Rather, it must be determined by something that possesses that larger meaning. The simple phrase does not possess it, just as the word "love" does not possess the idea contained in "love is blind". Considered in itself, the part does not possess the meaning of the whole; otherwise it would be the whole. The part is made to serve the whole through the whole, by existing as part of the whole.

Shakespeare conceives the whole before writing, and it is the intelligible whole that determines and shapes every part of the play, i.e., the letters, the words, the phrases, the sentences, the paragraphs, the scenes, the acts, etc. The intelligible whole that Shakespeare conceives is not in the book, but remains within him - it is part of his interior. But existing natures (beings) have their own interior; they have their own nature (only an intelligent creature, man, is intelligently conscious of that interior).

Now, as we move towards the subatomic level, we are moving towards a level that is real, but not as rich in property. The realities we discover at this level have a greater openness to determination (potentiality). For example, the electron is more open to determination (more potential) than the atom, the atom more open to further determination than the molecule, and larger more complex molecules have more potential than a flower, etc. In other words, the atom has less potentiality (more definition) than the electron (the electron is a part of it; if it is not a part of it, it is potentially a part of it, but actually a whole unto itself, but poorer in property than an atom). A protein molecule has less potentiality than a carbon atom, and a horse has less potentiality (more meaning) than a protein molecule.

Now just as the idea of the entire novel determines the configuration of each part, not vice versa, so too does the substantial form of a material being communicate its own intelligible configuration to every part of that being. The parts do not determine the whole, and the whole is not an effect of the parts, for that would suggest the parts are prior to the whole, which means they would be wholes unto themselves. But they can only be parts if they cease to be wholes. If four beings resisted the pressure to relinquish their existence to become parts of a greater whole, but combined with one another, the result would be four beings, not one.

Now, once a novel or play has been read, we finally come to understand it; for we only understand something when we know it as a whole. All the parts of the novel serve the whole, the single idea that exists in the mind of Shakespeare. But after a time, the reader forgets the details. Nevertheless, he knows the novel or play as a whole: "I know that book, I've read it before", he says. "So I'd like to read something I don't know. Let me look for another book." After a few years, he might decide to re-read the novel. His initial knowledge of the whole begins to acquire a greater precision, perhaps one he once had, but lost over time.

It is the knowledge of the whole that is always the condition for the possibility of knowing its parts. At the beginning, it is knowledge of a relative whole (i.e., the sentence in relation to the words, the paragraph in relation to the sentences, or the chapter in relation to the paragraphs) that is the condition for the possibility of understanding the parts we are reading. Unless I understand each word within the order of the whole sentence, I do not understand what I am reading. The words have meaning, that is, a direction or movement forward towards an end. Each move forward brings me closer to the whole idea (either of the sentence, or of the paragraph, or of the chapter, or of the whole novel). Each whole enables me to understand each part of it completely.

The entire meaning contained in "love is blind" allows me to grasp the particular nuance given to the word "love"; it enables me to understand something about love, in particular, something the author wishes to convey to me about it. By itself, the word "love" does not convey that larger meaning. But consider our previous example: "A certain kind of love is blind, for it is passion that has a tendency to blind the intellect, and so the kind of love that blinds is an emotion, not an act of the will". My understanding of "love is blind" is much more complete, it is far more nuanced and somewhat richer, in light of the whole for the sake of which it was phrased. If, as a result of a loss of memory, I cannot retain the words in order to discern the movement or direction in the writing, I end up knowing each part in isolation from the whole. Hence, I cannot grasp the whole.

But the whole idea determined each part, which is why each part together moves forward to convey the overall meaning. If my memory works, I remember the whole word, the whole two words, the whole three words, the whole four words, and the meaning, which always exceeds them individually, gradually comes to light. The words only exist in view of the whole, and the whole determines the sequence of the words, providing them with their moving power, that is, their ability to carry the reader along.

Now, the greater the potentiality or openness to determination a thing has, the greater is its poverty, and the greater a thing's poverty, the less causal power it enjoys. In other words, the greater the indeterminacy of a thing, such as the letter 'a' in comparison to the meaning of a complete novel, the less it has to impart. It has, rather, a greater openness to receive a richer determination.

As reality moves towards the quantum level, it moves towards a level of greater poverty or indeterminacy - which is consistent with the popular designation of Heisenberg's uncertainty principle as the 'indeterminacy' principle. To deny causality on this level is not entirely irrational, for in light of the principles we've been discussing, perhaps it is to be expected. But the quantum level is no more the cause of what takes place on the ordinary macroscopic level than the letters of the alphabet are the cause of the novel.

It is the idea of the novel (the story) that is the final and formal cause of the novel; the words and sentences are determined by it and are ordered to serve it, that they may communicate it. In other words, the story is not an emergent property; rather, it is the parts that express the entire idea that emerge as an effect of a prior cause.

This order that the analogy of the novel uncovers is an order that exists with respect to every "whole", every being, every substance on the periodic table as well as every living entity. An empiriometric understanding of the physical universe at any level is genuine and real, but it is not and cannot be an ultimate explanation, that is, an explanation in terms of first causes. The empiriometric sciences are an intelligible account of secondary causes (i.e., the heart really pumps blood, DNA really brings about certain traits in an organism, etc.) that presuppose the existence of intelligible natures in the first place.

Our understanding of the relationship between quantity and the essential nature of things begins at the pre-scientific level, and when we do science, we always do science within the framework of a large network of pre-scientific knowledge. At the pre-scientific level, "what a thing is", that is, its nature, is always prior to quantity.

Chapter 19: Aristotle on the Soul

Aristotle's understanding of the soul is very different from that of Plato, who was a dualist; this means that he regarded the soul as one substance, the body as another distinct substance. Hence, for Plato, man is two substances. This is not the case of Aristotle. Man is one substance; he is a psychosomatic unity (psyche: soul; soma: body).

We have already reasoned that if a thing were alive by virtue of its matter, all material things would be living. But clearly this is not the case. And so a thing is alive by virtue of a principle that is not matter, that is, an immaterial principle. This principle is not a substance, but the formal principle of a substance.

Consider the doctrine of the four causes while we employ an analogy from the realm of art or production. A computer engineer gets an idea for a unique type of computer. The first thing he does is to produce a blueprint. He then purchases the matter in order to produce the parts of this computer. He then begins to build his motherboard, sound card, video card, etc. After a week of work, he finishes his computer.

Now the agent cause in this case is the computer engineer; the material cause is the matter that went into making the parts; the formal cause is the very idea of the computer, and the final cause is the ultimate purpose of the computer.

Now, looking at this computer, let us ask ourselves: "Where is the form of the computer?" The answer is not in the computer, but in the mind of the engineer. The form is the "idea" (*eidos*) that he originally conceived. Without that "idea" or form, there is no computer. The engineer could not have gone to work organizing the matter into a unique computer without the idea that governed his action. It was the form in his mind that directed the organization of the matter. The form in his mind was the organizational or unifying principle of this new computer.

Now, imagine if that computer were able to build itself, without the help of the engineer. Imagine it creating its own parts, placing them in their proper place, etc. We'd be astounded at such a thing. But that is exactly what happens in living organisms. They self-organize. The fetus in the womb, for example, takes non-living matter from the mother and builds its own spinal cord, brain, organs, etc.

The reason is that the form is not in the mind of some person. Rather, the form is in the organism itself. That is why it is called an organism; note how the word 'organism' is related to the word 'organized'. The form is the organizational or unifying principle of the building process; the "idea" in the mind of the computer engineer was the organizing source or principle of the building process. What is the principle of the bio-molecular unity in the living organism? In other words, what is the organizing principle of the living thing? According to Aristotle, it is the form within the organism, or what he calls the "substantial form". It is the function of the form to unify, or to organize, or to form matter. Recall in school when your teacher asked you all to "form a straight line". The command to "form a straight line" or "form a circle" was a command to organize yourselves into a particular form. Wherever we have form, we have unity. The soul is the "substantial form" of a living thing, and so the soul is the organizing principle of the living substance. That is why a corpse decomposes. It has been transformed. It is no longer a unified substance; it is lacking form, that is, a substantial form.

For Plato, forms are subsistent things that are eternal and which exist in some other world, an intelligible world of ideas. This sensible world is not fully real, for Plato. It was only created after the pattern of the world of forms. For Aristotle, this is not the case. Forms exist in substances. A thing is "what it is" by virtue of its form. The soul of a living substance is its substantial form, and so it is not that the soul is somewhere inside the body. Rather, there is no body without the soul. It is more true to say that the body is in the soul than it is to say that the soul is in the body.

Let us employ another analogy, one that makes reference to the structure of an army. An army has an ordered and organized structure. The principle of that organizational unity is the General (5 star). He has the plan, the strategy, and this plan is communicated to the 4 star General, then to the Lieutenant General, who is in charge of the Corp. The plan does not come from the companies. The companies receive their plan from the captain, who receives it from the colonel, who receives it from the brigadier general, who receives it from the major general, who receives it from the lieutenant general, who receives it from the General of the Army.

If the army is a unified whole, it is so by virtue of one unified plan or idea (form), and that one idea has its source in the General of the Army. Kill the General, and there is no unifying principle; the entire army would be left without a single plan of action. The companies would be left without organization, without unity or form, and so they could no longer work as a unity, but as individual companies with their own plan.

In the same way, the form is the organizing principle of the living body, and that form is in the organism. Just as the companies do not organize themselves, but receive their plan of action from a single principle (ultimately the General), so too the parts of the body are not the source of the organizational unity of the body. Rather, they receive their organization, their unity, from a single principle, namely, the substantial form.

The corpse is like the army without a General; it lacks organizational unity, which is why it decomposes (de-composition; lacking composition or unity). Each part does its own thing, goes its own way, so to speak. There is no longer a single form that unifies the entire substance, and so a corpse is not a single substance, but a conglomeration of many substances.

In sum, the soul is the substantial form of the body. It is the life principle of a living substance. It is that which makes the substance to be the kind of thing it is. Just as you cannot talk about a structured army as one thing, and a plan as another—for without the plan, there is no structured army—, in the same way you cannot talk about the body as one thing, and the soul as something else, for example, as something inside the body. Without a soul or form, there is no body.

Chapter 20: First and Second Act

Consider the following problem: Am I alive because I am breathing? Or, am I breathing because I am alive? If the answer is that I am alive because I am breathing, it would suggest that a living thing is its "activity". You might agree and point out that certain activity, such as metabolism (the interplay between catabolism and anabolism) constitutes the thing, such as the cell; for without metabolism, the cell is dead. Hence, a cell is alive because there is a metabolism. Since metabolism is a living activity, it would follow that activity (metabolism) determines the "thing" (i.e., the cell). In other words, the "thing" is primarily an activity - or series of activities (metabolism, breathing, growing, reproducing, etc.).

If a thing is nothing other than its activity, then there is no underlying or enduring 'thing', only various activities, like metabolism, breathing, etc. The "thing", i.e., the organism (i.e., dog) would seem to be nothing other than the name given to the final product; but there would be no entity as such, only activity. In other words, there is a predicate (growing, breathing, eating, etc.,) but no real subject. For example, "John is a thing that breathes" would be a misrepresentation of the facts. There is no single thing, "John". Substance is but a name.

If the answer to our original problem is that I am breathing because I am alive, then "things act". In other words, entity precedes activity. This thing "barks and runs" because it is first and foremost a dog that has a single life principle, determining it to be the kind of thing it is; that thing swims and breathes through gills because it is first and foremost a fish, which is a single thing that has a life principle.

The cell metabolizes, but metabolism is a self-perfective activity, which means it is an activity of a cell (entity) carried out for the sake of its own perfection. Self-perfective activity presupposes a subject of the activity that is distinct from its activity.

Activity is the realization of a thing's capabilities. There is no action without a subject to carry out the acting. It is the hand that waves, it is the finger that wiggles, it is the "person" that thinks, it is the organism that metabolizes, it is the cell that divides, etc. And that is why we ask the question: "What" is it that is growing? "What" is it that is breathing? When we ask such questions, we are asking: "What is the subject of those activities?" Thus, when a person shakes hands with or hugs another, he is not shaking a shake, or hugging a hug; he is shaking a hand, or hugging a person.

Some Points on the Powers of the Soul

We have seen that for Aristotle, the soul is the organizing or unifying principle of a living organism. Now wherever there is unity, there is form. Hence, the soul is the substantial form of the body. This implies, among other things, that it is not a separate substance, as it was for Plato. Rather, body and soul together constitute one living substance. Hence, man is a psychosomatic unity.

Now, we come to understand the nature of a thing through its activities, for a thing acts according to its nature, and so the acts of a thing reveal the thing's nature. For example, we understand that a plant is a living kind of thing because it grows, among other acts. Growth is an activity that belongs to living things. We understand that an entity is an animal because it moves from one place to another and can detect sounds, etc. The kind of activity a thing performs, such as locomotion and hearing, depends upon the kind of thing it is. Plants do not move from one place to another, nor do they detect sounds, for a plant is not an animal, but a plant, and it does not belong to the nature of a plant to be able to run, jump, hear or see, etc.

If a plant is actually growing (activity), then it follows that it has the power (potentiality) to grow. If I am actually typing, it follows that I have the power to type; if you are actually thinking, then it follows that you have the power to think. Activity, in other words, is the realization of a power (potentiality). And so it is the powers of a thing that are the immediate principles of the thing's activity. We call these powers faculties. These faculties or powers are actual potentialities, and so powers do not belong to the material principle of a substance, but to the formal principle of a substance, that is, they inhere in the substantial form of the organism; the substantial form or soul is the principle of actuality of a living thing. The substantial form of a plant, for example, has three distinct powers that are the proximate principles of the three distinct activities of growth, reproduction, and nutrition.

Now plant life is not the most complex kind of living thing in the physical universe. The next level up on the hierarchy of being is that of animal. This level includes the vegetative, but for Aristotle, this does not necessitate an added soul. An animal is one unified substance, having one substantial form, not two -- otherwise it would be actually two beings. But this one substantial form has many powers. Along with the powers of nutrition, reproduction and growth, the substantial form of a dog, for instance, has the powers of external and internal sensation. But higher than the animal level is the human level, which includes all the levels below it and surpasses them in the two specific powers of intellect and will.

Chapter 21: Happiness and the Good Life

Now that we have a better grasp of the nature of the soul, let's return to the question of happiness and what constitutes the good life. Aristotle's ethics is first and foremost an ethics of the good life. How does one achieve the good life? In order to answer this question, we must have some understanding of what is meant by "the good".

We begin with a description of "the good" as it is commonly understood by most of us. We speak of a good pen, a good computer, a good pair of skates, a good car, a lousy car, a lousy computer, etc. If we look carefully, we see that the good of a thing has to do with its operation. When a thing has a *proper* operation, the good of the thing and its well-being consist in that operation. The proper operation of a pen is to write, and so a good pen writes well. The proper operation of a knife is to cut food, so a good knife will cut well. The proper operation of a car is to drive efficiently, safely, smoothly, etc. So, a good car is one that drives well, that is, efficiently, safely, smoothly, etc.

Now, a substance operates or acts according to its nature. We know that a plant, for example, grows, reproduces and nourishes itself. A good plant is one that does these things fully, according to its innate capacity and is not hampered by disease or some other impediment to its well-being. Thus, it will look healthy and strong. An animal, however, is more than a plant; it has more power or powers. Specifically, an animal has the powers of sense knowledge (external and internal sensation) and the powers of sense appetite (concupiscible and irascible), as well as the power of locomotion. So, it is not enough for an animal to be able to grow, reproduce, and eat. A good animal will be one that functions according to the entire capacity of its nature. Hence, a good animal will sense well, be able to move well, possess a healthy appetite, etc. A good dog has an acute sense of smell and hearing, runs and fetches sticks, eats enough to sustain it, etc. Man, though, is much more than a brute animal. Man is specifically different than a brute in that he has the specific powers of intelligence (the ability to apprehend the natures of things) and will (desiring not merely sensible goods, but intelligible goods, such as truth, happiness, beauty, leisure, virtue, friendships, marriage and family, etc.). So, it is not enough that human beings sense well, run fast, and eat the right foods, etc. A good man is one who functions according to his nature, which is a rational nature. Hence, a good man is one who reasons well and chooses well.

A Note on Happiness

Aristotle said that every agent acts for an end (final cause). The ultimate end sought in every one of our actions is happiness. As Socrates knew so well, all men desire happiness. But the question is what exactly constitutes a happy life? Happiness will have something to do with a good life, and the good of a thing is in its final cause (the ends towards which a thing naturally tends).

Is it possible for a human person to achieve everything he has set out to achieve in life and in the end find himself unhappy? The facts suggest that it is indeed possible. If this is true, then it follows that happiness is not necessarily doing what you want to do, and that is a very striking point, if you think about it. It means that I am aware that I want happiness, and I have no choice in the matter, and yet what I think I want in life may not be what I want at all.

Is it possible to have a wife/husband, children, house, and a good job, and at the same time still be unhappy? Many of us have the intuition that, yes it is possible for such a one to find himself unhappy. If this is true, then it follows logically that happiness is not necessarily having a wife/husband, children, house, and a good job, etc.

Happiness, for Aristotle, is not a passivity (a passion), that is, it is not something that comes to us from the outside. Rather, happiness is an activity, that is, it is an interior achievement. It is an activity rooted in human choices. In other words, if someone is genuinely unhappy (which is more than being not pleased or feeling sorrow), it is because he has not chosen well. And if one is happy, it is only because he has chosen well. A good man is one who reasons well and chooses well; hence, a good man is a happy man. Happiness, according to Aristotle, is going to result from making choices that promote the fullness of one's nature; and human nature has specific powers that are open to being disposed well or perfected, namely, intellect, will, as well as two sensitive appetites: the concupiscible and irascible appetites. Human happiness or well-being is to be found in the perfection or right ordering of those human powers.

These particular powers of the soul are perfected by habits, which are dispositions that incline a power to a particular activity so that it is carried out easily and with pleasure. A good habit is a virtue, while a bad habit is a vice. Thus, happiness is activity in accordance with perfect virtue. Now virtue is two-fold: intellectual virtue (wisdom, science, understanding of first principles) and moral virtue (prudence, justice, fortitude, temperance). Moral virtues are habits that make their possessor morally good. Intellectual virtues, on the other hand, do not make a person morally good, but wise, or knowledgeable, or learned.

Contemplation

Happiness is the fulfillment of one's nature. But the highest power that renders us specifically different from brute animals is intelligence, that is, the ability to know, judge, and reason. And so human perfection or well-being will consist in the perfection of the intellect; as Aristotle writes: "All men by nature desire to know...For it is because of their wonder that men both now begin to philosophize and at first began to philosophize." The purpose of man's life consists in perfecting this sense of wonder. In other words, man's chief end in life, according to Aristotle, is to possess or contemplate truth, that is, to contemplate the highest things. The activity of contemplation is the highest activity in which a human person can engage. Consider the following words of Aristotle:

...the activity of our intelligence constitutes the complete happiness of man,... So if it is true that intelligence is divine in comparison with man, then a life guided by intelligence is divine in comparison with human life. We must not follow those who advise us to have human thoughts, since we are only men, and mortal thoughts, as mortals should; on the contrary, we should try to become immortal as far as that is possible and do our utmost to live in accordance with what is highest in us.

This is a remarkable insight. What Aristotle is exhorting us to do is to aspire after what is higher and larger than us, namely truth. But note how many people today choose not aspire to what is higher, but are in pursuit of what is in fact lower; consider the current preoccupation is genitalia in our culture. Consider how many shows and commercials are filled with sexual innuendo, as if the chief end in life is to achieve the perfect orgasm. The genitals are located below the waistline, and so most people are living for what is below, not above. Aristotle points out that our happiness lies in striving to be "immortal as far as that is possible", in other words, to emulate the gods.

The believing Catholic, Jew, or Muslim is able to see that what Aristotle says here is more true than he might have originally realized. We are immortal, as St. Thomas Aquinas will demonstrate. And so we really can strive to live like the angels, who eternally contemplate the beauty of God as He is in Himself. Indeed we must strive after immortality; for our destiny is know the highest being, which is God, and to contemplate the divine nature for all eternity.

But man is not an angel, that is, a pure spirit. Man is a rational animal (a psychosomatic unity). He has a host of powers in common with brutes; and it is precisely here where difficulties of the moral life come into play. Man has to contend with two sensitive appetites, namely the concupiscible and irascible appetites from which the entire network of human emotions arise. The concupiscible power has as its object a sensible good simply apprehended as such, i.e., a steak or a cold drink, etc. Often, however, we experience difficulty in achieving a good (the steak is very expensive). The good then becomes a difficult good, and it is this difficult or arduous good that is the object of the irascible appetite. The concupiscible appetite gives rise to the emotions of love, desire, pleasure, hate, aversion, and sadness; while the irascible appetite gives rise to the emotions of hope, despair, daring, fear, and anger.

Order vs. Disorder

Sometimes the appetites rebel against reason. But man, if he is to be fully human, must act in accordance with reason, that is, in accordance with what is highest in him. Sometimes a person might give up easily when things become difficult, or he might run when there is danger. Sometimes a person cannot hold a job because he has no self-control over alcoholic drink, or he has no control over his sexual appetite, and so can think of nothing other than sex. Sometimes it is reasonable to take risks, but fear might incline a person to take the safe path, and the result of his lack of reasonable daring is that the end demanded by reason is not achieved. The appetites, if they are not controlled, can wreak havoc in our lives; they can move us to do irrational things. Moreover, Aristotle pointed out that as a person is, so does he see. In other words, our character, which is determined by the moral choices that we make, affects the way we see and interpret the world. A morally deficient character will result in a disordered mind.

The good life begins by bringing order to one's life. A good life is an ordered life. In fact, "peace" is precisely an ordered life. The Greek word for 'peace' is *eirini*, derived from *eiro*, which means to join or tie together into a whole. The Latin word for 'peace' is *pax*, which means unity, order or harmony. The good life begins by bringing about a harmony between the appetites and reason.

A disordered life is a life in which the concupiscible and irascible appetites rule over intellect and will. Such people are governed by their appetites, which is really the same thing as to be governed by the emotions. To live a disordered life is to live like the brutes; it is a life that is more bestial than it is human. A fully human life is one in which the appetites, and thus the emotions, are governed by reason.

It takes a great deal of work to order one's life in accordance with reason, but this is precisely the key to a life of peace, that is, a happy life. The person who is governed by the passions never finds peace, but is always restless and swayed this way and that, like a dry leaf on a windy day.

What does an ordered life look like? It looks beautiful; note the order and harmony in a beautiful work of art. A person who has brought order to his life is one who is of noble character. Now the purpose of moral reflection is to determine the *kalon*, that is, the morally right course of action, which accords with reason. "Morally right" does not seem to fully translate the *kalon* as Aristotle understood it. The *kalon* is the morally good, or more accurately the morally beautiful or noble. Some actions are noble, others are ignoble. The morally good person will choose what is most noble, that is, he will choose in accordance with reason (with what is highest in us).

By virtue of the unity that exists between soul and body (matter and form), the morally beautiful character will manifest in the countenance, and so he or she will become physically attractive or beautiful as a result of that moral nobility. The converse is also true; a person of bad or ignoble character will not appear attractive for very long. It is not true that beauty is in the eye of the beholder; rather, beauty is in the eyes of the noble one we behold.

The happy man is the noble man. The reason this is true is that we can only bring order to our lives by perfecting the four principal powers of the soul that are open to perfection (intellect, will, concupiscible and irascible powers), and these powers are perfected by the four principle or cardinal virtues. The intellect is perfected by the virtue of prudence, the will is perfected by the virtue of justice, the irascible appetite is perfected by the virtue of fortitude, and the concupiscible appetite is perfected by temperance.

Prudence is the virtue by which we order our actions to their proper end, and the ultimate end is the contemplation of the highest things. An imprudent man makes choices that steer him off course, away from that end, making it impossible for him to achieve it. For example, if he experiences anger, he will simply act on it and likely bring about a great deal of harm to others.

An imprudent man does not know what the just course of action really is; he does not understand justice. He will lack the rest of the virtues, which is why Aristotle refers to prudence as the mother of all the virtues. Justice is in the will and is the constant will to render to another his due.

Fortitude is the virtue that moderates the emotions of fear and daring. The brave man is not the person willing to dive into a pool filled with poisonous snakes or jump from one speeding boat to another; these latter are instances of foolhardiness. Rather, fortitude is the virtue that binds the will to the good of reason in the face of the greatest evils, those that threaten one's very life. There is nothing reasonable about swimming with snakes or risking one's life unnecessarily in order to prove oneself, but there is something reasonable and noble about going into a burning building in order to save someone's life.

And finally, temperance is the virtue that moderates, in accordance with reason, the pleasures of touch. The most intense pleasures that need moderating are those associated with eating, drinking, and sexual activity, those activities ordered towards the preservation of the individual and the preservation of the species. Abstinence moderates the pleasures of eating, sobriety is the virtue that moderates the pleasures of alcoholic drink, and chastity moderates the sexual appetite, ordering it to its proper ends, which are the procreation of new life, and the expression of marital love.

What Aristotle argues here is really more in accordance with the facts. Recall the questions we asked earlier about whether being happy is necessarily the result of having a spouse, house, good job, etc. Only a virtuous person will be able to be a good husband/wife, a good parent, and a person committed to the good of the state. And so it is not enough to have these things in order to be happy. And it isn't doing what you want that renders a person happy, but willing the good, the noble, the beautiful. Happiness is activity in accordance with perfect virtue, and so it is impossible for a virtuous person (character) to be unhappy.

The Secondary Instances of the Good Life

The good life also includes secondary aspects that add to the happy life. Many people today confuse the secondary instances of the *kalon* with the primary, which is virtue. But happiness is found in virtue, not in these secondary instances, which only add to it, as salt adds flavor to food that is already good. These secondary instances include pleasure, good health and appearance, proper nourishment and sustenance, a full life span, friendships, sufficient wealth and enough time for leisure, and respectable family origin.

Finally, Aristotle underscores the importance of a proper upbringing. A child that is brought up well is well disposed towards goodness. It does not mean that he or she will necessarily turn out well. But a child that is habituated towards sense pleasure will mistakenly think that the purpose of his life is nothing but pleasure, which is a false notion of happiness. And a child that is habituated towards a quest for fame and power will mistakenly regard honors as the chief end or purpose of human life, or the principal means of happiness. But the pursuit of honors is fickle, and those people who are satisfied with the recognition of excellence rather than the excellence itself are deceived. Only a person brought up properly will recognize the *kalon* in the virtuous activity of the noble person. So it is true that good parenting does incalculable good. In fact, one could argue that in this light, parenting is probably the most important work in the maintenance of civilization.

Chapter 22: On the Distinction between Essence and Existence: An Introduction to St. Thomas Aquinas

Although Aristotle takes matter more seriously than Plato does, it can be argued that St. Thomas Aquinas takes matter much more seriously than does Aristotle. For Aristotle, essence is, as it was for Plato, the form. But this is not so for Aquinas. If the essence was simply the substantial form, then matter is outside the essence of a thing. But am I not essentially a material kind of being? For Thomas, the essence of a material thing includes matter and form. A human being, an animal, a rock, are essentially material things.

But what accounts for the fact that a substance is what it is? The answer is the substantial form. What accounts for the mutability of a material substance? The answer is its matter. Form exists in composition with matter, and matter is the principle of a thing's potentiality. What accounts for a thing's extension? The accident 'quantity'. And what accounts for one's ability to laugh? One's power of intelligence.

But what accounts for the very fact that a thing exists? There is nothing in the substance itself that requires it 'to be'. Prime matter is the material cause, rendering a thing mutable; the substantial form determines the matter to be a certain kind of thing, i.e., a rabbit, or gold. Quantity gives the rabbit or the gold parts outside of parts. Quality is the accidental form that qualifies the gold in a particular way, i.e., its color and texture, etc. But there is a distinction between *what a thing is*, and the very *act of its existence*. One can study "what" something is without knowing whether or not it actually exists. We can study certain frogs that are extinct—without knowing they are extinct—, that is, we can come to understand "what they are", but that very knowledge does not enable us to determine whether or not those frogs actually exist.

For St. Thomas, there is a real distinction between essence, which answers to the question "what is it?", and existence, which answers to the question "is it?" This is a departure from both Plato and Aristotle, for whom *ousia* meant essence or being.

For Aquinas, a being is a *habens esse*: that which has an act of existing. In other words, a being is not simply a substance. A being is a substance that has an act of existing. This means that for St. Thomas, the whole substance is in potency to existence; it does not have existence by nature. You and I have a received existence. Consider that it is correct to say: You are human (you are your essence); but it is not correct to say: You are existence (you are not your existence). Rather, you *have* existence. An existing being exists not by virtue of itself nor by virtue of its substantial form, but by virtue of its *esse*, that is, its received act of existing. The substantial form is the act of matter, but the *esse* of a being is the act of being. The act of being is the act of the substantial form (which is the act of matter), as well as the act of the accidents. In other words, without *esse* (the act of being), there is no being to speak of.

Recall that the definition of a thing expresses a thing's essence, and whatever belongs to a thing's essence belongs to it necessarily. For example, a triangle is a three sided figure; hence, a triangle is necessarily three sided; it cannot "not be" three sided. Man is defined as a rational animal; hence, all men, no matter who they are, are necessarily rational creatures and cannot "not be".

Whatever does not belong to the essence a thing will be excluded from the definition of the thing, and therefore will not belong to the thing necessarily, but only contingently, or possibly. Notice that metal, yellow, large, etc., are not included in the definition of triangle, even though some triangles are metal, yellow, and rather large. This means that a triangle is not necessarily metal, yellow, and large, but possibly so. As well, blond hair and blue eyes do not belong to the essence of man, otherwise all men would have blond hair and blue eyes, and anyone who does not is not a man. Hence, it is necessary that Mike be rational, sentient, that he have a will, that he have the potentiality to walk, the power to see, remember, etc., but it is not necessary that he be tall, blond, German, etc. Moreover, if the power to walk, see, or hear, etc., cannot be realized in a human person, it is not due to the person's nature, but to some deformation rooted in poorly disposed matter, i.e., eye damage, oxygen deprivation to the brain, no legs due to an accident, etc.

But if **existence** were part of the "what" of Mike, that is, part of his essence, then Mike would necessarily exist (since whatever belongs to the essence of a thing belongs to it necessarily). In other words, it would be essential for Mike to exist. And just as a triangle cannot **not have** three sides, and a human being cannot **not have** the power to reason, and a bird cannot **not have** wings, Mike could not **not exist**; he would have always existed, exists now, and ever shall be. But we know this not to be the case. The act of existing is received. Mike came into existence. He is not existence, rather he is human. A being is an existing nature.

Some Thoughts on Epistemology

Aristotle points out that "nothing is in the intellect that is not first in the senses." All knowledge begins in sensation, but it does not end there; rather, it ends in the intellect. Like Aristotle, Aquinas argues that there are three acts of the intellect: simple apprehension, judgment, and reasoning. The first act is the apprehension of the thing's essence, but for Aquinas, essence is not existence. I can know what a thing is, but that knowledge is not a knowledge of whether it is or not. So, how does one apprehend existence? By a distinct act of the intellect, its second act. This is called *existential judgment*: I know "what" that is, but I also judge "that" it is. The third act of the intellect is reasoning, for example, drawing conclusions from prior premises, which are judgments.

How is the first act of the intellect related to sensation? Briefly, the internal sense called the synthetic sense takes the separate sense data from each of the five senses and unifies it into a percept. A remembered percept is an image in the imagination, which is another internal sense. This percept is called the phantasm. For Aquinas, every individual person has his/her own active intellect—this was not the case for Aristotle. The active intellect abstracts (separates out) from the phantasm the intelligible content, that is, the essence of the thing. Now, this phantasm is not some static image in the imagination. The thing that we perceive outside of us acts in certain ways, and we come to know "what" a thing is through its activity. Thus, the phantasm is a moving one. The object of the intellect is the "what" of the thing that we perceive, its nature or essence.

The active mind abstracts all the intelligible content it can gather—which might be very minimal at first—and impresses it upon the passive or potential intellect. The potential intellect becomes actualized by that nature or essence. That is what Aristotle meant when he said that the intellect is in a sense all things; for the intellect becomes what it knows in an immaterial way. In other words, the passive mind becomes "informed" by the thing, that is, it receives its essence. The passive mind actualized is nothing other than the passive mind having become that thing's essence.

But the passive intellect does not just become a form. The passive intellect receives the essence of the thing known, and the essence includes matter. The essence receives a new kind of existence in the intellect. Outside the mind, the essence is particular, in the here and now, subject to quantity, etc. That tree has existence outside of the mind; it is there, now, actually green and brown, actually large and heavy, etc. And it is particular. But essence and existence are really distinct. The active intellect abstracts the essence from its individuating conditions, and after impressing the essence onto the passive mind, the essence acquires a new kind of existence (an intentional existence, or a logical existence). The essence exists universally in the mind. The tree outside the mind, however, has not changed. The tree is still there, a composite of essence and existence.

The essence is existentially neutral (it can exist in the mind or outside the mind). It need not necessarily exist in any particular way. The intellect, in knowing things, gives the essence a new existence (an intentional existence). The essence is capable of existing universally, because the essence is a potency to existence. It receives a different kind of existence in the mind, an immaterial existence, a universal mode of existence, an abstract mode of existence, unlike its existence outside of the mind.

A Note on Levels of Abstraction

Thinking is essentially abstract. The mind abstracts or —separates out the intelligible content from its object and considers it abstracted from individual matter (the particular thing). The concept or idea —man, for example, does not refer to any individual (particular) man. Our ideas, such as man, equine, tree, science, calculus, number, etc., are not material things; otherwise our ideas would be particular and could not be shared or communicated. All our ideas are universal. But the mind is capable of abstracting at various levels. Aquinas distinguishes between first, second, and third levels of abstraction.

The physical or empirical sciences take place on the first level of abstraction. What this means is that the mind abstracts from the particular or individual material thing (i.e., this bone, these organs, this tissue, etc.), but not from common sensible matter (i.e., bone, organ, tissue in general). The scientist studies this cadaver not in order to understand this cadaver, but to understand the anatomy of all bodies. But he does not abstract from bone, muscle, tissue, etc., just this bone, this muscle, this tissue, etc.

Ideas like cell, or branch, or oak tree, or photosynthesis, etc., are all ideas at the first level of abstraction. They do not refer to any particular cell, branch, or tree, but only cell, branch, or tree in general. Cells have quantity, and so too do branches and oak trees. But the idea of oak tree does not include any particular size.

But some ideas are more abstract than others. The mind abstracts even further when it considers quantity separated from its sensible matter. For example, a cell is generally round; the mind abstracts round or circular from sensible matter and considers the properties of the circle abstracted from sensible matter (i.e., the sensible matter of the cell, or the smooth, clear, hard glass of this clock). In order to understand the properties of the circle, one need not know anything about the properties of the glass, or the cell, or the properties of wood, or various metals that might possess a circular shape, such as a street sign, etc. The mind also abstracts discrete quantities or number from individual material things in order to consider number alone. In the real world, we find a multiplicity of substances or things, but the mind is able to separate out number alone from the concrete substance (whatever it might be), such as 2, 10, 50, etc. This is the level of abstraction on which the mathematician operates. This is called the second level of abstraction.

The mind is capable of abstracting even further. It can abstract from quantity and any other particular mode of being (accidents) in order to consider being simply as being. In this way, the mind considers the properties of being insofar as it is being. In other words, just as the mind can focus on the properties of water (chemistry, the first level of abstraction) or the properties of living things (biology, the first level of abstraction) as well as the properties of quantities such as triangles, circles, numbers, etc., (mathematics, the second level of abstraction), the mind can also focus on the properties of being in so far as it is being, not insofar as it is circular, and not insofar as it is living, or chemical, etc. This is metaphysics, the third level of abstraction. Metaphysics, or the philosophy of being, takes place at the highest level of abstraction; it is not possible to abstract any further, for there is nothing wider than being (beyond being is non-being, or nothing).

The more abstract the level on which the mind operates, the greater the certainty of its conclusions. The reason for this is that when the intellect abstracts, it separates its object from matter, and the more abstracted from matter, the clearer is that knowledge, which is why mathematics is clearer and more certain than biology.

On the first level of abstraction, we theorize, we posit a hypothesis, i.e., the cause of cancer. Experiment and empirical data are needed to verify the hypothesis. That is why certainty is more difficult to come by. To determine whether or not our hypothesis about the cause of a particular effect is actually so requires a great deal of labor, but once it has been empirically established, the knowledge possessed is universal in scope.

Operating on the second level of abstraction, as in mathematics, requires much less labor, and since we abstract from sensible matter, there is no need to empirically verify our conclusion. We simply work it out through mathematical reasoning; for mathematics is not about causes of any sort of motion, and so there is no exploration into the reasons for certain motions or changes. Mathematical entities do not move or change because the mind abstracts from movement and sensible matter.

But metaphysics, the highest level of abstraction, requires no empirical verification, and its conclusions enjoy the greatest certainty. For example, assuming one properly understands these principles, we are absolutely certain that "nothing can both be and not be at the same time and in the same respect." To deny it is to affirm it. Also, it is certain that "Nothing moves itself from potency to actuality except by something already in act", for if it were not so, being and non-being would be identical and contradictories would be true at one and the same time.

But the study of history, for example, involves no abstraction. It is not a science, for it does not result in the possession of universal ideas or necessary conclusions. History deals not in laws, but in contingencies, that is, particular historical events that need not have occurred. Certainty is very difficult, if not impossible, at this level. The historian will formulate a hypothesis, and like a scientific hypothesis, it will be in the form of a conditional syllogism, an instance of affirming the consequent (If p, then q; q; therefore p). This is the reason for its uncertainty or lack of necessity. Recall that affirming the consequent is invalid from a logical point of view, which means that the conclusion cannot be deduced with certainty from the given premises (it lacks or force of necessity). Thus, to come to an understanding of history requires a great deal of labor, i.e., a great deal of research and reading. History is thoroughly empirical. It requires evidence, either archeological evidence and/or documented evidence. Nevertheless, documented evidence is not always entirely clear and certain.

Faith (natural faith) is a necessary step in the learning process. Faith is trusting in what somebody tells you because you have evidence that the speaker is well informed about the subject and is honest. We have faith in our family doctor that the prescription he writes for us is not going to kill us; we put our faith in the Pharmacist that he or she didn't make a mistake on the dosage and that what we are given to take is going to help us—unless we studied pharmacology. We trust our mechanic when he tells us he fixed the brakes. We simply get in the car and wait for a red light, and then we'll discover whether our faith was well placed. The world of science relies heavily upon faith—no scientist can repeat every experiment and study done in the past, nor even the most recent studies. We trust that data has not been falsified. That trust has been betrayed very often in the past. In 1998, a British surgeon and medical researcher published a study claiming a link between the measles, mumps and rubella vaccine, and autism. It took years to discover that the claim was fraudulent. But in that time, some children died as a result of the faith placed in that claim.

Points to consider

The fact is we simply can't function without faith. We're just too limited. Children believe their parents when they are told that brushing their teeth is good for them. Thus it is reasonable to trust. If there is no "reason" not to trust the other, then there is no reason not to trust him. Hence, we trust him, or her, or the institution. Imagine a child who refuses to trust his parents and demands proof before doing anything: "I don't trust you that this food is edible, or that this toothpaste won't harm me". A marriage relationship is based on faith. One simply does not know whether this person really loves the one he says he loves, that he's not lying and using her. He says he loves her, and she trusts him, and she puts her faith in him. And that's the beauty of genuine love—it is based on natural faith. Faith is risky, but what kind of relationship is based on complete security? Certainly not love.

But with a little thought, we should realize that we readily put our faith in truth claims that we should approach with more caution. Very often people will say "this is bad for you, it causes cancer, I know this because I read it in the Star, etc." But what they read was not a double blinded peer reviewed study. They really don't know, they just believe what they read, without realizing that there's often an agenda behind these studies, either political or economic.

Truth is possible to attain at all levels of abstraction, but it is more difficult to attain at the lower levels; the more abstract the knowledge, the more certainty the knower enjoys. Reasoning, the third act of the intellect, occurs at all levels of abstraction, from natural faith (there is no "reason" not to trust him) to history (we infer this from that, etc.) to the physical sciences, all the way to mathematics and the philosophy of being. The higher up we go, the more "pure" is the reasoning (there is no faith in mathematics).

What about the claim that science has shown that our ordinary knowledge or way of knowing is unreliable, and that only the more precise knowledge of the empirical sciences is reliable? It is true that science often corrects our initial interpretation of the world. We might have thought that the sun rises, but through a more precise knowledge given by science, we are now certain that this is not the case. Many more examples can be put forward to prove the point.

What science does here, however, is it corrects a specific kind of interpretation (a hypothesis about secondary causes), not our general or pre-scientific knowledge, which is the pre-condition for science. For example, I can come to know that my cancer was not caused by too much sugar (my original hypothesis), but was the result of exposure to pesticides, etc. What science does not and cannot do is justify its initial assumptions about its pre-scientific knowledge of reality (i.e., that reality is intelligible in the first place and that things act for an end and with a definite order, etc.). In other words, the claim that the scientific process gradually does justify our initial knowledge by making it more precise confuses precision with certainty. The empiriometric sciences make our general knowledge—which according to the classical realist is more certain than scientific knowledge—more precise.

And so, when a scientist shows that a commonly held interpretation of a particular phenomenon is wrong (i.e., it is not the union of sperm and menstrual blood, but sperm and ovum that is the starting point of human life), he does not show that our ordinary knowledge is uncertain; rather, he shows that our ordinary knowledge lacks precision. The new advancement does not correct ordinary knowledge, but a previous attempt at a more precise knowledge, that is, a scientific interpretation of a particular phenomenon whose cause we wish to know. His new interpretation, which is empirically based and tested, is a more precise knowledge of something we know at the ordinary level (i.e., this baby is alive and is human). Scientific knowledge continues to rest on ordinary knowledge, because a "more precise" knowledge means a more precise knowledge of what we knew less precisely, but initially.

It does not and cannot mean that ordinary knowledge is uncertain until we acquire that more precise knowledge; for if ordinary knowledge is uncertain, then a more precise knowledge is just as uncertain, for it would participate in that original uncertainty; it is merely a more precise knowledge of an original uncertainty. For example, I see something that I am not certain is real; it could be a ghost. There is something unreal about the specter before me, but the more I look at it, the more I see that he has green eyes, is wearing a blue coat, has old shoes on that one might have worn at the time of the First World War, his hairstyle is not current, etc. These more precise details do not alter my original uncertainty about its reality. They only extend that uncertainty; it is a detailed knowledge of an uncertain reality. I am still not certain that those shoes are real, that the hairstyle is one belonging to a real being, that the coat is real, etc. Precise scientific knowledge participates in the reality of our initial and ordinary experience.

Chapter 23: An Existential Demonstration of God's Existence

Let us begin by defining our terms. First, the word "contingent", from the Latin *com* and *tangere*, ('to touch upon'); contingent means "that which need not be the case", or "something which just happens to be the case". A contingent being is a being that need not be. It is not necessary that the oak tree in your backyard be. It was planted by your grandfather, perhaps, but he need not have planted it. It just happens to be the case that he planted it. You can also purchase an ax and cut it down tomorrow. Hence, it need not be; it came into being at one time, and it can cease to be at one time.

You and I are contingent beings. It is not true to say that "you cannot not be". If that were the case, you'd have always existed. In other words, you and I are not "necessary beings", or non-contingent beings.

The question we wish to explore is whether there exists a non-contingent being. Just defining it does not show that it actually exists. So, we begin by assuming that everything that exists is a contingent being. A contingent being is a composite of essence and existence. It is "what" it is (i.e., human), but it "has" an act of existing.

Now, the act of existing that a contingent being "has" does not add anything to its nature or essence. For example, you and I can come to understand the nature of an *atelopus exiguus* (a type of frog) without knowing whether or not such a thing actually exists. Should the frog be discovered to actually exist, its being will not add anything to the nature of the frog as you understand it already.

And so a contingent being that actually exists is a composite of "essence" and an "act of existing" (*essentia et esse*). That is why knowing **what** a thing is does not tell me whether or not it is, and knowing **that** a thing is does not tell me **what** it is.

At this point, let us recall what an analogy is. Consider the following analogy: cat is to meow as dog is to ___? The answer, of course, is "bark". Or, 2 is to 4 as 3 is to ___? The answer, of course, is "6". Now think of the following analogy: Essence is to existence as potentiality is to actuality.

What this means is that a contingent being is a potential being that has been reduced to an actual being (it has an act of existing). 200 years ago, your oak tree did not exist. Now it actually exists; it has an act of existing. Now, one cannot say that it was impossible for the oak tree to exist. It exists now, in your backyard, which proves that it was possible for it to be. The oak tree is a possibility that has become an actuality. It is a unity of potency and act, or essence and existence. We can know what it is (essence), and we can know that it is (existence).

Now the act of existing is **an act**. The essence is related to the act of existing as potentiality is related to actuality. The *atelopus exiguus* does not actually exist any longer. It is extinct. They were a potentiality to be, and as actually existing beings they were composites of essence and existence. As a composite of essence and existence, the particular frog is a potentiality not to be (it can cease to be). To prove this, note that the *atelopus exiguus* is now extinct. They no longer have actual being. So too, your children do not exist. At this point, they are a potentiality to be.

Everything in the universe that exists is a contingent being. If one does not accept this, but argues that not everything is a contingent being, then the argument for the existence of God becomes much easier—for we are trying to prove just that, namely, that there is a non-contingent being besides contingent beings. So the question at this point is that if everything that is, is a contingent being, a possibility made actual, what is it that accounts for the reduction of all these beings from potentiality to actuality? In short, what is the efficient cause of the received act of existing (*esse*) of a contingent being? There are three possible options:

1. A contingent being brings itself into being (imparts to itself its own act of existing).
2. Contingent beings bring contingent beings into being (a contingent being imparts the act of being).
3. A non-contingent being brings things into being.

We can rule out the first option. A contingent being cannot bring itself into being. If a being does not have an act of existing, then it isn't a being; it is merely a potentiality. But a potentiality without an act of existing does not exist. It is nothing. And nothing brings itself into existence; for in order to bring oneself into being, one would have to exist before one exists, which is absurd; for if a thing does not exist, it cannot do anything.

Could contingent beings bring contingent beings into being? It is not possible for you or me to bring something into being from nothing, that is, it is not possible to impart the act of existing. All we can do is bring something into being from already existing material (produce something). Even reproduction, for us, is not creation. We do not create our children. We reproduce; we provide our kids with their genetic material, but we don't create them from nothing. We receive them. So, whatever contingent beings do, they must first exist in order to do it, and whatever contingent beings act upon must first exist in order for them to act upon it.

A contingent being can cause, but it does not impart existence. The reason is that whatever a contingent being does, it acts according to the limited powers of its nature. A plant cannot sense, because sensation is not a power that belongs to its nature. You can ask questions, because it is within your nature to apprehend the causes of things, for you are a rational animal. But the act of existence (*esse*) is really distinct from the essence, that is, it is outside the essence of a thing. The reason we are only capable of producing, which is to bring something into being from already existing matter, and are incapable of imparting *esse*, is that we can only act according to the limited powers of our nature and the act of existing is outside that nature. If I were able to impart the act

of being from absolutely nothing, I would have complete
dominion over being, which means nothing would limit me
(for outside of being is "nothing"); hence, I would be
omnipotent.

As a cause, a contingent being is a caused cause. For
example, a carpenter causes the house to be, and so a carpenter
is a caused cause, since a carpenter is a contingent being. But
no contingent being causes being or existence; hence, only a
non-contingent being causes being, that is, only an uncaused
cause causes existence. Only a non-contingent being can
account for the existence of contingent beings. A non-
contingent being is not a possible being, but a being that
cannot not be. A non-contingent being is a being whose
essence is to be. It is his nature to exist.

In order to have a universe of contingent beings, there
must be an uncaused cause. An uncaused cause does not *have*
existence. Rather, an uncaused cause *is His own existence*. This
uncaused cause is what we mean by God. In other words,
God's essence is identical to His *esse*; He is *Ipsum Esse* (Being
Itself), and so it is within His nature to be. And since like
produces like, or since the effect always has a likeness to its
cause, the *esse* of contingent beings is efficiently caused by none
other than that being who is His own "to be" (*esse*) itself. *Ipsum
Esse subsistens* is the sufficient reason for the very act of
existence of whatever is; without a non-contingent being, there
is no sufficient reason for the very act of existing of any
existing thing whatsoever. In other words, although there is a
great deal about this particular thing and what it does that can
be sufficiently accounted for—by an appeal to certain aspects
of its nature, certain parts of it, etc.,—, nothing within its
nature can act as the sufficient reason for its very existence,
and so it always remains forever more than what can be known
of it scientifically or essentially.

Chapter 24: Some Implications of God as Ipsum Esse Subsistens

God is that being whose essence is identical to His act of existence. God's essence is *to be*. Hence, it follows that God, who is *Ipsum Esse subsistens* (Subsistent Being Itself), cannot not be. God is His own to be, and therefore exists necessarily, while everything else exists as an actualization of a possibility. There are a number of implications that reason can draw out from this notion that God is His act of existing. Let us consider a few of these logical implications.

1. God is One:

There cannot be two beings whose essence is to be. In order to distinguish one thing from another, such as two pieces of chalk, we must look for that which is outside of what they have in common. If both pieces of chalk are white, we cannot say that this piece of chalk can be distinguished from that piece of chalk in that this one on the left is white, because they are both white. We have to find something that they do not share in common. If there were two non-contingent beings, then what would distinguish the one from the other? It would have to be something outside of what they are in common. What are they? Being Itself, that is, two beings whose essence is to be. But outside of Being Itself is non-being (nothing). Hence, nothing distinguishes them, and so they are not "they" (plural), but one.

2. God is not material:

If God is His own Act of Being, then God is Act. If His essence is not in potency to existence, but is His existence, then God is pure Act without any admixture of potentiality. Therefore, there is no prime matter in God, for prime matter is potentiality. Nor is God made up of any secondary matter (extended substance); for what is secondary matter (substance) is in potentiality to certain accidents, i.e., quantity, quality, when, where, etc. But there is no potency in God.

3. God is not a quantity, nor does He have quantity:

Quantity is divisible, and God, who is His own Act of Existing, cannot be divided into two, as was shown above (God is one). Also, consider the word "divisible" (able or potentially divided). But there is no potentiality in God. Also, what is Act is immaterial, and what is immaterial cannot be divided. Also, what is extended has parts outside of parts. A block of gold has parts outside of parts, for example the part on the left is outside of the part on the right, yet both parts share in the nature of gold. The nature is found whole and entire in every part. But if God is His own Act of Existing, He cannot have parts. Consider, this part of God is not that part of God. If this part of God is Being, then there cannot be anything outside of that part, for outside of being is non-being. If there are no parts outside of this part, then there is no "this part". This part is so only in relation to that part. Hence, there are no parts in God.

4. God is outside of time:

What is in time is subject to time, that is, actualized by time (time is an accident of a material substance; a secondary mode of being that actualizes the substance in an accidental way). But a Being who is His own Act of Existing cannot be in potency or be subject to anything. For there is nothing outside of Being; and He is Pure Being. Therefore God is eternal. What is eternal is not something that endures forever, time without end. What is eternal is simply present without a before and an after. In other words, all of human history is a present unit or point for God's "point of view"; there is no future, no past, only present.

5. God is not in place, therefore God is not in the universe nor outside of it:

To be in place, that is, subject to place requires quantity and figure. God has no quantity, as was shown above. Therefore, God has no place.

6. That God is present everywhere:

If God alone imparts the act of existing (*esse*) on contingent beings, then God is intimately and immediately present to anything that is. There cannot be anything between God and a contingent being. To impart being means to bring something into being from nothing, not from something mediate. Therefore, wherever there is something, God is more intimately and immediately present to that something than anything else could possibly be. In other words, God is more immediately present to you than the person sitting next to you; and even more present to you and me than we are to ourselves. Wherever there is being, there is God. Hence, God is everywhere without being subject to place.

7. That God has Intelligence:

A thing is known in so far as it is in act. For example, we know the essence of a thing when the intellect abstracts the essence from the material conditions of the thing. The passive mind becomes actualized by the essence, and this is to know—there intellect is in act. If God is pure Act, then God is perfectly intelligible to Himself. Also, act is perfection. The word 'perfect' means 'made through'. A carpenter making a table takes wood, which is at first potentially a table, and changes it, moving it from being potentially a table to being actually a table. It is actually a table when the form 'table' is finally in the matter; at that point, the table has been 'made through' or perfected. A thing is perfect in so far as it is in act, and imperfect to the degree that it is in potentiality (i.e., "your essay has a lot of potential" means more work needs to be done).

But God is pure Act of Existing. Therefore God is perfect. He cannot lack any perfection; for otherwise He would be in potency to further act. Thus, He would not be pure Act. Now, of all the perfections found in beings, intelligence is considered preeminent; for intellectual beings are more powerful than those without reason. Therefore God is intelligent.

8. That God's knowledge is His Existence:

God is entirely simple, that is, entirely without composition—He is pure act, without composition with potentiality. There is nothing in God that is distinct from His Existence. God's knowledge is not distinct from His Existence—otherwise there would be composition in God. Now, there is nothing outside of God's Act of Existing (outside of *Ipsum Esse* is non-being). Hence, God's knowledge is His Being. Also, if there was knowledge in God, and this knowledge was not His Act of Existing, then it would be related to His Act of Existing as potentiality is related to actuality. But there is no potentiality in God, as was shown above. Hence, God's knowledge is His Existence.

9. All other perfections in God are identical to His Existence:

Any other perfection, such as love, justice, wisdom, power, beauty, etc., are found in God, but they are identical to His Existence for the reasons stated above.

10. That there is will or volition in God:

If God knows Himself (and He cannot not know Himself) or understands Himself, Who is perfect and therefore supremely good (perfect), then it follows that He necessarily loves Himself. For the good is that which all things desire; and all things desire first and foremost their own perfection, that is, their own act. If God is pure Act without any admixture of potentiality, then God is unlimited Good (potentiality is the source of limitation in things). What is supremely Good without limits is, if known, necessarily loved. God is His own Act of Existing, therefore He is perfectly knowable to Himself. His Self-Knowledge is His Existence. Therefore He loves Himself necessarily. And since love operates through the will, there is will in God. Moreover, God's will is identical to His Existence; for God is entirely simple, as was shown above.

Also, God's willing and God's knowing is not a power or potency that can be actualized. God's knowing and willing are eternally Act, for His willing and knowing are identical to His Act of Existing. So God always knows Himself and loves Himself. He imparts existence on contingent beings not out of necessity, but through His own will. Whatever is, He knows, for it is His knowledge and will that cause other things to be. Hence, God does not learn as we learn, God does not discover as we discover. God does not move from potentiality to actuality, that is, from potential knowledge to actual knowledge. Anything that is, exists by virtue of God's knowledge and will. If God does not know it, it does not exist.

11. God's Knowing is the Cause of Being:

If God's knowledge is His Existence, then it follows that God's knowledge is the cause of whatever is. A thing exists because God knows it (and of course wills it into being). Existing things exist independently of our knowing them, but this is not the case for God. Whatever exists, exists because He knows it. If He stopped knowing something, it would cease to be. Moreover, it is important to note that God does not cause existence within the framework of time, or at the initial stage of a thing's existence, that is, "horizontally". Thus, it is important **not** to imagine God creating at the beginning of time as a manufacturer produces his product at the beginning of that thing's existence. Rather, whatever exists, is caused first by God and is preserved in existence by God (vertically, so to speak). Time (or the time line) depends upon motion in order to be, but motion depends upon an existing being that moves. At every instant of its existence, a "thing" is caused by God whose essence is to be. So, even if we were to assume that the universe always existed, everything that exists and that evolves and changes is still given existence at every instant of its existence and thus preserved in existence throughout its history; for no contingent being contains within itself the sufficient reason for its own unique act of existence (*esse*).

12. God is Omnipotent:

Since God is the First Existential Cause of whatever has existence, it follows that God has complete dominion over being. You and I might have dominion over the fish, the animals, the trees, etc., but we don't have dominion over being. We cannot impart being (bring something into being from nothing). Now, since there is nothing outside of being, and God has dominion over being, it follows that He has unlimited power. Hence, God is omnipotent.

13. God is Infinite:

If God is His own Act of Existing, then it follows that God is infinite (without limits). God is His own Existence, and outside of existence is non-existence (or nothing). Hence, there is nothing outside of God to limit Him. Hence, He is infinite. Moreover, potentiality is the principle of limitation in things. In a contingent being, essence is related to the act of existing as potentiality is related to actuality. But God is pure Act of Existing. Thus, He is unlimited by potentiality; His Act of Existing is not limited to a determinate mode of being by an essence distinct from *esse*. Hence, God is unlimited or infinite.

14. God is Supremely Good and cannot do evil:

Whatever exists is good insofar as it exists. Goodness is a property of being. Thus, to exist is good. That is why things struggle to perpetuate their existence. Evil is a deficiency, a deformity, or a lack of something that should be there. And so it follows that if God is His own Act of Existing, then God is

Supremely Good, or perfect Goodness. If He is infinite, then He is Goodness without limits. Thus, God cannot do or will evil. Whatever God does is good insofar as He does it.

15. Whatever happens to those who love God, He permits for their greatest good:

If God is omnipotent, and if God is perfect and unlimited Goodness Itself, then it follows that whatever happens to you and me in our lives is permitted by God ultimately for our greatest good. Omnipotence means that He can do whatever He wants, and perfect goodness implies that He wants only what is best for us. The two together imply that God wills our greatest good and is able to bring it about—if we allow Him to. Hence, whatever He allows to happen to us in our lives is permitted by Him ultimately for our greatest good.

16. God is Subsistent Beauty:

Every perfection that exists in God is identical to God's Act of Existing. Beauty is a perfection; it is a kind of order, a harmony that pleases when known. Beauty is a property of being. It follows that God is Subsistent Beauty. Hence, whatever is beautiful, i.e., a beautiful sunset, beautiful scenery, the beauty of the stars, or a beautiful face, etc., is really an imperfect reflection of God's perfect and infinite beauty. And if the human person has a natural and ever increasing desire to behold the beautiful, he has a natural desire to see God.

17. God is Justice:

Justice is a perfection (an unjust man is not regarded as a perfect man), therefore, in God, justice is identical with His Act of Existing. Thus, God is justice. Hence, we can conclude that ultimately, injustice is temporary. God cannot allow injustice to endure or have the final word. Nor is it possible for God to ever be unjust.

18. God is Truth:

Truth is the conformity between what is in the mind and what is (in reality). But what is, exists by virtue of being known by God and being willed into existence (as we said above). God's knowledge is the measure of reality, not vice versa. God is thus the measure of truth. Therefore, God does not have the truth, rather God is Truth. And so it follows that whoever loves truth, ultimately loves God, just as whoever loves justice—and not everybody does—, ultimately loves God.

19. God alone satisfies the will perfectly:

The object of the will is "the good". Whatever a person wills, he sees it as good. This is true because the good is "that which all things desire". Joy is the state that results from the satisfaction of the will, which is the possession of the good. Now, if whatever is in God is identical to His Act of Existing, and goodness is in God, then God is His Goodness; He is unlimited Goodness Itself. And if the object of the will is the good, then to see and know God as He is in Himself is to experience the perfect satisfaction of the will, which is an unimaginable joy. Philosophy cannot demonstrate through reason alone that the human person is destined to see God as He is in Himself, but reason does show that were we to possess God, who is Goodness Itself without limits, we would possess a happiness that is complete and sufficient unto itself. To have had the opportunity to achieve that eternal destiny and to have missed it by virtue of our own depraved character, is hell indeed.

20. Making God the end of all your efforts is eminently reasonable:

Love means to will the good of another (benevolence), and good is a property of being (to be is good and it is good to be). God's act of creating (bringing things into being) is an act of love, that is, a willing that the goodness of existence be enjoyed by the creature. Now, man is an intelligent being whose highest activity is to know and to love. Therefore, man's highest and greatest possible achievement is to know and love God. It follows that it is reasonable to spend every ounce of one's energy towards the attainment of that goal. A reasonable life is one directed ultimately towards the possession of God in knowledge and love. Any other goal incompatible with that end is simply irrational.

Chapter 25: Is God the First Existential Cause of Evil?

To deal with this question, we need to define our terms, namely good and evil. The good is that which all things desire (Aristotle). If a person desires something, he sees it as a good. What all things desire first and foremost is their own perfection; this is another way of saying that all things desire their own "to be", or their own "act of existing." If we were being attacked by someone swinging a machete, we would run. Why? Because we desire to be; in other words, good is really the same as being (it is only different inside the mind, not outside the mind). Good is a property of being, just as nutrition is a property of living things. And so we can say that whatever is, is good insofar as it is.

If good is being, evil is going to be a kind of non-being. More specifically, evil is a lack of something that should be there. In order to keep things simple, consider physical evil. It belongs to the nature of a bird to have wings; a bird without wings cannot fly. A bird ought to have wings. If it does not, it suffers from a physical evil or defect. Compare the words 'defect' and 'perfect'. All things desire their own perfection, but we do not desire our own defection. The word 'perfect' means "made through", but "defect" implies the opposite: "not completely made through". It is not a defect that man is born without wings, because it does not belong to his nature to have wings. That is why a child born without wings is not said to be suffering from a physical evil. A child born without arms, on the contrary, does suffer from a physical evil or defect. Evil is a lack, a privation of due being. That is why there is no such thing as pure or total evil; total evil would be nothing. Evil always exists in a subject that is basically good.

Now God is His own Act of Existing and is the cause of the received act of existing of everything that is. If good is a property of being, then God is supremely or perfectly good, and in willing to bring things into being, He is willing to communicate goodness to other things. One of those things is human beings. The human being is the kind of being that has intelligence and will, which means he can know the natures of things. As a result, he can choose freely between alternatives. Thus, he has the ability to make evil choices.

Free Choice

Free choice is fundamentally about alternatives. The will necessarily desires "the good"; it has no choice but to desire the good. If we were to see God as He is in Himself at this moment, we would necessarily love Him, because He is the fullness of good; for He is the fullness of being. Heaven is precisely that never ending possession of the supreme good, the vision of God as He is in Himself. So it is true to say that all things, whether they know it or not, have a fundamental desire for God.

Now, within the alternatives that are presented to us in our everyday lives, one does not find the fullness of good (infinite good); one only finds limited goods, for contingent beings are finite beings. For example, you are in bed and your alarm clock goes off; it is time to get up for school. You have alternatives.

1) You can get up and get ready for school.
2) You can get up, but stay home and work on a final essay.
3) You can sleep in and go to school late, etc.

Each alternative offers some benefits not contained in the others, and so you begin deliberating on the alternatives. The intellect presents to your will known goods contained in the alternatives, and your will is commanding the intellect to continue presenting them. But you have to decide at some point, and when you decide (from the Latin *de sacare*: to cut off), your will commands the intellect to cut off deliberation. Your choice is the last alternative on which you were deliberating when your will commanded the intellect to cut off deliberation. You decided; in other words, your choice was self-determined. And that's what it means to choose freely: self-determination.

That's the kind of being God has brought into existence in creating persons, the kind of being capable of determining itself. In order to deliberate and make a decision on an alternative, your intellect and will must be preserved in being. God is the First Existential Cause of your intellect and will, because they are your powers, and God is the existential cause of your act of existing. And so, God is the First Existential and Preservative Cause of your existing action of deliberation and decision.

But making an evil decision is our choice. An evil decision is the choice of an alternative that lacks something it ought to have; it is the choice of a morally deficient alternative. It is not as complete as the other alternatives. For example, a person gives birth to a handicapped child. The alternatives presented to him are the following:

1. Sedate the baby and starve him, so that he will die.
2. Feed the baby and care for him.
3. Give the baby up for adoption.

The person begins deliberating. He knows from natural law that human beings have an inalienable right to live, and that the value of this child does not depend upon his physical and mental quality. And so he knows that one must not choose to directly destroy human life, which is intrinsically good, for the sake of making one's own life more convenient. That rule or moral norm is in his mind, and so he deliberates. The first alternative bothers him slightly, yet it offers to make his life much easier. He will be free to take trips every summer; he will not have to make renovations on his house for the sake of his handicapped child, etc. The second alternative strikes him as the more humane, but along with that will come all sorts of personal sacrifices. All sorts of goods come from personal sacrifices, i.e., spiritual growth, good character, and the joy of a relationship with your child, etc. The third alternative contains goods that the others do not present, for example, a couple who are childless will be given a child to raise and love, but then he might feel terribly guilty knowing that others are asking the mother who the child's biological parents are, and he doesn't want to risk having people think bad thoughts about him. As he is deliberating, he decides not to consider the rule or moral norm, and his will commands the intellect to stop deliberating while it considers the first alternative. Thus, he chooses to euthanize the baby.

The first alternative is morally deficient; for it lacks due reverence for human life. Now the will was free to command the intellect to stop deliberating at any of the alternatives, because each alternative contained finite goods that the others did not, and so the will was not necessitated towards any one alternative.

God is the First Existential Cause of the action to the degree that the action has being, but the action is evil insofar as it lacks something, in this case due reverence for human life. God wills that man choose the better option, the one that is less defective, but He created man with the ability to determine himself. Man has chosen the deficient option for the sake of other goods that will come to him from that choice. And so, man is the first deficient cause of his evil actions, while God is the First Existential Cause of all of man's good actions, and whatever goodness there is in man's evil actions.

Thus, God is not the cause of man's evil actions. God cannot will evil because evil is not a being. There is a sense in which we can say that evil does not exist; it is a defect, a lack of due being, a kind of non-being. Now man does not will the evil alternative insofar as it is evil, but only insofar as it contains goods that he desires. But he is not drawn by necessity towards the deficient alternative. He chooses it freely.

Chapter 26: The Immortality of the Soul

Consider that a material thing is incapable of total self-reflection. A material thing can only reflect upon itself partly, that is, only a part can reflect upon another part. Take a piece of paper for example. It is not capable of perfect self-reflection. Only one part of the paper can actually reflect upon another part.

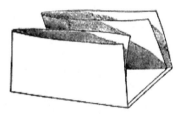

A mirror is something that reflects an image, but even a mirror does not reflect totally, but partially. We only see a part of ourselves in a mirror, never the whole of ourselves. Moreover, sensation, which is dependent upon matter (i.e., the organ of the eye, the ear drum, etc.), is not capable to complete self-reflection; the senses do not sense themselves sensing. In other words, matter cannot transcend itself. But thinking transcends matter. The thinking person is capable of complete self-reflection. For example, although I cannot imagine my act of imagining, nor see my act of seeing, I know that I am knowing. I also know that I know that I am knowing. I also know that I know that I know that I am knowing, and so on and so forth. In fact, I am really only present to myself in the act of knowing something other than myself. When I am in the act of knowing John or Dave, I am also, at the same time, aware of my act of knowing. I know that I am knowing him, or them, or it.

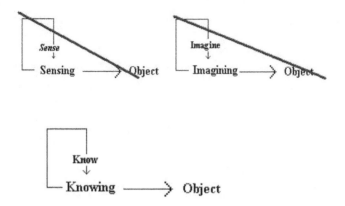

Try touching your sense of touch touching, or imagining your imagination imagining something. Can you smell your sense of smell smelling? But I know myself in the act of knowing; I know myself as knowing while I am knowing.

And so if a material thing is incapable of complete self-reflection, but the mind is capable of complete self-reflection, we can conclude that the mind is not a material organ. The intellect is an immaterial power; for the mind can act independently of matter.

Each person has his or her own active intellect. The intellect is a power, a potentiality with reference to activity, a faculty of the soul, like the other powers. But this power, unlike the other powers, acts independently of matter. Of course, the mind needs a phantasm, and so it depends upon the brain to provide one. But the active intellect abstracts the essence from the phantasm in order to impress it upon the passive mind.

Now, being is prior to activity (in order for a being to act, it must first be). So, if something acts independently of matter, then it can exist independently of matter. Hence, the intellectual soul of man can exist without a material body.

Every being, as well as a human being, is a composite of essence and existence. But the act of existing of a dog, or a cat, or a flower, etc., belongs to the whole dog, cat, flower, etc. So when the dog dies, it exists no longer; it has been transformed. What existed no longer exists. The whole thing has lost its act of existing, because the act of existing belonged to the matter/form composite.

But if a power of the soul can act independently of matter, namely the mind, and we have deduced that it can thereby exist independently of matter, then the act of existing (*esse*) of a human being belongs first and foremost to the soul. The soul not only communicates form, life, intelligible density, to the body, at the same time it communicates existence to the body.

Consider too that human beings have always speculated on the possibility of life after death, and they have done so because humans have a unique and unusual experience; we experience that we are both inside the world and outside the world at the same time. By knowing the world we live in, we transcend it. Yet we are in the world. By knowing the universe, a scientist experiences that he is both inside the universe and outside of it at the same time; he is outside of it in that he can transcend it in knowing it. We experience ourselves transcending matter, and this experience cries out for an explanation. Because we experience this transcending of all that is material, we tend to easily believe that there is something in us that can survive the destruction of the body.

Of course, this does not prove the existence of Heaven; all it shows is that the soul of a human being is a subsistent soul and that it survives the death of the body. It also shows that those who believe in life after death have not adopted a belief that is contrary to reason.

The Shortest Proof for the Immateriality of the Mind

In his work *Idea Men of Today*, Vincent Edward Smith provides the shortest proof of the immateriality of the mind. His argument runs something like this: The simplest of all ideas is "being", or "is". As such, being cannot be divided, for being has no parts. The instrument or tool that delivered the idea of being to the knower must be simple and without parts. Hence, the mind is an immaterial power, and it is indestructible; for one cannot destroy or divide or tear apart what is simple and immaterial.

Allow me to explain this further. The simplest of all ideas is "being", or "is"; for example, I know that I am, that you are, that the clock is, that my cat is, the tree in my front yard is, etc. The idea of being is not only the simplest of ideas, it is also the absolutely first idea; before I know anything more specifically or precisely, I at least know that it "is", that it exists.

Now, "is" or being cannot be divided. Consider a single line. This line is divisible, and when it is divided, it becomes two. A circle can also be divided. When we divide it, it becomes two halves.

As you can see, whatever has parts is divisible. Now, to be something with many parts is to exercise a kind of multiplicity (a single whole having many parts). Consider that a human being has a hand, a foot, a forearm, a torso, etc. Although the parts are continuous, each part is outside the other part. So, my hand is not my foot, my foot is not my torso, etc. Divide a line in two and we know that this part of the line on the left side of the division is not that part of the line on the right side of the division.

Now, being cannot be divided; being has no parts. What would it mean for this part of being to be outside of that part of being? To be outside of being is to not exist, because outside of being is non-being, and non-being is nothing. So, the idea of being cannot be a line, or a circle, or any other quantity. The idea of being is absolutely simple, without parts, and thus indivisible.

The instrument or tool that delivered the idea of being to the knower must be simple and without parts. Hence, the mind is an immaterial power, and it is indestructible; for one cannot destroy or divide or tear apart what is simple and immaterial.

Chapter 27: Some Thoughts on Nothing
Why the Universe Does Not Come From Nothing

I cannot begin, as I would like to, with "Nothing is..." because nothing "is not". It is natural for us to inquire of the nature of things, for we naturally want to know "what" something is. But there is nothing to understand about 'nothing'. "Nothing" has no properties, "it" has absolutely no intelligibility, which is why "nothing" cannot be designated as an "it". When we speak of "nothing", we are not really speaking about "nothing", because there is nothing about which to speak when it comes to nothing.

Thus, "nothing" is not a terminal from which something or some change proceeds. A terminal is a principle, a starting point, or that "from which" something proceeds, and as such, a terminal is intelligible. But "nothing" is not intelligible, for there is nothing to know when it comes to 'nothing'.

"Nothing" does not endure in a way that can be measured according to a before and an after, for there is nothing to measure. Nor does "nothing" possess any kind of extension, for extension is intelligible, it is meaningful, but 'nothing' is simply meaningless - it has no meaning, for there is no 'it' when it comes to nothing. What is extended, either spatially or temporally, has parts, but nothing has no parts. Thus, two things cannot exist side by side "in nothing", for there is nothing in which to exist. Nor can "nothing" be understood "in relation to" something; for something cannot be "related to" nothing, because to be related to nothing is not to be related at all. And so it is contradictory and thus absurd to speak of something coming "out of" nothing, or something coming "from" nothing. What we are doing when we speak that way is we are imparting to "nothing" a degree of reality so that it can enjoy a "relation to" something. But whatever has a "relation to", the terminal or end to which it is related is not nothing, but something, no matter how unusual or mysterious it might be.

To understand anything at all is to understand the way in which it "depends upon" something else. But it is impossible for something that does not contain its own sufficient reason to depend upon "nothing". To depend upon nothing is not to depend. So, that which depends upon nothing is independent. What is independent does not depend upon anything other than itself in order "to be" and to be understood; thus, it is sufficient unto itself. To know it is not to seek to understand it, but to understand it already. And so, something that does not contain within itself the sufficient reason for its own intelligibility or meaningfulness, but depends on something outside itself in order to be understood, does not depend on "nothing" in order to be understood, for if it did, then it would be unintelligible, at least ultimately, since "nothing" is unintelligible; therefore, if it does not contain within itself the sufficient reason for its own existence and its own intelligibility, the sufficient reason is to be found in "something", whatever that turns out to be.

But, as was said above, if it is independent and sufficient unto itself, to know it is not to seek to understand it, because to know it would be to understand it, since the sufficient reason for it is within it or is it. To seek to understand the sufficient reason for it would imply that it is not really known at all, but misunderstood to be something that depends upon something other than it, in order to be understood. In other words, we are seeking in vain to understand it. It does not need to be understood in relation to something other than itself.

As was said, the sufficient reason for it is either within it or is it. If we seek to understand it (for example, as we seek to understand the universe by seeking its origin), then the sufficient reason for it is either outside it (outside the universe), or is an aspect of it (an aspect of the universe itself). It cannot be discovered in "nothing", for there is nothing to discover in "nothing". Furthermore, to say that the sufficient reason is to be discovered in "nothing" will imply that its sufficient reason is to be found within itself (ie., within the universe or some aspect of the universe). But, it is clear that indeed we seek to account for the very existence and intelligibility of the universe, thus its sufficient reason must be found within it, that is, in some aspect of it - if not outside of it, and if not in nothing.

Now, an aspect of a thing is a "part" of a thing. If the sufficient reason for the whole is found in a part of the whole, then that part of the whole cannot really be a part of that whole, but is in fact a whole unto itself. In other words, that part, which is regarded as the sufficient reason that accounts for the whole, is really the whole itself, or a whole unto itself distinct from the whole whose sufficient reason we are seeking. As an analogy, consider a puzzle piece. That piece of the puzzle is only a part; it does not provide us with a picture of the whole puzzle, otherwise it is not a part, but the whole puzzle. The piece of the puzzle is not the sufficient reason for the entire picture of the puzzle. The part only accounts for that part; it possesses only what it possesses, nothing more; to possess more than what it possesses is contradictory.

Thus, the sufficient reason for the "being" of the whole is not contained in a part of the whole. If it were, the part would not be a part of the whole, but a distinct whole unto itself - or it would be the whole itself, and thus not a part of the whole. The reason is that "being" has no parts. A being with extension has parts, but 'is' has no parts. What would it mean for "is" to have parts? Consider an extended whole that has parts, such as a pie cut into four pieces or parts. We can say that this part is not that part (this section over here is not that section over there). Thus, a whole with parts is divisible. But 'is' cannot have any parts, for that would mean that this part of 'is' is not that part of 'is'. But outside of 'is' is 'is not' or 'nothing'. Thus, 'is' cannot be divided. But a part is divisible from the whole. Thus, a part is, by its very nature, a part of a whole and exists because the whole exists. In other words, a part 'is' because the whole of which it is a part 'is'. And so the part does not account for the existence of the whole, but vice versa; for a part is less than the whole, and that is understood to be so the instant we know what it means to be a part and what it means to be a whole.

And so, the sufficient reason for the whole (for its very being or 'is') is not going to be found in an aspect of the whole

(a part, or at some level of the whole), otherwise that aspect is
the whole, not an aspect or part. If the sufficient reason is not
the whole - for if it were, we would not seek its sufficient
reason, we would possess it already in knowing the world - ,
then much less is it an aspect of the whole; rather, it is a
distinct whole that contains what it imparts. Thus, the whole
(i.e., the entire universe) is related to "it", and this "it" is not
"nothing". What is it? It is the sufficient reason for the whole
that we are seeking to understand. It contains within itself the
sufficient reason for itself and everything else that is related to
it as its origin. Whatever this is, it is not "nothing". It cannot be
what we are seeking to understand (i.e., the universe), because
the very fact that we are seeking to understand the whole (i.e.,
the universe, its origin, etc.) implies that it is not the sufficient
reason for its being and its intelligibility.

Chapter 28: A Note on Final Cause in Human Action

Recall that final cause is two-fold: a) End of the generation (proximate end), and b) End of the generated (ultimate end). In a typical accidental change, for example in the realm of art, the end of the generation coincides with the formal cause. Recall that the formal cause is: *that for the sake of which there is coming to be.* The sculptor is carving for the sake of realizing the form in the matter. He will stop working (end) when the form is completely realized in the matter. When that occurs, his work is perfected (*per.* through; *factum.* made). The end of the generated is the ultimate end, the ultimate purpose for which he made the sculpture, or clay pot, or painting, etc.

It is the end of the generation (the proximate end) that tells us what is in the mind of the sculptor. His idea is the form he intends to impose on the matter. Thus, the proximate end—at least for us observers—reveals "what" it is he is making. In other words, the essence of his act (what he is doing) is determined by the proximate end (i.e., He is making a flower pot; she is going for a leisurely jog, etc.). And since the proximate end is the formal cause, it is the proximate end that determines the action to be the "kind of act" it is, at least proximately. We know what someone is doing through the proximate end that is intended. The ultimate end (end of the generated), however, will give us deeper insight into the nature of his act. For example, a man is making a gun, but his ultimate end will tell us whether this 'production' is part of a murderous plot, or whether it is simply artistic expression, or perhaps is carried out for some non-violent practical purpose (i.e., a starter's pistol).

In sum, the form determines the substance to be what it is, but an action has a form as well, and it is the end which is the form of the act; for the end determines the action to be the kind of act it is. To get a better handle on this, consider two men, each firing a gun at a human being in their respective neighborhoods. In one case, the shooter is firing a gun at a man in order to stop him (he's running at the shooter with a knife); the other shooter is firing a gun at a man in order to kill him. The ends in both cases are entirely different, and that is why the two acts are essentially different. The former is a self-defensive act; the latter is a murderous act.

Now, there are many actions a person performs, each one defined by its end (both proximate and ultimate). But the totality of one's actions, that is, one's entire life, is also directed to an end, which is an ultimate end. The ultimate end of a person's entire life that he intends ultimately in doing all that he does will determine the kind of life he is living. In other words, the very meaning of his life is given by this ultimate end.

Consider now the question whether it is possible for a person to have a life inundated with pleasures and still find himself unhappy, and whether a person can achieve everything he has ever set out to achieve and in the end remain unhappy. Indeed, it is possible to have achieved all that one has set out to achieve and yet be happy, just as it is possible to have a pleasure filled life yet be unhappy.

But the person who has achieved everything he has set out to achieve in life is a happy person, it logically follows that his happiness is not the result of having achieved everything he has set out to achieve. To show this, imagine two ladies who both graduated from university with honors, married with a family, and each one has become a family physician and lives in a large house. However, one is happy, the other unhappy. If that is a possible scenario, then it follows that the happy woman is happy not by virtue of the fact that she graduated with honors, became a doctor, is married with children, etc. If that were so, the other would necessarily be happy as well.

So, what is the reason for her unhappiness? The two lives are virtually identical from the point of view of their activities and achievements. But one says her life is without meaning, the other says her life is meaningful. It follows that their lives must be radically different from another point of view. If they are radically different in kind, and if the kind of life one is living is determined by the ultimate end (just as the kind of act one performs is determined by the proximate end), then the two lives are radically different in kind because each of them has a radically different ultimate end.

How do they differ? Let's say that one lady has devoted her life to her own personal fulfillment, which is a more respectable way of saying that she is devoted to herself ultimately. If the other lady (the happy one) has also devoted her life to the fulfillment of her personal dreams, then ultimately her life is no different in kind. But if her life is radically different in meaning, it must follow that her ultimate end is not 'herself', but something outside herself. Let's say the ultimate end of her life is to serve not her own will, but the will of God. Thus, the two lives are radically different in kind. The one life is secular and ultimately self-centered; the other is religious and 'other-centered'.

Does this account for their radically different internal states? I would submit that it does. Two people can have very similar achievements, i.e., graduation from a prestigious university, a career in medicine, marriage and family, financial success, etc., and live very similar lives in appearance, and yet feel radically different about their own lives. The one may be unfulfilled, bored, and unhappy, while the other is fulfilled, motivated and full of joy. The difference, I will argue, lies in their ultimate ends, which are not identical. The one life is directed beyond the self to something larger than the self, the other is directed ultimately to the self, or to the fulfillment of his/her will.

This is an artificial scenario, to be sure, and does not constitute proof by any means. But let us return to a point about knowledge and will. When we know something, we become what we know in an immaterial way. The object of our knowledge exists in us 'intentionally'—not physically. Knowledge is thus a way of existing. I exist as that tree, or dog, etc., without ceasing to be myself. In knowing anything, I become larger. We all have a desire to know, for we all desire to become larger. But there is another way to become enlarged that is even less self-centered, and this is through the will. I know that person as another being of the same nature as myself, and through self-knowledge I know that he too wants the best for himself. I can freely choose to join my will to his and will the best for him as I will the best for myself. In this case, I go outside myself, so to speak, and become him, that is, another self.

This is self-expansion, but different from that of knowledge. In knowing him, he becomes me (exists in me in a new way) without ceasing to be himself, and without my ceasing to be myself. But in love (willing the best for him for his own sake, not for my sake), I exist as another self outside myself, in him, without him necessarily even knowing about it. I have become two, and if I love another person for his own sake, I have become three, four, etc. It is in man's nature to become another through knowledge and love, but to become another through love requires a free act of the will. I will argue that happiness directly corresponds to the self-enlargement that is genuine love of another. Thus, happiness is an activity, not a passivity; it requires a free act of the will that is directed outside the self towards other human persons.

No matter how rich in wealth or achievement a person's life is, if it is directed ultimately for the sake of personal fulfillment, the person in the end will be deeply and radically unsatisfied. He will only find his own fulfillment when he ignores it and concerns himself with the happiness of human persons outside himself.

Can a person have as his ultimate end the happiness of others (plural) without concerning himself with God? The problem here is that in this case, one's ultimate end is not single, but plural (others); it is singular in idea only (i.e., humanity). One's ultimate end must be an end that is a real being, not an idea. A person's greatest happiness is going to be in knowing and loving the highest being. If I really love each human person (not just an idea, like "humanity"), then I love the Real Being that is the origin of that 'exemplar', namely God Himself, who is the origin and end of all beings. Happiness is only found in loving God and neighbor.

Chapter 29: The Emotions and the Virtues that Perfect Them

The emotions have an innate need to guided by reason. When the passions or emotions are disposed by virtue to readily obey reason, the human person thereby becomes more passionate, not less. When they are not so disposed, that is, when the passions rule over reason, the result is an emotionally disordered human being. Such a person is emotionally unstable, that is, emotionally unhealthy, or emotionally immature. That is why happiness is a matter of virtue (the emotionally unstable are not happy).

According to Aristotle, it is not true that if one knows the good, one will do the good (Socrates and Plato). Rather, it is more true to say that if one does the good, one will know the good. In other words, it is by possessing the virtues that one comes to know from within, through a connatural knowledge, what is the right or most noble (*kalon*: morally beautiful) course of action. That is why Aquinas pointed out that there are two ways of knowing what the right thing to do is: scientifically (the science of ethics) and connaturally. Both are important. But it is with regard to this connatural knowledge only that one may speak about emotions as a way of knowing. Emotions in themselves are not ways of knowing, rather, they are sensitive appetitive reactions that follow upon knowledge (sense and or intellectual knowledge). But when disposed by virtue, they provide connatural knowledge; without virtue, the emotions actually blind the intellect.

Let us focus our attention at this point on which virtues perfect which emotions. To speak of virtue perfecting an emotion means that an emotion is disposed by a quality (good habit or virtue) to readily obey reason. For example, a person who cannot help "flying off the handle" every time something does not go his way is a person whose emotion of anger is not disposed to readily obey reason. Moreover, the emotions help us to execute reason's demand, that is, they "move us" in the right direction; but emotion indisposed to obey reason is like unchanneled water that floods and destroys a village.

Temperance and the Emotions of the Concupiscible Appetite (love, desire satisfaction or pleasure; hate, aversion, sadness)

The virtue that perfects the concupiscible appetite and its emotions is temperance and its parts. The object of the concupiscible appetite is the sensible and/or intelligible good (the pleasant), or the sensible and/or intelligible evil (the unpleasant).

The first emotion is love. This emotion is fundamentally the love of self. If I say I love pancakes, I really mean that I love what the pancakes do for me, i.e., they please me. The passion of love is not love in the highest and most human sense of the word (benevolence, which is an act of the will); for we don't destroy what we love, but we destroy pancakes when we eat them.

Now food and drink exist for our own individual preservation, so it is good to eat, and it is fitting that food tastes good. But if we love the pleasure it brings too much, we will eat and drink excessively, and that will begin to destroy us, i.e., overweight, diabetes, clogged arteries, etc. And even if our excessive love of food and drink does not harm us physically, it harms us morally, for our life becomes centered around the pleasures of food and drink, and eventually we are no longer concerned with the higher goods, i.e., spiritual goods, i.e., truth, beauty (in art, poetry, literature, etc.), the good of others, the common good of the civil community, etc.

Temperance moderates the love we have for the pleasures of touch, in particular those associated with food and drink, and sexual activity, which are the most intense pleasures. Temperance disposes the emotion of love to obey the demands of reason. But temperance also affects the emotion of hate. If a person loves himself too much, that is, loves his own satisfaction excessively, he will hate immoderately whatever causes him displeasure. For example, we all hate needles, but to hate that sensation so much that we refuse a reasonable vaccination is unreasonable and thus disordered; so too, we might have an aversion to hospitals, but we should work hard to rise above it so that we can visit our sick family members, for example.

The emotion of sadness or sorrow can be excessive if we lack temperance. To be so overwhelmed with sorrow because you had to go without a meal is disordered. A man who has a disordered satisfaction that food brings will experience excessive sorrow when his food is delayed, or when it is not prepared to his liking—those in the food industry are very familiar with these kinds of people. And so fasting, to some degree at least, is reasonable and morally required.

Food and drink is not the only thing that brings emotional satisfaction. Human beings have a sexual appetite, ordered towards the preservation of the species. This desire is especially vehement, which is why it needs to be disposed to obey reason. That part of temperance that moderates the sexual appetite is chastity. The unchaste person has a disordered love of sexual gratification; he or she is ruled by the appetite for sex, and this leads to excessive sorrow when that appetite is not fulfilled, and it leads to incalculable harm to self and others (moral and physical harm) when it is fulfilled outside is proper context, which is marriage (for example, sexually transmitted diseases, out of wedlock pregnancy, infidelity, emotional hurt, divorce, pornography and female exploitation, sexual addiction, etc.).

We also have a natural love of ourselves and our own excellences. That love too needs to be moderated in accordance with reason. Humility is the virtue that achieves this. A humble person knows his talents as well as his limits. Many gifted people, however, suffer from an excessive love of themselves or their own excellence. This vice is pride. The prideful person is riddled with disordered passions. He will have a disordered desire (which is an emotion) for recognition, or he will have a disordered satisfaction (which is an emotion) in his achievements, whether that is a career, or winning an argument, or winning a game, or publishing a book, etc. He will have a disordered delight (satisfaction) in being "better" than others, and that disordered passion will blind him to the excellences of others—he will not desire to notice them (disordered desire). He will love "the spotlight", "the limelight", and he may love excessively his own looks (vanity). He or she will begin to dress immodestly, because she wants to be the object of others' attention; for she loves herself excessively and wants others to notice her and adore her as well, so she dresses so as to turn the gaze of men towards her. But those who do not love themselves excessively will dress modestly, and they will have the awareness of the need for modesty, an awareness that is lacking in the immodest (vice or disordered passion blinds the intellect).

The person who lacks humility will have an aversion for humbling situations and lowly tasks (scrubbing floors, etc.), and will experience excessive sorrow when humiliated in some way. That sorrow will also lead to anger. For example, a true saint will not be terribly disturbed at someone who calls her a "good for nothing lowlife", for she will readily agree. A proud person will be incensed at such a remark. A proud person will experience a tremendous aversion at being corrected by someone else, but a humble person will experience gratitude at being enlightened by another.

Although anger is an emotion of the irascible appetite, it does require moderation or restraint, and it belongs to temperance to restrain. An intemperate or indulgent person often exhibits uncontrolled or disordered anger when his passions are not satisfied. Meekness is that virtue that moderates the passion of anger to readily obey reason. Note carefully that it is reasonable and praiseworthy to experience anger at an injustice, either against the self but especially against another person; not to experience anger is "vicious" (a vice), it is a sign that one is indifferent to justice. The vice of anger refers to anger that is contrary to reason. There is no "reason" to be angry that the local bakery has run out of your favorite donuts, for example, but it is reasonable to be angry that you are being ignored by the waitress because you are black, or brown, or Muslim, etc. The former is contrary to one's appetites, the latter is contrary to justice.

Fortitude and the Emotions of the Irascible Appetite (hope, despair, fear, daring, anger)

The virtue that perfects the irascible appetite and its emotions is fortitude and its parts. The object of the irascible appetite is the difficult sensible and/or intelligible good (the difficult pleasant), or the difficult sensible and/or intelligible evil (the difficult unpleasant).

Let us begin with the emotion of fear. Fortitude disposes the emotion of fear to readily obey reason. Fear arises when we encounter a difficult evil that we judge is insurmountable. In battle, a soldier will experience fear, for there is no way to avoid the enemy's aggression, and it might very well lead to his death, but he stands his ground and defends his country and the goods that his country has spent decades achieving (freedom, education, democracy, a sound constitution or charter of rights and duties, etc.). At times, the difficult evil is surmountable, so he experiences the emotion of daring (I will attempt a daring rescue that may cost me my life). But the brave soldier (fortitude) will moderate his daring so that his behavior is not reckless or foolhardy.

Now sorrow is an emotion of the concupiscible appetite, but difficult evils can generate sorrow. This sorrow will often move a person to give up on that difficulty when reason demands that one stay the course. Patience is that part of fortitude that disposes the emotion of sorrow to readily obey the dictates of reason; i.e., it is reasonable to be patient with a child, he's immature, doesn't know any better, etc.

The passion of hope bears upon the difficult good that is judged to be obtainable. It is noble for us to stretch forth in hope towards achieving great and honorable ends. The virtue of magnanimity disposes the passion of hope to obey reason in this movement towards the honorable. The excess of magnanimity is threefold: 1) presumption, which is the mistaken and audacious assumption that "I can do anything I put my mind to"; 2) inordinate ambition, which involves aiming for something that is well beyond my capacity (I am determined to be an engineer, even though I've never passed a math course in my life); and 3) vainglory (the desire to be famous, to be the object of public attention). The defect of magnanimity is pusillanimity. The pusillanimous person does not hope enough, his passion of hope is flat, so to speak; he settles for a very unheroic life that aims at nothing noble and honorable (i.e., I just work, watch TV, eat what I want, vote for the one everyone else is voting for, don't get involved, don't bother speaking out, so just leave me be, etc.). But consider a father who works long hours building houses, for example, so that his children can have what he did not have. That can be a heroic albeit uncelebrated life.

Not everyone has the means to do great things at great expense, but those who do will find that rather challenging. Magnificence is the virtue by which one disposes the emotion of hope to do great things at great expense. The defect of this virtue is stinginess. In this case, one's passion of hope bearing upon great things is flattened; one becomes stingy. The excess of magnificence is extravagance. Here one spends money on oneself, and so one's hope is in oneself (which is easy), not directed out towards difficult and honorable goals at great expense.

There are a number of things we need to do every day, and some of these things are difficult and demand perseverance. For example, cultivating the virtues is a difficult and lifelong task that requires perseverance. It is easy to give up when things become difficult. Some people, however, do not give up when it is reasonable to do so. For example, working on a Rubik's cube well into the night when one should get some sleep is unreasonable and thus pertinacious (pertinacity is the excess). One could say that such a person has too much love for the pleasure of achieving a difficult task, and so from this angle one is intemperate. It could also involve the vice of pride, or excessive love of one's excellence (one cannot accept defeat).

These virtues bring order and stability to one's emotional life. The two specific powers of the human person, however, are intellect and will. The moral virtue that perfects the intellect is prudence, and the virtue that perfects the will in its relations towards others is justice and all its parts. One can only achieve temperance and fortitude through prudence, which is the mother of all the virtues. It is the virtue of prudence that humanizes the emotions by cultivating the virtues of temperance and fortitude. Now the science of morality is part of the virtue of prudence, and so for a more complete understanding of what constitutes emotional well-being, we will need to treat in a special way the virtue of prudence.

Some thoughts on how emotion affects judgment

Passion arises from a judgment, but passion in turn narrows one's perspective, at least momentarily. That might be a good thing in certain circumstances. At a certain moment, I might be required to act decisively and with reason, and the emotions that arise out of an objective assessment of the situation have the effect of focusing my attention on the problem at hand. But when it comes to a much larger vision, or when it comes to discussing a more general problem that requires a much wider grasp of things, we need to be less "caught up" in our emotions; we need to be more stable emotionally. And so if a person is, in general, emotionally unstable (emotionally disordered, i.e., lacking the virtues), that habitual disorder is going to affect his or her ability to evaluate situations. His perspective will be habitually narrowed and twisted, and almost everything will be understood in reference to the self. He or she will see and judge everything in light of how it affects the self.

Consider a person who is lazy, unmotivated, immature, who would like to live as he did growing up, when his parents took care of him. He is uncomfortable going out into the world to take on his responsibilities. He is afraid, and he stubbornly wants to remain in the comfort of a childlike existence. How will he perceive the world? He will perceive the world as a fearful place. How will that affect his perspective with regard to other things, such as the political environment? It is conceivable that he will be attracted, for example, to the political candidate who promises to raise taxes, to increase the size of the welfare state, to increase the size of government, and who talks about taking money from the wealthy so as to redistribute it to the poor, etc. That will have great emotional appeal to him. If his self-love is excessive, he may not care how his lifestyle choice and his desire for a future that includes higher taxes will impact others.

Consider the person who has initiative, who is courageous enough to face the world, enter into relationships with others, make sacrifices, who is determined to contribute to the common good, to take his place in the world, etc. As he begins to experience success, he will experience the greater and more enduring joy of moral integration. He has a degree of good moral character, for he is a person of responsibility, and he experiences the rewards of his hard work, economically, psychologically, morally, physically, etc. That is going to affect the way he perceives the political landscape. He is a more just person, one who is committed to the good of the social whole and who is just in his dealings with the individuals he meets. And so his emotions of the concupiscible and irascible appetites are properly ordered, for they are in line with (submitted to) the will for a good moral order that includes himself but is much larger than himself, for it bears upon the common good of the civil community. He will know "well-being" from within, from the inside, to a much greater extent than lazy lout, who knows little more than the fleeting pleasures of food and drink and anything else he can get his hands on. And so he (the morally noble person with initiative) will not necessarily be attracted to the political candidate who promises a larger welfare state. He will know from within that the bar is too low, so to speak. He will be drawn to the candidate that has a plan to make it much easier to be a responsible and independent citizen.

Now, with more experience with human frailty and illness, we would hope he realizes that not everyone is able to achieve what he has achieved. Some people are visited with tragic circumstances that are beyond their control. His perspective will be balanced by that consideration. But if he loves his success too much, if he becomes too cocky and fails to appreciate his limits and the role of good fortune in all of this, he might become indifferent to the sick and suffering and too quick to judge their predicament. So too, his emotional state, his emotional complacency, might be so excessive that his vision is far too narrowed and that he too sees everything in reference to himself.

Disordered passions blind the intellect, which in turn leads to imprudent decisions, very often to unjust decisions, and these in turn have very costly social repercussions. Disordered passion blinds us above all to the limits of our own perspective. The result is that we are not aware of just how limited our point of view is—we think our view is much larger and all-encompassing than it actually is, and that is why we feel so right.

At that point, it is more difficult to listen to others, we may be tempted to dismiss them, even demonize them (we continually witness this in politics). But as we get older, we should begin to see that reality is much more complex than we once thought. If that happens, we become much less self-righteous. At least that is what should happen. Very often it does not, because of the passion of pride, which is the disordered love of one's own excellence. One cannot tolerate the feeling of being wrong, for it conflicts with one's rather inflated image of oneself. And so if one insists on enjoying the passion of satisfaction in being right, then one is unwilling to listen and have one's viewpoint enlarged. The other's perspective does not "feel" the same as my own, for it comes across to me as uncomfortable, it conflicts with my own, and it implies that my own is limited and that I am limited, and because my passion of self-love is excessive, I find it hard to entertain the possibility that it is true to reality.

This eclipse of a healthy sense of the limits of our own individual perspective and that narrowing that emotion causes in turn increases the passion to defend a particular point of view. But most importantly, "as a person is, so does he see", said Aristotle. He provides the example of a coward (one who has disordered fear) who sees the brave man as "rash" or "foolhardy". The coward does not see and evaluate correctly, for his judgment is distorted by his own self-knowledge, for he sees himself as the measure of what is reasonably brave, he does not see himself as a coward. But he fails to maintain the course of reason because of his fear. He has allowed himself to be governed by fear, not reason, and so he flees when he should stay the course and defend the defenseless, so to speak. Or, consider the foolhardy man who needlessly performs daring and risky actions when it is reasonable for him not to— since he has a wife and three children at home that need him. He sees the brave man, who acts according to the demands of reason and thus moderates the emotions of fear and daring, as a coward. And so the foolhardy man also does not see clearly nor evaluate correctly. It is the man of fortitude who evaluates correctly, for his emotions are in line with reason, and so he is emotionally inclined towards the most reasonable and noble course of action.

Chapter 30: A Note on Connatural Knowledge

Connatural knowledge is knowledge through inclination. The word connatural comes from two Latin words: *con* or 'with' and *natus* or "birth". When a mother gives birth, the child comes forth out of her interior. We speak of things having a nature, an interior, an essential quality (essence). The French word 'savoir' means "know how", as in how to do something, but 'connaitre' is used to describe the kind of knowledge that we have of individual human persons. One can know a great deal about a person (the science of psychology) without really knowing the person (connaitre). To know a person is to know him "from within", so to speak—in contradistinction to a knowledge "from without". This knowledge "from within" is a result of the mutual indwelling that love brings about: the lover exists in the beloved, and the beloved exists in the lover.

A morally good man who does not know the science of ethics can know by a kind of connaturality (or knowledge through inclination) what the right course of action is in a given circumstance. He knows from within, for he is inclined to choose the morally noble course of action because he possesses the virtues, which are dispositions inclining a person to act in a particular way with ease. This is what Aquinas is referring to in the following: "Now rectitude of judgment is twofold: first, on account of perfect use of reason, secondly, on account of a kind of connaturality with the matter about which one has to judge. Thus, about matters of chastity, a man who has learnt the science of morals judges rightly through inquiry by reason, while he who has the habit of chastity judges rightly of such matters by a kind of connaturality."

A person can know about religion without being religious, and a person can know the faith from within, from having lived it, without being learned in the science of theology. The latter knowledge is connatural knowledge, whereas the former—theological knowledge—is not necessarily connatural. Hence, Aquinas writes: "Accordingly it belongs to the wisdom that is an intellectual virtue to form a right judgment about divine things through inquiry by reason, but it belongs to wisdom as a gift of the Holy Spirit to form a right judgment about them on account of a kind of connaturality with them…Now this sympathy or connaturality for divine things is the result of charity, which unites us to God,…"

How this works is difficult to understand, but the following is an attempt to explain this way of knowing. Aquinas points out: "Whatever is received into something is received according to the mode of the receiver" (*Quidquid recipitur ad modum recipientis recipitur*). As this pertains to knowledge, it is true that "a thing known exists in a knower according to the mode of a knower." An apple known exists in the cognitive powers of a dog according to the mode of a brute animal, and the mode of knowing of a brute animal is limited to sensation, which bears upon material singulars. But the apple known exists in the mind of man according to the mode of a man, which is why it exists in him universally and immaterially—for the mind is immaterial. In order for us to know the nature of a thing, the intellect must abstract the intelligible content (essence) of the thing from its individuating conditions and impress that intelligible content upon the passive mind. And so, my passive mind becomes the essence of the being outside me, without changing that being. My mind becomes conformed to the thing it knows (the mind becomes what it knows, in an immaterial way).

But how does a person who is not learned in the science of ethics judge rightly about moral matters, such as matters pertaining to chastity, or fortitude, or justice, etc.,? Chastity, for example, is not an individual substance whose form or nature needs to be abstracted from its individuating conditions. Rather, it is an idea that needs to be incarnated in individual instances—note that this direction is the opposite of what usually takes place in our knowledge of things. And so it is the human person who needs to be changed, that is, conformed to the virtue in question, and the result of being so conformed to that virtue is the ability to judge rightly concerning matters pertaining to that virtue, through a kind of connaturality. The reason for this is that a thing is inclined to act according to its nature or form. For example, a substance having the form of a plant is inclined to grow, reproduce, etc. A substance having the form of a dog is inclined to see things and desire them, etc. Things act according to their natures. Similarly, a person conformed to chastity, justice, fortitude, etc., will be inclined to act chastely, justly, and courageously, etc. And because we possess self-knowledge, the virtuous person knows from within, by knowing his own inclinations, what the right thing to do is.

To understand this better, consider an Olympic figure skating or gymnastics competition. To the rest of us who are not skaters, the competitors all look equally skilled, for the most part at least. But to the judge, who was a former skater or gymnast, there are obvious grades of perfection within the ranks of the competitors. The judge is able to correctly judge of the quality of each skater by a kind of connaturality; he or she knows "from within", for he or she has become athletic, has acquired the skill or quality of being a skater or gymnast, and possessing that quality from within enables him or her to judge rightly concerning matters pertaining to that specific sport. So too, a person who has become musical will be able to judge the performance of a piece much better than one who is not at all musical, and a person who is a skilled artist will be able to judge a work of art much better than one who is not at all artistic. Even a critic who has no artistic talent will be able to judge a work of art properly as long as he has a great love of art, for love brings about a mutual indwelling. Some people say they "live and breathe" art, or music, or sports, etc. In other words, it is within them. Their knowledge of what constitutes great art, or music, or literature, etc., stems from their very depths.

Similarly, it is the virtuous man who knows from within what is genuinely virtuous. Now, it is in this way that emotion can become a source of knowledge; for it is virtue that disposes an emotion or passion to readily obey reason. To possess the virtues is to have brought order to one's passions, and this order or conformity to truth renders a person able to judge rightly concerning moral matters. So it is not emotion pure and simple that enables a person to judge rightly, but emotions disposed by good habits (virtues) that render one able to judge by a kind of connaturality. Finally, connatural knowledge is for the most part pre-conscious; in other words, one knows, but one does not always know why one knows what is right and noble.

Chapter 31: Inclination to God and the Moral Sense

There are a number of ways of knowing involved in a person's sense of moral duty, that is, his sense of the natural law. Involved are intuition, connatural knowledge, self-knowledge, and reasoning. And a large portion of that knowledge, in most people at least, is not explicit and conscious, but remains implicit and pre-conscious, albeit very real.

Aquinas argued that every human being, whether he realizes it or not, possesses a natural knowledge of God; it is a confused and general knowledge—this is true even for the "atheist". It is this knowledge that is the source of the moral sense, a natural awareness of a moral order that includes a host of duties. This moral sense can be dulled or intensified, depending upon how we choose to respond to its commands in the deepest recesses of our conscience, that is, whether we choose to obey it out of reverence for a good we know is larger than ourselves because it embraces everyone, or whether we choose to disregard it for the sake of the delectable. The evidence for this natural knowledge is in man's behavior, in his search for 1) the sufficient reason that explains the existence of things, and 2) in his desire for happiness. Allow me to explain what this means.

God and the Intuition of First Principles

I would like to begin with the principle of sufficient reason, which runs thus: "Everything which is, to the extent to which it is, possesses a sufficient reason for its being so that it is capable of explaining itself to the intellect. In other words, whatever is, has that whereby it is."

Consider the example employed in an earlier chapter, that of a broken window. You come home one evening and find that your living room window has been smashed. You immediately wonder how that happened. In other words, you seem to know that there is a sufficient reason for this window being broken. Now, "whatever is, has that whereby it is"; and so this broken window has that whereby it is broken (i.e., the reason), either in itself or in another. If it has "that whereby it is" in itself, then it contains within itself, within the very notion of "broken window", the reason for its being broken. If that were the case, then just knowing that this window is broken is enough to know the sufficient reason for its being so, and thus you would not ask the question: "Why is this window broken?" The reason would be contained in itself, and so it would explain itself. But that is clearly not the case, which is why you wonder how the window got broken.

Notice, however, that you do not wonder how you are able to carry on an intelligent conversation with a friend; there is nothing about that which you find puzzling. The reason is that the "sufficient reason" for the conversation is contained within your friend's very nature, for he or she is a human person, that is, a rational animal. An individual with a rational nature is capable of communicating concepts through language—that's what it means to be rational. But a flower is not capable of such communication, and so if a flower were to pose a question to us, we'd be wonder struck.

If that which is has that whereby it is through another, then it depends upon that 'other'. Thus the broken window has its sufficient reason in something outside of it.

Now when we see something existing, or an inanimate thing moving, we naturally inquire of the reason until we possess the sufficient reason, at which point we are sufficiently satisfied. The reason for the moving ball is the pitcher's act of throwing (the efficient cause). Knowing the efficient cause, however, is not always sufficient. If a neighbor tells us that the boy down the street threw the ball through the window, we continue to search for the reason until we find the sufficient reason—a "throwing arm" is insufficient. It is not enough that his arm was moving and caused the ball to move through the air, thus breaking the window. We know that arms don't throw things; it is the agent as a whole that throws things, and so we naturally want to know "why" he threw the ball in the first place. In other words, we're looking for the final cause of the action (the end, or purpose). If it is determined that he threw the ball to his friend during play and the pitch was wild and thus he accidentally broke the window, we now possess the sufficient reason. But if that is not the case, we continue to search for the reason. If we learn that he threw the ball at the window because he was angry with you and wanted revenge for an injustice he believes you committed, then we are coming closer to the sufficient reason that explains the broken window.

Now, consider the principle of identity: each being is what it is (a carrot is a carrot, an oxygen atom is an oxygen atom, etc). There is quite a bit packed into that first self-evident principle. In knowing anything at all, I know first and foremost that it is (it exists). Being is first in my knowledge of anything. I may not understand who or what is approaching, but I know generally and confusedly that something is approaching. After a while, I come to realize that it is an animal. After a bit more time, I realize that it is something possessing a canine nature. Finally, I realize it is my pet dog that was lost. That realization is accompanied by a sense of relief.

In this apprehension of my approaching dog, I know "what" it is (a canine creature), and I know "that it is" (my dog has existence). The formulation of the principle of identity—"each being is what it is"—contains two apprehensions: the simple apprehension of a being's nature or essence (what it is) and the judgment of its existence (that it is). But my dog's existence is not contained in her nature (canine)—otherwise I would not have been worried that she might have been killed; for whatever belongs to a thing's nature belongs to it necessarily. Thus, the ability to think belongs necessarily to a rational nature, "3 sides" belongs necessarily to a triangle, etc., and so if behind this door there is a human being, it is necessarily the case that he or she has a rational nature and thus cannot not be rational, and if there is a triangle behind this wall, it may not be made of wood and painted yellow, but it necessarily has 3 sides (it cannot not have 3 sides).

Existence, however, does not belong necessarily to my pet dog's nature; otherwise my dog would necessarily exist, and could not not exist (just as a triangle cannot not have 3 sides, etc.). In other words, the sufficient reason for my dog's existence is not contained in its nature, but is outside of it. More to the point, the existence of anything that I apprehend, whether it is a human, a cat, a plant, or a mineral of some kind, etc., is not contained in the nature that I grasp through simple apprehension. I apprehend existence through a distinct act of the intellect, namely existential judgment.

And that is precisely why we wonder why there is anything rather than nothing at all. We want to know the ultimate meaning of things, the purpose of life, the origin of existence, etc. We do so because *the sufficient reason for the existence of things is outside the things themselves that we know, and so we are constantly seeking to discover the causes of things.* Sure, we now know why your eyes are blue, and why your cells multiply, and why you should moderate sodium in your diet, etc, but we continue to seek for more answers to our questions, for we want to know why you and everything else exists *in the first place.* We have a desire to know the ultimate causes of things, the first causes, and being (existence) is absolutely first. To know the cause of the origin of the whole is to understand the whole.

Of course, most people do not have all this worked out in explicitly formulated concepts and first self-evident principles, but they do, nevertheless, have a knowledge of the "insufficiency of being", even if it is only a preconscious one. But there is more to this. If I possess—even confusedly and pre-consciously—a knowledge of the insufficiency of things to explain their very existence, then I know that *things depend on something outside of them in order to exist* (to be and continue to be). In other words, if the sufficient reason for their being is not within them, it is outside of them, in another. And since the most obvious agents of a living thing's generation are its parents who are themselves beings whose sufficient reason for being is outside of them, whose parents in turn are beings whose sufficient reason for being is outside of them, and so on, etc, I am aware (even confusedly and perhaps pre-consciously) that all things depend for their existence on a being who contains within himself the sufficient reason for his own existence, that is, a being whose existence and essence are one and the same, and who is thus independent.

If I were to provide an analogy, think of a chandelier hanging above your head in a ballroom, but you are positioned in the room such that you cannot see the ceiling, only the chandelier and the links of the chain by which it is suspended. Now in your mind, it matters not how many links in the chain there are; the ceiling could be so high as to require hundreds, even thousands of links. Nevertheless, each link is dependent upon another (i.e., the one is holding up the link below it because it is being held up by the one above it, which in turn is being held up by the one above it, etc.). The very fact that there are hundreds of dependent links makes no difference to your knowledge of the insufficiency of the links as an explanation for the chandelier being suspended above. Multiplying them into the millions, even trillions, does not in the long run satisfy you by offering you the sufficient reason for its suspension. You know that there must be a ceiling from which the links are attached—millions of dependents do not amount to an independent.

And so, one does not even need to see the ceiling, but one knows nonetheless that there is a sufficient reason for the chandelier being continually suspended above our heads, which is why if we want an explanation for its suspension, we look to see the ceiling, or whatever it is that is radically different from the dependent links in between. Whatever it is, we know it is a stable origin that enjoys an independence not belonging to the links.

Now, it is not necessary to think of this in terms of a long series of causes stretching back into the past; that would be to misunderstand the point being made. If the sufficient reason for a thing's very act of existence is not contained within it, then there is no need to search for it in another being in the same predicament (i.e., a parent). Every being in such a predicament is immediately dependent upon this efficient cause who is the sufficient reason for the existence of all things.

Human beings have a more or less confused knowledge of this, and they've always had this knowledge; this sufficient reason for being is what we call God. But those who refuse to do so, i.e., atheists, are nonetheless still in search for "the origin" that they expect will explain and thus provide the sufficient reason for the very existence of the universe. In other words, their search for this sufficient reason shows that they understand, even if only pre-consciously, that there really exists a sufficient reason, otherwise there would be no "reason" to search.

The Desire for the *Bonum Universale*

There is also another angle from which we can look at all this. You and I are moved to act, to pursue, to search, to work, to accomplish, etc. Whatever we choose to do, we do so for the sake of an end (final cause).

Consider any activity whatsoever—your neighbor fixing his car, for example. Why is he doing that? He's acting for an end, namely, that the car will continue to function. And why would he want the car to function? So that he can get from one place to another. And why would he want to drive from his home to, let's say, his workplace? Well, he wants to work. Why does he choose to work? In order to support himself, etc.

As we can see, it is the end that gives meaning (direction) to one's activity, and it is an end that is the reason (the cause) for the previous movements or actions. The end is the final cause, or that for the sake of which there is activity. The final cause (end) is the mover that moves the agent to action. The ultimate end is the ultimate reason, that is, the ultimate mover of one's actions.

So let us ask the question: "What is the ultimate reason why we do anything at all"? The answer is happiness. We seek happiness, and the happiness we seek has certain characteristics. We seek a happiness that is enduring and unqualified; for example, were we to achieve that happiness, we would not say to ourselves: "I want this to come to an end". We want a happiness that endures. We want a happiness that does not depend upon contingent factors like the weather. We seek a happiness that is complete, that is desired entirely for its own sake and not for the sake of something else, and one that is sufficient unto itself, not one good among others, but a final good that transcends all others. That's why we continue to seek, regardless of how much we already possess, for our current state of happiness is always qualified, incomplete, and not entirely self-sufficient.

The human heart (will) is restless. It is always searching for more, no matter how much it already possesses. Now if we seek this unqualified good (end), it must mean that we know it in some way; for we do not desire what we do not know—the will can only tend towards what the intellect presents to it. So what is it that we know, which is behind the will's tendency towards it? We know there is a universal good, an unqualified good, otherwise we would not desire it. We may not know clearly and explicitly what that is, but we know it confusedly and generally at least, which is why we continually tend to it.

This is the good that we love before and above all things, and this ultimate end is the reason why we recognize the goodness in all other human goods in our life, i.e., our friendships, our work, our leisure, our insights, etc., just as our neighbor sees all those things that contribute to his achieving his end, which is the functioning of his car, as good; for example, he sees his tools as good, his garage as good, his tires as good, oil as good, etc. They are all good in view of the good of a functioning automobile, but a functioning automobile is good in view of his work, which is good in view of his very life that his work helps to sustain.

My life and all other human goods are good because they are related to the ultimate end, which I naturally love more than I love myself—for I am not the *bonum universale*, for if I were, I would no longer seek anything outside myself. Indeed, my life is good for its own sake, but it is also relatively good, that is, *in relation to* higher goods that are specific to my nature.

For example, it is good to be alive, and so I know that food and shelter are good for the sake of that life. But I seek more than just living. Indeed, it is good to be alive for its own sake, but I also want to live in order to continue to possess truth, to love, to raise my children, pursue justice, etc. I pursue a life rich in human goods, but behind all this is a pursuit of something supremely good, a self-sufficient happiness that I do not find within myself or as yet in the world. I certainly desire my own perfection, my own fullness of being, but that desire is for something other than me. In possessing it, I seem to be aware that I will possess perfection and thus happiness— otherwise I would not pursue it. I desire a universal good, an unqualified good that will bring me an unqualified happiness.

This self-sufficient happiness, which is the ultimate end of everything I do, coincides with the sufficient reason for the being of all beings. My search for the sufficient reason for being and my search for happiness converge towards the same point. Being Itself (that being whose nature is to be) and the universal good (the possession of which constitutes my perfect happiness) are one and the same.

This one end is God, whether we are explicitly aware of it or not. In fact, Aquinas' five demonstrations of God's existence are simply ways of showing that what we already know confusedly and generally is in fact what we mean by God. To repeat, although an atheist rejects the idea of God's existence, he pursues nonetheless the origin that he expects will explain and provide the sufficient reason for existence. Perhaps he thinks that sufficient reason is going to be located in a particle, or in an equation for a theory of everything, etc, but it is the difficult work of philosophy that involves attempting to determine whether these or other such things constitute the sufficient reason for the existence of things. Similarly, a person might believe that his greatest happiness, the ultimate end, is the possession of power or unlimited wealth or fame, etc. So too, it belongs to philosophy to test that supposition through reasoning. Regardless of this, what is clear is that these people, and everyone else, are aware of a sufficient reason for being and a *bonum universale* (universal good), for their actions reveal such an awareness.

The Moral Sense

There is much more to this pre-conscious and confused knowledge of the universal good than what we've unpacked up to this point. We experience reality as intelligible, good, and beautiful, even though its goodness, intelligibility and beauty are limited. Now, all these properties (intelligibility, goodness, and beauty) have to do with order. This is especially obvious in the case of beauty; a beautiful symphony is ordered, harmonious, and radiant with meaning. We speak of beautiful days, beautiful sunsets, beautiful skies, etc. If there is beauty to reality, there is an order to reality.

That is why we have a sense that the origin, the sufficient reason for existence, is intelligent, good and beautiful; for we all know intuitively the principle of causality, that for every effect, there is a cause, and the effect cannot possess what the cause is lacking, for that would suggest that something comes from nothing (or that nothing and something are identical, which is absurd). And that is why human beings, from as far back as we know, have an awareness of a God (or gods) that is in some sense personal (intelligent and volitional) and who is deserving of acts of sacrifice and thanksgiving. He is the origin of the order found in things, considered in themselves and taken as a whole.

Now the world we live in is characterized by movement. Things are in motion; there is change in the universe, and every agent moves for the sake of an end, a final cause. A thing's final cause tells us the good of the thing, that is, it tells us what completes it. A plant moves, but its motion is towards its own completion, i.e., a rose develops in order to be a rose most fully and completely. That is why we understand what constitutes a good and healthy rose, a good and healthy dog, etc. Without that knowledge, we couldn't treat diseases in plants and animals, for we can only know a pathology in light of the good of the thing.

Now I know from within that I am inclined to an ultimate end, namely happiness. I also know from within that I am inclined towards a number of ends (human goods, such as life, the possession of truth, the knowledge and appreciation of what is beautiful, personal friendships, marriage and family, a just social order, etc.). I also know that this and that person over there are of the same nature as myself (human), and I know through observing their behavior that they too are inclined to these goods, and ultimately to the universal good, because everything they do is also for the sake of happiness. We all experience our own lives and the lives of one another as fundamentally good.

And so I know that the good is much more than my own private good; I know that it is much more than your private good. I know, therefore, that there is a common good that is larger than my own private good, just as each player on a soccer team is aware of a common good, which is the team's victory; each player will share in the victory and will be glorified by it. This common good, however, is larger than the individual player's private good, for example, the player's individual scoring record. Note that the team's strategy is ordered for the sake of victory (the common good). Every action on the part of the individual players is ordered towards the common good, and a player's acts are judged to be good to the degree that they are ordered to the common good, which is victory. To score is good because it contributes to the end to which all their actions aim, but if a player were to get carried away and begin performing dazzling tricks with the soccer ball, which then leads to the other team scoring a goal, his actions would be judged by his teammates as bad—albeit skilled. Were he to continue in that vein, he would eventually be benched, because his behavior is harmful to the team (and thus every player on the team, including himself). His actions lack order towards the good of the whole, perhaps as a result of having an inflated ego, a passion for praise, etc. He has the potential to be a great player, but does not achieve excellence because his actions on the field lack due order towards the good of the whole, that is, the common good.

Each one of us has a sense of a moral order which
includes us (our own good), but which is also larger than us
considered individually (it embraces the good of everyone). I
know from within that I am a moral agent, and that I have a
natural inclination towards the universal good that I can't do
anything about (I necessarily will my own happiness), but I am
aware that I have the freedom to make choices that establish
me in a certain relationship with my ultimate end, this personal
God, who is the origin of the order of creation. If I sense that
He is personal, even confusedly and pre-consciously, then I
sense He has a will and that the order of creation manifests His
will, just as the order I behold in a work of art is an expression
of the will of the artist.

Plants and animals are not moral agents. The movement
of a plant is such that as long as it is watered and planted in the
proper environment, it will mature and become what it is
inclined to become by nature. So too is this the case with
brute animals. Both plants and animals achieve their own
good naturally. But human beings, on the other hand, have the
ability to freely determine themselves towards their own
fullness of being or in a way that arrests that maturation. A
moral agent can choose to fulfill his nature or destroy it.

As a moral agent, I have the ability to think and make free
choices, thus determining myself to be a certain kind of
person, that is, shaping a moral identity for myself. This is
what we mean by moral character. By my free choices, I
determine myself to be a person of good character, or a person
of deficient (evil) character. I am either the kind of person
who freely chooses to love the moral good before the
delectable good—which involves freely choosing to love your
good and everyone else's (the common good), thus God's
goodness expressed in the order of creation—, or I am the
kind of person that loves my own private pleasure (the
delectable good) over the moral good.

The human person detects within himself a law, a
command or rational dictate, to which he feels called to obey,
and it is a command to respect the order of creation in all
things, in himself and in the social order. He knows from

within that he respects that moral order by freely choosing to do what he understands to be good as such, as opposed to what is simply pleasurable for him.

For example, I know that you are of the same nature as myself (through simple apprehension), and I know from within that it is good for me to be alive (I desire to live). Now I desire to possess certain property for the sake of preserving my life, for example, I own a pair of shoes, a jacket, my own lunch box, etc. I know that you too possess property for the same reason, and that it is good for you to do so—in other words, it is "right" (Latin: jus) and ordered for you to do so, not disordered—property is ordered towards the preservation of life, which in turn is ordered towards knowledge, personal relationships, and other human goods, and finally the ultimate end (the *bonum universale*). The social order, which includes the economy and the order of justice, exists for our shared good (common good), and I know that I would not want you to take my shoes and lunch box just because you happen to like them (I need them), and so I know from within that I ought not to take yours (because I know that you are of the same nature as myself), even though possessing them would bring me some kind of emotional satisfaction.

If it is right and ordered for you to own them, it is wrong and disordered for me to take them simply because I like them. If my emotions are moving me to take your property when you are not looking, simply because I desire them, I now have a choice before me: to resist that temptation for the sake of an order larger than me, or give into it, thus choosing my own emotional satisfaction (pleasure) over the order of justice. In choosing the latter, I am choosing to treat myself preferentially. Although I know you to be equal in dignity to me, I am treating you in a way that fails to respect that equality, and thus that order. I am twisting that order, elevating my desire for emotional complacency above your right to own and share in the good. I am aware that I am violating a natural law, that is, a natural command or dictate of reason to respect an order that is larger than me.

Think of how a crook behaves when he is caught and confronted—he often reacts with violent indignation. And how does a criminal behave when he discovers he's the victim of a theft? Also with violent indignation; thus he is aware that theft is a violation of a right, but he is indifferent to the rights of others and incensed when confronted with the truth of his disordered character.

Just as a bad but skilled soccer player behaves without order towards the good of the whole, so too a morally bad person chooses without due regard for the good of the whole, that is, the entire moral order. In doing so, he goes against his deepest awareness of that order, that is, he violates his conscience. He is disordered within himself, for his emotions are not disposed to submit to the demands of reason, thus he is intemperate, and he lacks the fortitude to sacrifice his own love of the delectable good for the sake of the good of the whole. Moreover, he is an unjust person, for by his own will he is a disordered part of the social whole.

Now the human person naturally loves God more than he loves himself. I know, for example, that I am not the "universal good". I also naturally love the good of the whole more than the good of the part. For example, if someone comes towards me swinging a baseball bat, I naturally raise my arms to defend myself. I am placing a part of myself in harm's way in order to protect the whole, thus I naturally love the whole more than the part, for the whole is a greater good than the part, which is good on account of the whole. Similarly, I see that I am part of a larger social whole (not a mere part, to be sure), and I naturally love the social whole more than myself. All this is natural and inevitable; there is no moral nobility in this. But as a moral agent, I must now freely choose in accordance with that natural inclination. For me to choose my own private satisfaction over the good of the social whole (which reflects back on me for my well-being, as a team's victory is also the good of the individual player), that is, for me to choose to disobey my knowledge of the natural law, my awareness of the command to revere that order of creation, is for me to choose in a way that is contrary to my own natural inclination (my own good). In other words, immoral choices put me on a path to self-destruction. Furthermore, I never do experience the "pleasurable good" that I choose above the moral good, at least not in any lasting and significant way, because the delectable good and the moral good are not necessarily opposed; rather, the former (*bonum delectabile*) is the fruit of the latter (*bonum honestum*). Immoral choices only succeed in bringing fragments of the delectable good, temporary pieces that lack breadth and depth, which is why immoral choices lead to greater restlessness, not greater peace. An immoral person is his own worst enemy, not to mention an enemy of the civil community as a whole.

Consider that by virtue of the close relationship between the moral sense and the sense of God's existence, it is no coincidence that moral reasons are and have always been at the root of atheism. To violate that moral order of which my conscience makes me aware is to dampen that voice, to suppress that sense of a natural and personal command or dictate (natural law). To eradicate that sense completely is, I suspect, difficult to do, and even more difficult to dampen that sense consistently, which is why those of depraved character will expend a tremendous amount of energy trying to show that God does not exist and that to believe in God is delusional and infantile. It is also no coincidence that atheists and agnostics who choose to obey the directives of that moral sense as it is made known to them in the deepest recesses of their conscience, very often will eventually come to a more explicit awareness of God's existence and become great converts.

All that we've elaborated and made explicit up to this point is known, more or less confusedly, vaguely, and pre-consciously, by every human person who has reached a certain level of reason. What is particularly disturbing, however, is the increasing number of people who choose every day to place their own pleasure (*bonum delectabile*) above the moral good (*bonum honestum*), in little acts of theft, lying, deception, cutting corners, insurance fraud, etc. In doing so, they not only place themselves on a path of self-destruction (personal disintegration or dis-integrity), they also create disorder in the world, for their disordered actions have wide and costly social repercussions to which they are frankly indifferent. But they know this fundamental conflict within themselves, they are aware of it and are ashamed of it, they don't love it, which is why they spend a great deal of energy trying to hide it, for they know that others, persons of virtue in particular, would find them unsightly and repugnant, as they find themselves unsightly and repugnant.

Chapter 32: The Virtue of Prudence

The mould and mother of all the virtues is prudence. It is defined as the intellectual virtue which rightly directs particular human acts, through rectitude of the appetite, toward a good end. Emotional well-being comes about through a certain structuring of the entire network of human emotions, one that results from a proper disposing of the emotions by the virtues. If we are correct, then prudence is the mother of emotional health. And if virtue is the secret to looking beautiful, then prudence is, in many ways, the mother of beautiful character; for it is prudence that determines the mean of reason in all human actions and situations.

Prudence, however, is not merely an intellectual virtue; it is also a moral virtue. A moral virtue is a habit that makes its possessor good. One may be brilliant and learned without being morally good, but it is not possible to be prudent and not morally good. The prudent man is one who does the good, as opposed to one who merely knows the good. There are many moral philosophers and theologians around, but prudent persons are probably not as common. It is much easier to talk about virtue, especially prudence, than it is to actually be virtuous. And one who does not behave well cannot be said to be prudent, even though he happens to be very learned. We will understand this better as we take a closer look at just what prudence is.

The more abstractly we think, the more certain we are of our conclusion. Thus, mathematics is a very certain science, more so than say biology. When was the last time we heard of a revised mathematical equation? But theories are normally revised in the physical sciences; for the objects of mathematics are more abstracted from matter than are the objects of the science of biology. Similarly, we enjoy a relatively high level of certainty when dealing with very general moral issues such as murder, euthanasia, lying, etc., but as we approach the level of the particular, that is, a more concrete level, we very often become less certain about what we ought to do, because the concrete level contains so many variables that render decision making much more complex; for there is much more to consider.

This does not mean that there is no truth on the concrete level of moral decision making, or that on this level the moral good is merely relative (i.e., relative to how you feel or what you want, etc.). Nothing could be further from the truth. Rather, it means that a special virtue is required by which one might see and readily make one's way through these murky waters to the right end. Prudence is the application of universal principles to particular situations, and so an understanding of universal moral principles is absolutely necessary. But since prudence deals in particulars, in the here and now of real situations, a number of other intellectual qualities are also necessary if one is to choose rightly, qualities that one does not necessarily acquire in a classroom setting. St. Thomas refers to these as integral parts of prudence, without which there is no prudence, just as there is no house without a roof, walls, and a foundation.

Integral Parts of Prudence

Understanding of First Principles (human goods and precepts)

The good is that which all things desire. Now all things desire to be most fully. Thus, 'good' is a property of being. But man is conscious of that towards which he tends. He knows himself from within. The ultimate reason why we do anything at all is the ultimate end, which is an end to which we are inclined naturally and which has the properties of completeness, self-sufficiency, and indefinite endurance. But we are also naturally inclined to more proximate ends, which are sought for their own sake in relation to still more proximate ends (such as pencils, automobiles, computers, etc.). The human person knows that he tends not simply towards one limited intelligible human good, but a number of them. These basic intelligible human goods are principles, that is, starting points; they are motivating principles of human action. Each one is a natural inclination within the human person, and each one contributes to our perfection as human persons.

The human person has a natural inclination to preserve his **life**; for he sees his life as basically good. Human existence is a rational animal kind of existence. It is basically good to be as a rational animal, created in the image and likeness of God, in the image of knowledge and love (intellect and will). Human life is specifically "cognitive" life, a life having the potential of self-expansion through knowledge and through love. Everything else in the physical universe exists to serve human life and is valued according to its ability to do just that. Thus, everything in the physical universe is instrumentally good, while the human person alone is basically good (he alone was willed into existence for his own sake).

This human person, who is fundamentally, intelligibly, and intrinsically good, desires to possess **truth** for its own sake. Knowing is a mode of existing. In knowing anything, one becomes what one knows ("the intellect is in a way all things"). Knowledge is a kind of self-enlargement. Man always desires to be more fully, and he exists most fully as a knower, as a see-er. His ultimate purpose in life clearly has something to do with knowing, which is his highest activity and, according to Aquinas, "the highest mode of having". As Josef Pieper writes: "Knowing is the highest mode of having because in the world there is no other form so thoroughgoing. Knowing is not only appropriation which results in "property" and "proprietorship." It is assimilation in the quite exact sense that the objective world, in so far as it is known, is incorporated into the very being of the knower." (*Happiness and Contemplation*, 65-66)

This human person we've been talking about has, at the same time, a natural inclination to **contemplate the beautiful**, to see it, to intuit it, to behold it. And so he visits art museums, gazes at the sunset or the beautiful face of a child, and he even contemplates the beauty of divine providence. His ultimate purpose has something to do with intuition, especially the intuition of beauty, and this is something that Plato understood well (Cf. *The Symposium*, 210e-212b).

Man is a **maker**. He brings all his sense and intellectual powers to bear upon the project of producing works of art, such as paintings, poetry, sculptures, buildings, monuments, etc., just for the sake of creating, or just for the sake of playing, such as golf, cards, chess, etc. Indeed, there is a permanent and underlying element of contemplation in all of this. It is man the knower who leisures. The person who plays has the cognitive power of complete self-reflection, and so he contemplates the marvel of his own skills and delights in the awareness of their gradual perfection. He contemplates his gifts and detects the giver underneath them. A good player is awed by the laws that he can detect behind an ordinary game of chess, for example, and the players delight in the intuition of the beauty of the execution of a well-planned strategy that resulted in a touchdown or a goal or a home run. Even spectators contemplate and discuss these plays typically after the game. Contemplation permeates the leisure of play and art carried out for its own sake. If it did not, no one would leisure. What brute animal leisures?

Man is a **social and political animal**. The human person is not thrown into this world as an isolated individual, but as a person. He is born into a family and is inclined to relate to that family and find his place in it; for he discovers himself through others, especially his parents and siblings. He is also born into a nation, and he is inclined to relate to the social whole, and to find his place within that larger whole.

He tends to establish friendships. He is glad to "see" his friends, to "hear" their voices. Ultimately, he wills to share the good that has come to him. Above all, he desires to share what he "sees" or knows with others. And others desire to share with him all that they have been gratuitously given, especially what they possess in knowledge (for knowledge is the highest mode of possessing anything). These others enable him to see what he was unable to see before. The perspectives they bring to him enlarge him, and they likewise are enlarged by what he brings them.

His friendships are not merely utilitarian. Rather, the highest kind of friendship he seeks is benevolent friendship

(*EN* 8. 3, 1156b6). He has only a few genuine friends with whom he can share himself on such a profound level. But he inclines towards them, because goodness is self-diffusive, and the more he is given, the more he wills to share what he has been given, and this is above all the case with what he "sees" or beholds, that is, what he knows, what he intuits or contemplates. Delighting in the presence of friends is nothing less than seeing. It is a form of contemplation.

Man is a **religious** animal; he aspires after what is higher than himself because he is aware of a thirst within himself, among other things. The human heart is restless, and it will remain so until it rests in the vision of God. For man beholds his own finitude and the finitude of creation. He aspires to what is beyond the temporal to the eternal, yet he cannot transcend the limits of his nature; but he dreams about it (as we see in Plato). He seeks to know the giver behind the gift of his existence, that is, behind the gift that is creation. As a spiritual nature, he is open to the whole of reality, the whole of being (universal being). He seeks to know the "whole of reality", that is, to possess the *bonum universale* (the universal and total good). We know from revelation that he is not going to attain it on his own. He might think, as Plato did, that death will free him from the temporal in order to enter into the realm of the "really real" so as to contemplate subsistent beauty. And that might very well be the case. But revelation tells us that this can only happen through God's initiative. He cannot, of his own nature, attain God. If he is to attain the *bonum universale*, it can only be through another gratuitous giving (distinct from creation), which we call divine grace.

Man is inclined to **marry**, to give himself completely to another, to belong to another exclusively in one flesh union. Even a marriage consummated by sexual union is a kind of knowing. Mary says to the angel Gabriel: "I do not know man" (Lk 1, 35). The giving of oneself in the marital act is a revealing of oneself to the other. One allows oneself to be known, and one gives oneself in order to be known by the other in a way that is exclusive and thus closed off to others. Marriage is a special kind of knowledge of persons; love wills that the other see or behold what it knows, especially conjugal love. And both husband and wife will to beget human life, because goodness is effusive, and their unique conjugal relationship is good. They desire that a new life, the fruit of their love, share in what they know, namely the relationship they have with one another (as well as with others, with creation, and with God).

Man is inclined to seek **integration** within himself, an integration of the complex elements of himself. This is because he seeks to be most fully, and one (along with good, beauty, and true) is a property of being. He is inclined to bring about a more intense unity within himself, namely harmony between his actions and his character as well as his will and his passions. Bringing order to the passions (cultivating temperance and fortitude) is a means to an end. A person aims to be temperate and brave for the sake of possessing the highest good, the possession of which is threatened by excessive sensuality and/or by inordinate fear and daring.

These are the primary principles of practical reason; they are the starting points of human action, the motivating principles behind every genuinely human action that we choose to perform. Now the very first principle of morality is self-evident and is presupposed in every human action. That principle is: *good is to be done, evil is to be avoided.*

It is from this principle that more specific precepts are derived. A specifically human act is one that is motivated by one or more of these intelligible human goods. Scratching an itch is not a specifically human action, for even dogs and cats scratch themselves when itchy. But asking a question is a specifically human action, for behind it is a will to know and possess truth, which is an intelligible human good. So too, stopping the car in order to behold a beautiful landscape or the majestic beauty of the Rockies is a specifically human and humanly good action.

Now evil is a privation, a lack of something that should be there; it is a deficiency or lack of wholeness. Thus, an evil will is one that is deficient, whereas a good will is whole and complete. Thus, a morally good action is one that involves a will open to the entire spectrum of intelligible human goods, whereas a morally evil action involves a deficient willing, a will not open to the full spectrum of human goods. A person is good if he wills the good, not merely his own good, for "human goods" are not limited to this individual instance which is himself. Nor is it limited to one's immediate family or relatives, etc. If a person is good willed, he wills the good wherever there is an instance of it.

From these principles, more specific or **secondary moral precepts** can be derived and, moreover, are naturally known to some degree or another by every human person. For example, everyone (more or less mentally sound) throughout the world and throughout history understands that justice is good and ought to be done. As precepts become more specific, however, and as they are applied to specific situations, disagreements begin to arise.

God is to be loved above all things. If God is Goodness Itself, the Supreme Good, then "relationship" with God is the greatest human good.

One ought to render due honor to one's parents. The family is the society through which we enter this world. We owe a debt to our parents that cannot be fully repaid. Relationship with this first society is humanly good and of the highest importance.

One ought to reverence the marriage bond; for marriage is an intelligible human good and the basis of the family.

Do not harm others. I experience my life as good, because I'm inclined to protect it. I also know that the other is of the same nature as myself and thus sees his life as equally good. And so I know naturally that I ought not to inflict harm on others, because they are basically good. Thus, one ought not to do anything that harms the common good of the civil community, and one ought to direct one's life towards the common good.

If others are intrinsically and humanly good, then one ought not to willingly harm or destroy another for the sake of some other human good; in other words, one must not do evil to achieve good. And since human goods are intrinsically good, that is, ends in themselves, then one ought not to treat another human person as a means to an end.

Since others are equally good, since they are essentially equal, it follows that one ought not to treat certain others with a preference based purely on feelings of partiality, etc, unless a preference is required by human goods. In other words, one ought always to treat others in a way that respects their status as equal in dignity to oneself.

Now the common good can only be achieved in communion with others, so if we ought to revere the common good, one ought not to act individualistically for human goods, but in community with others.

And since man is a rational animal who desires his own fullness of being (good), he ought to act rationally. Hence, one ought not to act purely on the basis of passion, either on the basis of fear, aversion, hostility, or desire for sensible goods, but one ought to act on the basis of reason, in pursuit of intelligible goods and in accordance with all the precepts of natural law. To act purely on the basis of emotion is to act as a brute, without the guidance of reason. For example, a real threat to human goods, such as a charging pit bull, would give rise to fear, and it is reasonable to allow that emotion to move us in the direction to which it inclines us. We might evaluate the threat as somewhat surmountable, in which case we ought to run for our lives. Such behaviour is reasonable and motivated by the will to preserve our lives. But refusing to go to school because one finds new social situations uncomfortable is to choose to act on the basis of feelings of fear and anxiety (assuming, of course, that there is a choice, and that there is no serious phobia that prevents a person from making a free choice). So too, refusing to walk to school because there is a dead skunk on the road that gives rise to feelings of aversion, or because one feels lethargic, are examples of behaviour not grounded in reason. Practical reason demands that good be done, but good is not being done because one values feeling good over intelligible human goods (the lower over the higher).

It is possible to act on the basis of the emotion of desire without reference to intelligible human goods. Eating is a desirable action and it serves intelligible human goods, for example human life, family, and friendships. But to willingly eat merely for the taste of food is unreasonable and not fully human, it is gluttonous. For example, a person who is not at all hungry nor in need of nourishment and sees no reason to eat, but who grabs a can of icing and begins eating it for the sweet taste, is behaving in a way that is not specifically and fully human, but less than human. It is human behaviour insofar as it is willed, but it falls short insofar as it fails to realize intelligible human goods.

Engaging in a mood altering behaviour, such as drug use, in order to feel as if one's life is all together (integrity) when in fact it is not, is again to engage in behaviour that is not humanly good. Actually taking steps to bring order to one's life is the more human albeit difficult option.

And since each person is intrinsically good and one (integral), and since one desires to be integrated, one ought not to violate that integrity. Hence, one ought not to lie (which is an immediate violation of integrity), and one ought to choose in accordance with one's best judgment on what to do here and now (conscience), and one ought to relentlessly pursue that truth of what is right and wrong, to make sure one's acts conform to the demands of the natural law.

Memory

If prudence were merely the knowledge of universal moral principles, we could stop here. But it is much more than that. Prudence requires a sensitivity and attunement to the here and now of the real world of real people. It requires a great deal of experience. That is why Aquinas lists memory as an integral part of the virtue of prudence, for experience is the result of many memories.

There is more to memory than the simple recall of facts. Memory is an ability to learn from experience. And so it involves an openness to reality, a willingness to allow oneself to be measured by what is real. This quality of openness is not as widespread as we might tend to believe at first. Some people just don't seem to learn from experience, that is, they don't seem to remember how this or that person reacted to their particular way of relating to them, for they continue to make the same mistakes in their way of relating to others. It is as if they have no memory of last week, or last month, or last year. They lack a "true to being" memory because they do not will to conform to what is real, but have made a stubborn decision to have reality conform to the way they want the world to be. That is why the study of history is so important for the development of political prudence; for how often have we heard the old adage that those who do not learn from history are condemned to repeat its mistakes?

Docility

Those who lack memory will more than likely lack docility, another integral part of prudence. St. Thomas writes:

> ...prudence is concerned with particular matters of action, and since such matters are of infinite variety, no one man can consider them all sufficiently; nor can this be done quickly, for it requires length of time. Hence in matters of prudence man stands in very great need of being taught by others, especially by old folk who have acquired a sane understanding of the ends in practical matters. (ST. II-II. 49, 3)

Docility is open-mindedness, and so it requires a recognition of one's own limitations and ready acceptance of those limits. Proud people who hope excessively in their own excellence will tend to make imprudent decisions because they fail to rely on others by virtue of their inordinate and unrealistic self-estimation. A person with false docility seeks the advice of others, but only those deemed most likely to be in agreement with him, or of those of similar depravity and who are thus unlikely to challenge the overall orientation of his life.

Shrewdness

The shrewd are highly intuitive, subtle and discreet. A shrewd teacher will pick up subtle clues that reveal just who it is he is dealing with in his classroom and what the needs of his students really are, which allow him to determine quickly the approach best suited to their particular way of learning. The shrewd are also able to detect evil behind a mask of goodness, so as to be able to plan accordingly. Some people are dangerously unsuspecting of the motives of evil and so they miss the clues that suggest a more ominous picture; for we tend to see in others what we see in ourselves, and if our motives are good, it is hard to suspect others of malice. Moreover, excessive empathy has a way of clouding intuition.

But just as memory and docility presuppose a good will (right appetite), so too does shrewdness. It can be the case that the inability to see is rooted in a will not to see; for sometimes people would rather not think about what the clues could mean for fear of what they might discover about someone, which in turn will affect their security in some way. As the old saying goes: "There are none so blind as those who will not see". It can also be the case that a person has not learned to listen to his intuition or perhaps confuses a negative intuition with judging the heart of another and so dismisses his intuitive insights, especially negative ones. On the other hand, it is possible that a person wants to see evil where there really is none. This is not shrewdness, but suspicion, and it is often rooted in a spirit of pride.

Reasoning

Once a person sizes up a particular situation, he needs to be able to investigate and compare alternative possibilities and to reason well from premises to conclusions. He will need to be able to reason about what needs to be done, that is, what the best alternative or option is that will realize the right end. Prudence thus presupposes a knowledge of the basics of logical reasoning, both deductive and inductive. If a person cannot see through the most common logical fallacies and lacks a critical mind, it is highly likely that he will frequently make imprudent decisions.

Foresight

Foresight is the principal part of prudence, for the name itself (prudence) is derived from the Latin *providere*, which means "foresight". Foresight involves rightly ordering human acts to the right end. This of course presupposes that the person is ordered to the right end, which is the possession of God through knowledge and love. The greater his love for God, that is, the greater his charity, the greater will be his foresight: "Blessed are the pure in heart; for they shall see God" (Mt. 5, 8). For it is through charity that one attains God, and it is through this supernatural friendship that one grows in a connatural knowledge of God. The more a person is familiar with the city towards which he directs his steps, the more able he is to see which roads lead to that end and which roads lead away. The more a person is familiar with God, the more readily able he is to discern behaviour inconsistent with that friendship. An impure heart, that is, a love of God mixed with an inordinate love of self, will affect one's ability to "see". An inordinate love of self will cause certain alternatives to have greater appeal, but these alternatives (means) will not necessarily lead to the right end. A prudent man sees that, but the imprudent do not. And if they lack true to being memory, they will continue to fail to see it.

Circumspection

It is possible that acts good in themselves and suitable to the end may become unsuitable in virtue of new circumstances. Circumspection is the ability to take into account all relevant circumstances. Showing affection to your spouse through a kiss is good in itself, but it might be unsuitable in certain circumstances, such as a funeral or in a public place. Telling certain jokes might be appropriate in one setting, but inappropriate in another. Circumspection is the ability to discern which is which. This too, however, presupposes right appetite. A person lacking proper restraint (temperance) will lack thoughtfulness and the ability to consider how the people around him might be made to feel should he take a certain course of action. The lustful, for example, lack counsel and tend to act recklessly. An egoist is also less focused on others and more on himself, and so he too tends to lack proper circumspection.

Caution

Good choices can often generate bad effects. To choose not to act simply because bad consequences will likely ensue is contrary to prudence. But caution takes care to avoid those evils that are likely to result from a good act that we contemplate doing. For example, a priest who is about to speak out publicly against a piece of unjust legislation might anticipate offending members of his congregation. Out of cowardice or an inordinate love of his own complacency, he might choose not to say anything at all and thus risk harming others through his silence. A prudent priest, on the other hand, will speak out when not doing so will harm others, yet caution will move him to prepare his congregation with a thorough preamble so as to minimize the chances of misunderstanding. One must never do evil that good may come of it, but one may at times permit evil on condition that the action one is performing is good or indifferent, that one does not will or intend the evil effect, and that the good effects of one's action are sufficiently desirable to compensate for the allowing of the evil effect.

The Potential Parts of Prudence

Good Counsel

Counsel is research into the circumstances and the various means to the end. A person not entirely pure of heart, that is, whose charity is very defective, will have more options before him, poorer options that nevertheless have some appeal. The better the character, the less will these poorer options present themselves; for they will drop out of the picture very quickly. This can be compared to a person who is physically healthy and has good eating habits and one who is unhealthy with poor habits. A typical menu will be more appealing to the one with poor eating habits, while the former deliberates over a few options, the healthier options on the menu. We've all heard the expression, "Where there is a will, there is a way". Good counsel, resulting from a greater hope in and love for God, generates the energy and imagination needed to discover the best alternative to achieve the best end.

Good Judgment

Judgment is an assent to good and suitable means. *Synesis* is good common sense in making judgments about what to do and what not to do in ordinary matters. It is possible to take good counsel without having good sense so as to judge well, but to judge well on what to do or not to do in the here and now requires a right mind, that is, an understanding of first principles and precepts and indirectly a just will and well disposed appetites (both concupiscible and irascible appetites). Without these, one's ideas will likely be distorted, and one's judgment regarding the best means will be defective; for as Aristotle points out, as a person is (character), so does he see. He writes:

> ...what seems good to a man of high moral standards is truly the object of wish, whereas a worthless man wishes anything that strikes his fancy. It is the same with the human body: people whose constitution is good find those things wholesome which really are so, while other things are wholesome for invalids, and similarly their opinions will vary as

to what is bitter, sweet, hot, heavy, and so forth. (Just as a healthy man judges these matters correctly, so in moral questions) a man whose standards are high judges correctly, and in each case what is truly good will appear to him to be so. Thus, what is good and pleasant differs with different characteristics or conditions, and perhaps the chief distinction of a man of high moral standards is his ability to see the truth in each particular moral question, since he is, as it were, the standard and measure for such questions. The common run of people, however, are misled by pleasure. For though it is not the good, it seems to be, so that they choose the pleasant in the belief that it is good and avoid pain thinking that it is evil. (*EN* 3, 4. 1113a25-1113b)

Gnome refers to the ability to discern and apply higher laws to matters that fall outside the scope of the more common or lower rules that typically guide human action. It involves good judgment regarding exceptions to ordinary rules. For example, in some schools, students ordinarily are not permitted to use electronic devices in a classroom, but a possible exception to the rule might be the case of a student with a serious learning disability and who is highly sensitive to the slightest distractions. One may be able to think of similar examples on a more judicial level.

Command

Command, which is the direct application of good counsel and judgment, is the principal act of prudence; for it cannot be said that one who takes good counsel and judges well, but fails to act, is a prudent man.

Vices Contrary to Prudence (Impetuosity, Thoughtlessness, Inconstancy, Negligence)

Impetuosity is the vice contrary to good counsel and amounts to a failure to adequately consider all available means to a particular end. Consider the teenager who is tempted to skip class, or lie for something or other, or become sexually intimate with someone. Rather than thinking things through and considering other alternatives, he skips a major test, or lies to get out of it, or immediately surrenders to the temptation to be sexually intimate for fear that further consideration will ruin the prospects. Impetuosity often results from an impulsive will or inordinate sense appetite, or from contempt for a directive (i.e., contempt for one's parents or the Church). Impetuosity is a defect of memory, docility, and reasoning.

Thoughtlessness is a defect of practical judgment and amounts to a defect of circumspection and caution. Consider the young person who curses in a public place, totally unaware of how his actions might affect others, or the young girl who, caught up in the excitement of having an older student take interest in her, gets into his car and drives off with him. Thoughtfulness, on the other hand, is a necessary condition of gratitude, which in turn is a prerequisite of the virtue of justice.

Inconstancy is contrary to command, the principal act of prudence, and is a failure to complete a morally good act by refusing to command that an act be done, a refusal rooted in inordinate love of pleasure. Consider the person who just can't get around to doing what he knows ought to be done, because of laziness or attachment to some pleasure.

Negligence is also contrary to command, but it differs in that it is a defect on the part of the intellect to direct the will in carrying out some good action. These vices involve a defect in understanding, foresight, and shrewdness.

Prudence and the Importance of Thinking

Adolescence is a period fraught with danger because it is a very emotional stage of human development, and unchanneled emotion has led many young people to decisions that they are now forced to live with for the rest of their lives, all because they chose not to think before choosing. Excessive emotion tends to cloud judgment, often inclining us to see what we want to see, and pushing us to make decisions before we have completely thought them through. And so now we have young adults who will never be parents because of scarring of their fallopian tubes, or as a result of contracting HPV, which led to cervical cancer, which in turn necessitated a radical hysterectomy. Some adults suffer from personality arrest and have the emotional maturity level of a young adolescent because of chronic abuse of mood altering substances. Many young adult females are living below the poverty line because they are single mothers and believed it when they were told "I love you".

It is very important that young people use the memory they already have in order to consider the possible consequences of decisions they are about to make. It is also very important to turn towards those who truly have their best interests in mind, namely parents. No matter how smart or sophisticated we might think we are, there is so much that we don't know and that only time and experience can teach us. Those unfortunate people described in the previous paragraph, who have been irreparably damaged by bad decisions, are almost always the type of person who holds his or her parents in contempt.

Prudence and Ethics

As we said above, prudence is both a moral virtue and an intellectual virtue simultaneously, for a moral virtue renders its possessor morally good. A prudent person is one who makes good decisions. A bright and learned person who makes foolish decisions, who is arrogant and subject to outbursts of anger, for example, is hardly someone whom we would hold up as an example of prudence. A person may study and grow in knowledge of the science of ethics without a corresponding moral growth, that is, while holding on to some very serious vices.

Thus, prudence is not quite the same thing as being a moral philosopher or theologian. One may be very learned in these disciplines, but lack prudence, at least to a certain degree. Perhaps we can compare this situation to the person who has studied art history and who knows about proper technique, materials, how this or that artist paints, by whom he was influenced, etc., but who is himself a poor artist. A moral thinker might have good counsel and judgment with regard to general moral issues; he may be a good problem solver and know how to apply universal moral principles to more or less general situations. But, as Aquinas writes: "In wicked men there may be right judgment of a universal principle, but their judgment is always corrupt in the particular matter of action" (*ST.* II-II. 51, 3, ad 2).

For prudence requires more than an understanding of first principles and precepts. It requires true to being memory, docility, circumspection, discursive reasoning, foresight, and caution as well as a shrewd mind. An expert in moral science might lack the humility to be docile, or lack experience with certain people and the intensity of charity necessary to develop a shrewd mind. His arrogance may render him relatively blind or dark of mind, for the "Lord looks upon the arrogant from afar" (Ps. 138, 6). He may lack patience, and he may have an exaggerated sense of self-importance and a hint of narcissism typical of professors today, and he may carry a great deal of resentment. Such a lack of humility destroys virtue, and without right appetite one is not prudent, for prudence requires a just will, a patient disposition rooted in charity, a humble self-estimation, a spirit of forgiveness, honesty with oneself, self-awareness, an awareness of temptation, etc. Without these, one will lack good counsel and good judgment, at least with regard to highly contingent matters.

For there is a realm that exceeds the range of the science of morality, just as there is a large realm that exceeds the limited range of a wireless router. Moral science helps to sharpen judgment, for not all moral matters in the here and now are strictly speaking prudential judgments, such as abortion, active euthanasia, contraception, adultery, lying, etc. The reason is that there are no circumstances that change the nature of these actions, which involve in themselves a deficient willing, that is, willing that is incompatible with complete openness to all human goods, such as human life and marriage, and justice. But a special virtue is required for the here and now precisely because of this limited range; for as we move outside of the realm of the universal and into this rather murky territory of the variable and particular, decisions on what to do and how to proceed become more difficult, far less certain, and they require very well developed sensibilities, intuition, experience, rightly ordered appetite, both rational and sensitive, especially a will formed by charity. It is not always easy to demonstrate the correctness of good prudential judgments; for some people don't see, for their reasoning is grounded in what they know, which in turn is rooted in who they are; for as a person is, so does he see (*EN* 3, 4. 1113a25-1113b).

A prudent person, on the other hand, is a good person. He has practical intelligence, or practical wisdom, and although one may have speculative wisdom without being morally good, including the science of ethics that settles for general statements about what is variable, one cannot have practical wisdom without being morally good. The more noble a person is, the more wise will he be in the practical sense, that is, in the concrete decisions he is required to make daily in the here and now. As one grows in holiness, that is, in charity and faith, one grows in clear-sightedness that is the offspring of purity of heart. One begins to contemplate God here in this world, for one comes to know God connaturally. One contemplates the genius of his providence and the depths of His love, which the pure of heart know from within. St. Thomas writes: "Now this sympathy or connaturality for Divine things is the result of charity, which unites us to God, according to 1 Cor. 6:17: "He who is joined to the Lord, is one spirit." Consequently wisdom which is a gift, has its cause in the will, which cause is charity, but it has its essence in the intellect, whose act is to judge aright, as stated above" (*ST.* II-II. 45, 2). That is why the saint enjoys a level of contemplation and wisdom that is unavailable to the theologian or philosopher who is lacking in charity. The light of contemplation in turn enhances one's ability to determine the mean of reason in fortitude and temperance and all their parts as well as the mean of justice, and the fire of charity renders one more just, brave, and temperate, which in turn spawns a greater prudence.

Chapter 33: Sexual Activity in Perspective

Many of us struggle to understand the nature of certain things because we have a tendency to focus on them in isolation from the whole of which, in the real world, they are a part. And because we tend not to re-integrate what we have come to understand within the context of the whole, the result is a body of disintegrated knowledge that allows us to maintain ideas that, when fully unpacked, lead to contradictions and absurdities. We remain unaware of these inconsistencies because we fail to do the unpacking. As an example, the typical biology student will maintain that he is alive because every cell in the body is alive (not vice versa). But for some reason, it never occurs to him to reflect upon his own experience of himself as a single, unified, living thing—and not a multiplicity of billions of living things—and ponder the incompatibility between that experience and his reductionistic biology.

This same tendency to consider "the part" in isolation from the whole without re-integrating that part within the whole—to which it belongs in the realm of the real—seems to show itself in all areas of knowledge, for instance, in the area of morality, particularly sexuality. But if we are to make any real sense of the morality of sexual acts, sexuality has to be understood within the context of the "whole" of which it is a part. So I'd like to begin by looking at the hierarchy of material substances within the physical universe as a whole.

We know naturally that there is a hierarchy of material being in the physical universe. This means that some substances are superior to others, that is, they have more power. The lowest level on the hierarchy is the mineral, the level of inert matter. On this level, a thing is moved by something outside itself, which in turn moves something outside of it; this kind of motion is transient. Up from the mineral level is the vegetative level, characterized by self-movement or immanent activity. Plants grow from within (incretion), they reproduce, and they engage in nutritive activity, taking inert matter from the soil, for example, and transforming it into living matter. Up from the vegetative level is the animal level, specifically characterized by a more immanent activity, namely sensation and sense appetite. Here, the animal knows material singulars, such as this tree, that piece of meat, the cat on the road, etc., without destroying it in the act of perceiving it. Up from the animal level is the human level, which is specifically characterized by intellectual knowledge, which is the knowledge of the natures of things. Human beings possess universal ideas (i.e., art, education, truth, love, person, etc.,), not merely particular images. As such, they come to know things as they are in themselves.

To understand this more fully, consider that an animal—that has the power to sense material singulars—really only pays attention to what has reference to itself and its own appetite for survival. Iconographers have to be very careful after having finished painting an icon that they do not leave it where a cat could get at it; for the cat will smell the egg used in the paint and begin licking the icon, thus destroying it. My dog chewed the spine of a 1941 edition of *The Basic Works of Aristotle* that I purchased many years ago in an old used bookstore, because she perceived "meat" in the cover. The cat does not know the icon as it is in itself, but only insofar as it has a reference to its appetite (self), so too my dog has no clue what a valuable book is, much less the works of Aristotle. If that cover was made of a material that does not arouse the appetite, she would have paid no attention to it.

But human intelligence is the ability to grasp what a thing is not insofar as it has reference to me and my own appetites, but as it is in itself. I know the other not insofar as he is of some benefit to me, but simply as he is in himself, namely, a human kind of being of the same nature as myself. And because I know him as he is in himself (his nature), without reference to me or my needs, I can will the best for him for his own sake, not for my sake—whether I choose to do so is another matter altogether. So too, works of art, ancient historical texts, or aspects of the natural world are all things that I can know, appreciate and reverence for their own sake without them having any direct reference to me and my sense appetites.

But what is interesting about the hierarchy of material being is that there is a hierarchy within each level of the hierarchy. Some chemicals are more stable than others, and some plants are more stable, more beautiful, and more complex than others (most of us would much rather receive a rose than a bacteria). There is clearly a hierarchy within the animal kingdom; a horse, for example, is superior to a worm. Now, what we notice when we examine this more carefully is that the lower a being is within its own hierarchy, the more it approaches the highest being in the level below it. For example, students will often argue that the Venus flytrap is a sentient creature (an animal) because it appears to sense the presence of a fly and traps it. It is indeed a plant, not an animal, but it is so high up on the hierarchy of vegetative life that it is easy to believe it is a sentient creature. Some animals are so low on the hierarchy of animal life that it is difficult to discern whether or not they are merely plants. Similarly, the higher primates have a remarkable resemblance to the human, making it very easy to mistake their behaviour for intelligent behaviour.

There is a kind of hierarchy on the human level as well, certainly not like what we find on the level below it—there are no various species of man as there are species of animal. There is, however, a kind of moral or "character" hierarchy established by human persons themselves through their own free choices. And likewise, the lowest on this level will approach the highest on the level below it (the animal level). There are human beings who are intelligent, good looking, and very personable, but who are almost entirely bestial in character. Think of the sociopath who has absolutely no benevolence for others whatsoever, but pays attention to others only insofar as they are of some use to him. We call them predators, wolves in sheep's clothing, or sharks, etc., for they resemble the higher beasts who only pay attention to that which has a reference to themselves and their own appetite for pleasure and survival, and experience no remorse for destroying others for their own benefit. On the other end of the scale is the saint who is willing to give his own life that others may live.

What does this have to do with marriage? Animals do not marry. They do not and cannot love another for the other's own sake, but only with the kind of love that is a passion of the sensitive appetite, and that passion is a love of something for the sake of what it does for the animal (i.e., food, drink, warmth, etc.). The human person, on the other hand, is inclined to marry. Young people today, although they might not completely understand what marriage is, have a genuine desire to marry. But what is it precisely that they desire in their desire for marriage? They have a hard time articulating what it is, but when pushed, they eventually do so; she wants someone to give himself entirely and completely to her, and she wants to give herself entirely and completely to him. Marriage has something essentially to do with intelligent love, and so it is a giving of the self. All specifically human love is a giving of the self, whether it is a giving of one's time, one's attention, one's property, etc. But not all love is a total giving of oneself, nor must it be. But it is very possible for a person to want to give his entire self—which includes his own body—to another and to desire that the other receive that total self-giving, and to want that other to reciprocate so that he may freely choose to receive her complete and total self-giving. If this complete and mutual self-giving is to be a genuine giving of the self, and not a taking (a mere passion), then it means that this love is a loving of the other for the other's own sake, not for the sake of the self.

That is precisely what marriage is: a mutual and total giving of one's entire self (body) to one another. It is an irrevocable self-giving precisely because it is total; for if I hand someone an umbrella but hang on to a part of it, I can revoke that giving by pulling back, for I've only given a part while hanging on to another part. But if I give all of it without hanging on to even a part of it, I cannot retrieve it. If a couple genuinely give themselves entirely to one another, that self-giving is an irrevocable gift, for no part of me has been held back.

That is why a genuine marriage is an indissoluble one body union that results from a mutual and total giving of the self. The two have given one another an irrevocable identity of "spouse", which cannot be undone any more than one can undo one's identity as a parent—not even the killing of one's child erases the identity of parent. And because marriage is a mutual and total giving of one's bodily self to another, it is till death, for only death can take my body from another or the other's body from me. Thus, to intend a temporary union is not to intend a marriage. Moreover, because a couple that intends to marry intends a one flesh union, the intention not to have children renders the marriage invalid; for a child is the fruit of the one flesh union of husband and wife. To intend not to have a child is to intend not to be one flesh. Now this **intention not to have** a child is not the same as **not intending** to have a child; for a post-menopausal woman who wishes to marry can indeed be married, but she will not intend to have children, for it is impossible. But that does not mean she intends not to; for she does not need to intend not to, because it is impossible for her to conceive new life.

Now because marriage is a one flesh union, the couple must be able to actually achieve a one flesh union. In other words, they must be able to receive one another's bodily self giving, and they do so in the act of sexual union. If the couple is not able to perform the sexual act, they are unable to be "one flesh".

The act of sexual union is a marital act, it is the physical expression of what the couple have brought about on the level of their wills, namely a complete and mutual self-giving, given for the sake of the other, not for the sake of the self. And so if the sexual act is to be a genuinely human act—and thus a fulfilling act—, it must be the expression of that very unique and exclusive conjugal love, and at least open to the procreation of new life, that is, it must not be accompanied by the intention not to have children. In other words, although a couple may not necessarily intend a child in the act of sexual intercourse (if they engage in the act during an infertile stage of her cycle), they ought not to intend not to conceive; thus a contracepted act of intercourse is not an act of marriage and is thus morally deficient.

The problem with the current cultural understanding of the sexual act is that it is the result of trying to understand it in isolation from the whole, that is, the entire human context. A part can only be understood in relation to the whole, and sexual activity is not a whole unto itself, but only a part of a larger meaning, namely marriage, which in turn is part of a larger meaning. The vehement pleasure associated with sex has diverted our gaze much like the misdirection of a good magician, diverting the audience's attention away from what is really taking place before them. The result is that the meaning of the sexual act is reduced from a genuinely human act of marriage that embodies the two intelligible human goods of "one flesh union" and procreation that constitute marriage, to a quasi-animal act that is simply a response to a sense appetite (the pursuit of pleasure). And just as all brute animals only pay attention to that which has a reference to themselves in some way, the pursuit of pleasure as the principal end of the sexual act changes the meaning of the act to one that involves knowing and loving the other for what the other does for the self sensually. In other words, non-marital intercourse is an abuse of the sex act, for it is an abuse of a person, and because the sexual act is the act of marriage, non-marital intercourse is an abuse of marriage.

Marriage is not a private, but a public affair. The reason is that the family is the fundamental unit of society, just as the living cell is the basic unit of the organs of the living body. Friendships are private matters, and the state has no business concerning itself with the private friendships of its citizens. But marriage, by virtue of its life giving character, is an institution, an organization that exists for the public welfare, and so the state has the right and duty to make laws governing marriage. But to do so properly, that is, in a way that will not reduce marriage to a private friendship with insurance benefits, the state must understand the specific nature of marriage and hold it up as the normative ideal that young people naturally desire and aspire to. Not everyone can be married, because not everyone has the psychological maturity and moral capacity (i.e., the virtues) to actually give himself or herself completely and entirely to another. Some are just too low on the moral hierarchy of human existence and live in ways that closely resemble the beasts who do not and cannot marry—although discerning that can be very difficult, because many are very cunning and hide their true character. But many can be married and want to be, and one of the most serious responsibilities of the civil community is to create the social and legal conditions that will nurture and help preserve that aspiration in young people. The very survival of the civil community depends upon it.

Chapter 34: What is Wrong with Reductionism?

Many young people who have good minds for science and math tend to think with a reductionist habit of mind. A reductionist will tend to see the whole (i.e., the world of nature, trees, animals, flowers, human beings, etc.) as nothing more than the sum of the parts that make it up. Reductionism goes hand in hand with scientism, which is the view that the only valid knowledge is scientific knowledge of the empiriometric kind (i.e., physics, chemistry, etc.).

Although the reductionist habit of mind makes for good science, it is a flawed method of explaining things ultimately. In other words, it makes for bad philosophy.

Let me begin by making a point about number. Number is multitude, organized, identified and measured by unity. Multitude, however, is plurality, pure and simple, and as such it is *unorganized*. Think of a continuous extension, like a quantity of milk. To number it, we need a unit, such as a litre. Now, in itself a plurality is unknowable, but it is known only when measured by unity. To reduce a plurality to unity is to number it, and our material world can accordingly be organized into unity. I will return to this.

Consider as well the following point: man has two interiors. The one is physical (i.e., we can look inside his body). But no matter how much we search the physical interior of a man, we will never know what is contained in the other interior (the interior he refers to when he speaks of his "mind" or "heart"). The human being has to manifest it by acting—in this case, speaking. There are also two interiors of any substance, such as a carbon atom. The only way to grasp the interior of a carbon atom is to observe how it acts; its activity reveals its nature. It does not have a conscious interior, like the human person, but it has a determinate nature. The interior of the atom is not the parts that constitute it. Rather, the interior is the nature of the atom.

But that is just what reductionism denies. Reductionism says that this "thing" is nothing *other than* the parts that make it up. So, there really is no single "it". "It" is a word, but "it" is nothing other than a sum of a multiplicity, namely, parts.

But if I understand "parts", does that not presuppose that I understand "whole"? If I know of the "parts of a thing", does that not presuppose I know "thing"? If I did not understand "thing", I would not understand "parts of the thing". So, if there is no "thing" or "it", there are no "parts of it". We could not speak of "real parts" if there is no "real whole" or "real thing".

But the reductionist claims that you, as well as anything else, are nothing other than the constituent parts. But what are the parts? The reductionist would say that each part is nothing other than the sum of its smaller constituent parts. What is an organ but the cells that make it up? And a cell is nothing other than the parts that make it up, that is, the parts that constitute it.

Of course, we have the same problem. How is it that I am able to grasp the notion of "cell" if the cell is nothing other than those constituent parts that make it up? What is the "it" that is constituted? The answer: the cell. But is the cell a determinate part? Does it terminate into a definite intelligible part of a larger whole? And is the whole thing (i.e., the cat) something determinate, that is, terminated as a definite intelligible whole, a thing in itself? One's answer is either yes, or no.

If the answer is yes, then the cell, or the organ, or the cat or man, is more than the multiplicity of parts that constitute it. The parts are reduced to a unity. That unity is called the cell, or the organ, or the man. That unity renders the multiplicity of parts intelligible. A raw multiplicity is unintelligible unless it is reduced to a unity. That is why we number things. An extension, for example, is measured by a unit called a yard. But a yard is numbered by the unit called a foot, which in turn is numbered or reduced to a unit called an inch. Hence, a foot is 12 inches. A number is a measure of quantity. Without a number, the quantity remains unorganized and thus unintelligible. Unit imparts intelligibility to a multiplicity.

A multiplicity, however, does not give itself unity. The unity comes to it from the outside, from outside the multiplicity. A multiplicity considered in itself is not a unit, and a unit is not a multiplicity. A unit is one. An inch terminates or determines an extension, giving it determination (definition, intelligibility). A litre measures or terminates a quantity of liquid. A pound terminates a quantity of weight, allowing us to determine the weight, to know its weight (i.e., this person is 200 pounds; that milk carton is 2 litres; that table is 5 feet, 6 inches, etc.). At this point the plurality is organized into an intelligible quantity.

One may object and claim that it is not true that "a unit is not a multiplicity; a centimetre is made up of millimetres. Hence, a centimetre is a unit, but it is a multiplicity at the same time."

A centimetre, however, is a unit (one one hundredth of a metre) that measures a meter, but because the centimetre is an extension, it too can be measured; to do so, we simply have to divide it further. A millimetre is one one thousandth of a meter. And so the unit of measure, like the centimetre, is not outside of the multiplicity spatially. Rather, it is outside of "multiplicity", that is, it is not itself a multiplicity, but a measure of multiplicity. As extended, it is a multiplicity that is open to being measured or numbered. To do so, we need a smaller unit of measure, i.e., the millimetre. But the unit allows us to number multiplicity (quantity, or the multiplicity of parts outside of parts). But "one" itself is not a multiplicity. Multiplicity does not number or measure multiplicity, a unit does.

A single cell, similarly, is an intelligible thing. A scientist sees it as a biological unit, certainly a part of a larger whole (the organ), or a whole unto itself, if it is a single celled bacteria. He begins to analyze it and study its constituent parts.

Now, if the answer to the above question ("Is the cell a determinate part?" "Does it terminate into a definite intelligible part of a larger whole?") is no, then the cell is nothing other than "its" constituent parts, i.e., proteins, amino acids, etc. These in turn are ultimately nothing other than atoms of elements, which in turn are nothing other than subatomic particles, which in turn are nothing but smaller subatomic particles, etc.

The result is that "thing" is not anything in itself. It is always other than "itself". A man is not a thing in itself, a dog is not a thing in itself, a flower is not a thing in itself, a single celled organism, like a bacteria, is not a thing in itself, an atom is not a thing in itself, etc.

Everything is other than "itself". There is no "itself". Nothing has any "interior"; *nothing is what it is*, but is "other than" what it is. Nothing has any determinacy; nothing, therefore, is knowable. Everything is unknowable; for we cannot know what is indeterminate.

Once again, science becomes a fiction, a construct. This will mean that science does not uncover the intelligibility of nature, because nature is not intelligible, it is absurd and unknowable. There is nothing *in itself* to know. And that is why genuine reductionists who take their conclusions to the very end are post-modernists who deny the existence of truth. Man is the measure of what is true and good, even though there is no "man" (no "thing" in itself).

But then one has to ask: "How is it possible to understand change?" Take the concept of evolution, for example. When we speak of evolution, we speak of something evolving. But if there are no "things" in themselves, then "nothing" evolves. I can only understand change when I understand that something enduring has changed in some way, i.e., you sat in the sun and became tanned. Your color changes, but you are the subject of the change that endured. "Tanned" is the predicate (John is tanned). But there is no "you", no cell, no organism of a determinate species, so what, therefore, evolves? In other words, change can only be understood against the backdrop of that which endures, that which is unchanging. Reductionism is thus incompatible with evolution.

And so, reductionism leads to the conclusion that categorical propositions are impossible. They are not real. For example: "John is a man" or "the cell divides" are nothing more than linguistic constructs that create the illusion of "thing". The principle of identity as well is a construct, and logic, in the end, can be nothing more than a construct.

The reductionist, however, "reasons" to conclusions from given premises. He says things like: The mind is nothing but the brain, and thinking is nothing but firing neurons, or neural biochemistry, and therefore man is not essentially different than brute animals, etc. Some reductionists, not all, proceed further and will conclude from all this that we should stop treating ourselves as privileged creatures, etc. Notice the reasoning from premises to conclusions, even though logical reasoning, which depends on categorical propositions, is impossible if reductionism is true.

Note also their desire that everyone conform to the fundamental truth that "man is nothing more than...", the truth which does not exist in the first place (since all science is a fiction). The truth is that there is no truth, just constructs. And if that is the case, it would seem that all constructs are equally valid and invalid at the same time (in other words, the principle of non-contradiction is also a construct). Which construct, therefore, is going to prevail? The one with the most power behind it.

If we wish, however, to hold on to our common sense and avoid this entirely irrational state of affairs, then let us return to the "yes" alternative above. If the single celled organism, for example, is a thing in itself, what is it that reduces the multiplicity to a unity, a determinate thing or entity that can be studied? It is something outside the multiplicity. One cannot appeal to the parts that make it up. The parts are organized into an intelligible whole (unity). The principle of unity is a principle that is outside the parts, a principle that embraces the whole and determines the parts to be what they are. In other words, we must proceed in the complete opposite direction of reductionism. It is the whole that explains the part or parts. Some principle belongs to the whole organism (or atom or bacterium) that determines it (and all its parts) to be what it is. We are back, once again, to the formal cause.

Chapter 35: Thoughts on Sensation, Intelligence, and Brain Activity: Can our knowledge be reduced to brain activity?

There is a real distinction between sensation and intelligence. Since, however, sensation is more evidently intertwined with matter, I would like explore this mode of knowing first; for if we can appreciate the immateriality involved in sensation, appreciating the immateriality in intellectual knowledge will be much easier.

The first point to be made is that sensation is an activity. This is such a significant point. The reason I say this is that if sensation is an activity, it involves an agent, a single substance or being. It is an agent who sees, who hears, who touches, who tastes, who imagines and who remembers, etc. I, who am a single being, perceive. It is not my eyes that see, rather, I see by means of the sense organ. So too, it is not my ears that hear, rather, I hear by means of the end organ of the ear drum. Moreover, I see by means of not only the end organ, for example, the eye. "Organ" includes, as in the case of the eye, the cortical center of the brain, and also their connecting link, which is the optic nerve. By extension, it is not my brain that perceives, nor is it my brain that is aware. Rather, I am aware, and I sense by means of the organ of the brain. In short, the brain is a part of me, part of a larger whole that has the power to perceive—which is an activity.

Now, the agent who is able to sense is, logically, the kind of agent who has the potentiality to sense, or the power to sense, for example, the power to see, to hear, to smell, etc. Thus, sense organs are not enough. There is both power and organ. The reason is that an activity is an "act" or actualization, and "actualization" means that a capacity or potentiality is reduced to actuality (or act or activity). Activity is the realization of a potentiality. The agent is the first act (for there is no seeing without a seer, just as there is no running without a runner). But "activity", such as that of seeing, is "second act". Between first and second act is the power or potentiality to activity (that is, the power to see, taste, touch, imagine, etc.).

A camera is a mechanism, but it is not a single agent that sees; a camera does not see, it does not perceive. There is no activity on the part of the camera, only passivity (something happens to it). In fact, when we use a camera, the camera is simply an extension of our own activity, that is, it is an instrument of our own activity; it is an extension of ourselves. But sensation is an activity of a single agent, a single being that has the power to see. Thus, sensation is rooted in a *psychosomatic composite* (a substance that is a matter/form unity). A sense cannot function without both a power and an organ, and so any damage to an organ will impede an agent's ability to sense.

A plant does not see or touch (the Venus flytrap does not feel), it does not have the power to see, or touch, or taste, or hear. Sensation is a vital act, an immanent act of a living thing, not an inanimate act of an inanimate substance. For example, rusting is not a vital act, burning is not a vital act, causing moisture is not a vital act; but sensation is a vital act (an immanent act), an act of a living thing or living being. Sensation is an agent's awareness of a singular material thing that is other than the agent, a material singular that is outside the agent.

Now, there is a passive element to sensation; there has to be. Something has to move the power from potentiality to actuality or activity, and the object of sensation is a material singular, so it is going to be a material thing that acts upon the senses. So in sensation, what occurs is that the sense organ is acted upon (passivity), and the agent senses (acts) by means of the organ.

Because sensible things are actually sensible, they can be immediately sensed by a sense power. To be sensed, they need only impinge upon a sense power, since a sensible thing is already (actually) sensible in itself, and so there is no need for an active power to render or reduce it to the state of being actually sensible. So, although man requires an agent intellect to reduce what is potentially intelligible to being actually intelligible, there is no "agent sense".

The senses must be acted upon (passivity) if they are to know, as color must act upon the eyes if I am to see, and as compression waves must act upon the ears if I am to hear. So, the senses are passive powers, faculties or potencies—faculties or potencies are not perceived by the senses, they are known by the intellect. The senses must be moved to activity. The eye, as well as any other sense, when passive (before it senses), is not determined. The senses, then, when not actually sensing anything, are indifferent as to what they are to report. For example, the eye is indeterminate or indifferent as to what color it will see (of course, it is not the eyes that see, but I see by means of the organ). To say that the organ is indifferent is to maintain that it is in itself indeterminate or unspecified, and therefore, to know one definite object, the sense must be determined or specified.

That which specifies the sense is called a "sensible species". Thus, the reason I see a rose, and not a rabbit, is that the object known (a rose) specifies my act of knowing. This sensible species is produced by the object outside of me, which is acting upon the sense organ. Moreover, since every effect has a likeness to its cause, the sensible species (the effect) carries the "likeness" of its producing cause (the physical object); it does so because the species is emitted by the object. A sensible species is a physical radiation emanating from the sensible thing, and without it, my senses would not be moved to act. This sensible species is thus a precursor of sensation; it is not a sensation floating through space on the lookout for a cognitive agent. As a vital act, sensation is an immanent act; it is in the knower; but the species itself is not known (See Azar, *Man: Computer, Ape*...pp. 177-178).

Sense knowing is an activity, and so what must be explained is the transition from the passive aspect of sensation to this activity. Prior to the activity, the senses are not active, only passive. It remains passive until awakened by an external object, until it receives a species (a determinant) from the object. Sensation occurs upon reception of this determinant, this specification. Once activated by the species, the sense performs its act of sensation (See Azar, p. 178).

Yet our knowledge is a knowledge of things, not a knowledge of the sensible species. If it were a knowledge of the species (a knowledge of what is happening within us, or what is happening to our sense organs), then to perceive is not to perceive things, but our own self, or some aspect of our self. We would not know things; we would not know the sensible world, but only what is in us. And if that were the case, we would not even know that we don't know the sensible world but only ourselves, and we wouldn't even be able to distinguish between an optical illusion and a normal perception that is not illusory. Thus, when a person argues that we can't know whether or not there is an extramental world, or that optical illusions prove that our senses are unreliable, they in fact show the opposite in the very distinction they are making.

A machine is not an agent who acts. A machine can be acted upon, but there is no *transition* from being acted upon to acting. The machine is not perceiving, because the machine is not a single being, not a single agent with **the power** (potentiality or faculty) to see, or touch, or imagine, or desire, etc.

To study the biochemistry of sense perception is to study this passive aspect of sensation. But the scientific study of this passive aspect of sensation involves sensation on the part of the one doing the studying (the scientist)—the scientist must be perceiving (acting, activity). He is studying one side of sensation, the side he's unaware of as an ordinary sensing creature in the act of perceiving—we're all unaware of that aspect. But to study the passive aspect of sensation is not the same thing as studying sensation (which is a study involving reflection and reasoning), and much less is it the same thing as the actual awareness involved in the act of sensation—we're all aware of ourselves sensing (thanks to the central sense, or synthetic sense), but few of us are familiar with the biochemistry of the eye and what occurs when one sees. A strict study of the passive aspects, that is, the biochemical conditions of sense perception, *without knowing sensation from within*, would not provide us with a knowledge of the activity of sensation—we wouldn't know what it means to sense. That can only be known from within, and that self-knowledge is not scientific knowledge, but pre-scientific knowledge that is presupposed in every scientific mode of knowing. I know that I perceive, that I sense, that I see, that I taste, etc. And so the one cannot be reduced to the other (sensation cannot be reduced to neuro-biochemistry); the one is related to the other, the one is a necessary condition for the other, but not a sufficient condition. In other words, sense perception cannot be reduced to its material conditions; to reduce it to that is to destroy it, to eliminate it.

That is why a mechanistic approach to human nature (reductionistic materialism) cannot account for sensation; only a psychosomatic anthropology can account for it. You are a psychosomatic unity (a matter/form unity), you are a multiplicity insofar as you are a material and quantified thing (i.e., with many parts), but you are a unity insofar as you are a being, an acting agent (one is a property of being, for whatever is, is one).

Now the word 'object' is derived from two words: *ob*: against, and *iacere*: to throw. An object projects itself or emanates a likeness of itself towards a subject, and this emanation is the species or determinant that impinges upon or specifies the external senses. By impressing itself upon the senses, this emission activates the sense power from its state of non-sensing to sensing (Azar, p. 178).

G. J. Gumerman writes: "All materials at temperatures above absolute zero in the natural environment produce electromagnetic radiation in the form of waves. The electromagnetic spectrum is a continuum of natural and induced radiation in wavelengths varying from fractions of a micrometer to kilometers" (Quoted in Azar, p. 178. Gumerman and Lyons, *Science,* April 9, 1971, p. 126.). Every object produces its own "specific" radiation. Right now, in the room we are in, there are color waves that we are unaware of, as well as sound waves. We are simply not attuned to them, but turn on a radio or a television, and the fact is verified. Similarly, objects radiate their likenesses, and it is only cognitive or sentient beings that are attuned to them. The sensible species comes from the physical object, and thus it is a received species; in other words, it impresses itself upon the sense (it is an "impressed" species). Its function is to unite the knower with the known, that is, to make the external object present to the sense organ or power. What I perceive when I am in the act of perceiving something is not the species, but the material thing outside me.

That is what is so mysterious about knowledge (sense knowledge and more so, intellectual or conceptual knowledge); the sensible species unites knower with the known. The sensible species is therefore unlike anything in our experience. It unites us to the known not by calling attention to itself, as would any natural or conventional sign, but without calling attention to itself at all and in any way. A natural sign like smoke calls attention to itself first, and then it unites our mind to something else, namely, fire, which is its cause. So too, a conventional sign like a wedding ring calls attention to itself first, and then it unites the mind to that which it signifies according to convention, namely marriage. But a sensible species that specifies or determines the sense organ unites knower and known immediately, and thus it is a formal sign, a pure sign, whose sole function is to signify. It is purely and entirely intentional (tending the perceiver to its object immediately). If it were not a pure sign, our sense knowledge would be at best indirect knowledge. I wouldn't know things, but the sensible species, and then I'd have to somehow deduce that this sensible species was the result of some cause that has a likeness to it, for example, the actual object itself. But then we are back to square one, and we would now have to explain how I know the sensible species itself, i.e., by means of another species?

An "object" (according to the etymology of the word) is that which is presented to or "thrown against" a subject. You are a single subject, which is why we can speak about an "object" of sensation: subject and object are correlative terms. But a machine, like a computer, is not a subject (it does not have a subjectivity). It is purely and completely an object. It can be the subject of a change, for example, it can be moved from one place to another. But it is not aware of an object, much less aware of its awareness. At best, a machine becomes an instrument of a living perceiving subject, the one who is using it to take a picture. We designed the machine, so there is a sense in which we project a kind of subjectivity into it (it is made after the likeness of the producer, it is an instrument designed to memorialize a moment in time), but there is no subject if there is no single being. Only a single, knowing, entity, a cognitive being, can be a subject of knowledge, because only a knower has an "object" of knowledge. Moreover, each sense has a formal object: the formal object of the sense of sight is color, the formal or immediate object of the sense of taste is flavor, the formal object of the tactile sense is the pressure or resistance of external things, the formal object of the temperature sense is relative warmth or coldness of objects, the formal object of the kinesthetic sense is pressure within the body, etc. An object can only exist for a subject. Without a subject, there is no object of knowledge, no object as such, only existents (beings or things). They become objects (in the strict sense of *ob-iacere*) when a subject enters into the picture.

Now, in the act of sense perception, a knowing subject is modified in a way that can be studied by science. For example, his sense organs are modified, there are neurological changes in certain parts of his brain, his retina becomes colored, etc. But when a scientist takes it upon himself to study the biochemistry involved in sense perception, there is an ordinary, pre-scientific mode of knowing that includes self-knowledge, without which he could not make sense out of what he is studying—this is such an important point. Now this ordinary, pre-scientific knowledge that includes self-knowledge, which involves an intellect capable of complete self-reflection, is a pre-scientific mode of knowing that is perpetually self-conscious or entirely reflective (i.e., I know that I am knowing, I know that I am sensing, I know that I am seeing, I know that I am touching, that I am moving, that I am breathing, I know that I am, that I am one, and that my self-consciousness extends as far as my extremities, for I know that I am not the molecules and atoms in the immediate atmosphere surrounding my hands, feet, face, body, etc.). This pre-scientific knowledge governs the scientific process from within, so that at each moment, I (the scientist) know what I am studying, for I know that I am coming to understand the neurological conditions of sense perception and that sense perception is a cognitive act of a knowing being or subject. If I didn't have that pre-scientific knowledge, I wouldn't know what I am doing in studying the neurological conditions of sense perception. My study would lack a framework and a focus.

It is this that sheds light on the immaterial aspect of sense knowledge. Sense knowledge is not and cannot be entirely material. Sensation in the human person always involves intellection, which includes complete self-reflection (I know that I am seeing, I know that I am touching, etc.). Now, a material organ is not capable of total self-reflection; for no material thing is capable of total self-reflection. The reason is that a material thing has parts, and so reflection in a material thing is only partial: one part can reflect upon another part (but the whole does not reflect upon the whole). Take a piece of paper and fold it, for example. One part will be folded upon another, or reflected upon another. But a single part cannot entirely reflect upon itself. The instant a part is made to reflect, it is lifted off and away from where it was previously. So too, a mirror (which is a material thing) only reflects partially. Now the sense of sight cannot reflect upon itself, because the sense of sight involves a material organ. The sense of sight does not see itself in the act of seeing, nor can I touch my sense of touch touching. But I am capable of complete self-reflection, for I know that I am knowing.

Moreover, I know that I am sensing (I know that I am seeing, tasting, hearing, etc.). I as a whole and as a single being am aware of myself as a whole. I am aware of my thinking and sensing. That is the self-reflection of a single being that is indivisible and conscious of that indivisibility (I know that I am one being). It follows that my mind is immaterial; it is simple and has no parts.

The same cannot be said of the sense organ. The brain is not immaterial, nor is any organ of sensation, which is why the sense organ does not reflect upon the whole of itself—no sense can sense itself sensing. Nor do I imagine my imagination imagining. The brain is the organ of internal sensation, and as a material organ, it too cannot engage in complete or "whole" self-reflection, only partial self-reflection.

Sensation in the brute animal which lacks intelligence and thus lacks the capacity of complete self-reflection is still partially immaterial. In other words, sensation in the brute animal is not an entirely material process. It is the activity of an agent (**a psychosomatic unity**). It cannot be reduced to the objectivity of neural biochemistry—in sensation, there is a transition from passivity to activity, and the animal knows something outside itself without changing what it knows (there is no chemical reaction or chemical change, the organ is specified, but it is not changed or transformed into a different thing). The result is that the animal is aware of something outside of him.

Knowledge *per se* is not a change. Indeed, physical changes accompany both sense and knowledge. All human knowing implies some degree of physical change, because all knowledge begins in sense perception. But although all knowledge is accompanied by a physical change (my finger immersed in warm water becomes physically warm), this change does not constitute knowledge—a thermometer also becomes hot if immersed in hot water, yet there is no knowledge in the thermometer. So too, the camera receives an impression of the object being photographed, yet there is no sense knowledge of the object. Sensation involves change, but change is not knowledge. To be physically heated is not to sense heat; in seeing, there is a physical alteration in the organs: there is a contraction or dilation of the senses, and chemical processes occur in the rods and cones. In plant life, in order to become something other than itself, a plant must cease being itself (i.e., a tree becomes a wooden desk by first ceasing to be a living tree). In cognitive life, however, the knower becomes the known without ceasing to be. Knowledge opens up the subject, enabling him to become "intentionally" what he cannot become physically. Knowledge is not a physical becoming, but an intentional becoming; it is an immaterial becoming, even in the brute animal. An immaterial power of a psychosomatic unity is actualized—even though this actualization is inextricably linked to the changes in a sense organ. Without losing his physical identity, a cognitive being shares in the perfections of other things. In sensation, the perfections it shares are not as profound as the perfections shared in intellection—the animal only perceives the accidental modes of being of things (i.e., color, flavor, size, temperature, pressure, etc.). There is a much richer apprehension in intellectual knowledge.

The brute animal is aware that it is sensing, and the source of this awareness is the internal sense called the synthetic or central sense. This sense unifies the separate data received from each external sense, composing the data into a single percept (internal sensible species), so that the animal knows (sense knowledge) that what it smells, touches, and tastes, and sees, all belong to the same single object (i.e., the single apple or the meat, etc.).

There is simply no way that the sense activity of a single agent can be understood reductionistically or mechanistically. The reason is that to reduce a substance to a collection of substances, to a multiplicity, is to destroy the unity, or better yet, it is to forget the unity, to overlook it, that is, to have one's head so immersed in the multiplicity of the molecular or subatomic realm that one loses awareness of the initial knowledge of the thing, the initial apprehension of what this thing is, and the existential judgment "that it is" (and is one). When that is lost, one must account for sensation as an activity of a single substance or entity, but one cannot do that unless one knows already that single substance. Sensation is not a passivity of some accidentally unified "thing" (as if "thing" or "substance" is merely some kind of illusion, as the reductionist maintains).

Now, the intelligible species is another thing altogether. The intelligible content of a thing, the idea, the concept conceived within the mind, is of an entirely different nature. At least a percept can be remembered, and when it is remembered, one is aware that it is an image, an expressed sensible species, something particular that corresponds to the thing in reality. When I imagine John Smith, that image is a remembered percept that corresponds vaguely to his appearance when he came to see me a couple of weeks ago, and when he was in my class last year. But an intelligible species is altogether different. It is not an image, but a meaning. Simple or complex ideas have no image, they are not sensible. Take the idea "complex"—it is not a sensible; it does not look like anything at all. It is an intelligible idea. Consider the idea of metaphor, or the concept "analogy", or the complex idea "a metaphor is not an analogy". The idea "analogy" does not bear upon any particular analogous relationship, but covers them all. Most importantly, the apprehension of existence (being)—, which is not to be confused with the general idea of being—is not an image, it is not sensible, but it is the most intelligible aspect of things—before I sense a being's color, and before I apprehend "what that thing is" (its essence), I apprehend "that it is". The act of existence (*esse*) cannot even be made into a concept. I can have a concept of John Smith (i.e., he is human), but I apprehend his existence at the same time, and the apprehension of an act of existing is neither a sense perception nor the apprehension of a thing's essence—it is an apprehension "that you are".

Being cannot be made into a concept, for to do so is to make it a genus. Recall that the specific difference is always outside the genus ('rational' is outside the concept animal, otherwise all animals would be rational), but the only thing outside of being is non-being, which is nothing. So being cannot be a genus, it is not a logical entity like an idea. Being or existence (*esse*) is an act, and you and I have the ability to apprehend that act. But that is not an image, it is not a sensible. I cannot hear existence, I cannot see existence. I hear sounds of existing things (birds), I see the colors of existing things, and my mind gradually apprehends the nature of the things I perceive through intellectual abstraction, but I judge (apprehend) the very existence of the thing that is colored, moving, smooth and cold, etc.

The brain is active while I am thinking, because my thinking is always accompanied by sense impressions, sense memories, perceptions, internal images of words, etc. Although being is not an image, my imagination provides one nonetheless, such as the very image of the word 'being'. But concepts are not extended, they are not mutable, nor are they divisible (they are indivisible), etc. But once again, it is a single agent that knows, that conceives ideas, who understands the diverse natures of things (partially, imperfectly, to be sure), the interrelations between things, who perceives the motions of things but also understands the meaning of those motions (I perceive a moving thing, but I also understand that this motion is a person running for his life, or diving to win gold, or building to shelter his family, etc.). And so even motions are particular and universal; there is this motion here, and motion in general, like the motion of "chemical change".

Reductionism is in large part a knowledge issue. It is not about science, it is about knowledge (epistemology). There is an epistemological error buried in reductionism. It is rooted in a lack of awareness of the role of knowledge in the scientific process, in particular the role of pre-scientific knowledge.

A reductionistic method of producing knowledge of the constituent parts of a whole does not yield a knowledge of this unity that we possess from within, ordinarily and pre-scientifically—we know ourselves as one being. It only yields knowledge of a plurality (a multiplicity of parts). And I understand the plant or my pet cat, etc., as a single whole precisely because I know myself as a single whole. You and I correctly interpret an animal's writhing in pain because we know pain's reality from within, and we project this knowledge into the animal when we see it acting in a similar way to our own experience. Without that interior knowledge, writhing in pain would appear to be a kind of geometric folding and contorting (Smith, *Idea Men*, p 420). In the same way, you know yourself as an extended substance (through external and internal sense perception), but you also know yourself as a single entity, that is, as one being—and you know this through self-consciousness, and you become conscious of yourself when you know something outside yourself. That is part of the reason why you know things as unified things or beings. You know that apple as a single thing, that it is distinct and not continuous with the atmosphere around it or the table below it. Although the animal might not be aware of its own awareness (that requires an immaterial power that is capable of complete self-reflection, not just the central sense), and thus might not be aware of its own awareness of its state of pain, (but only aware of its pain), you understand that this animal is in a lot of pain. In the same way, it is this experience of your own interiority, this experience of yourself from within as a single and indivisible whole that allows you to understand that the cells in this frog, or in this man, are parts of the single being (whole) that is this frog or man.

So it is not reductionism that can account for self-consciousness, it is self-consciousness that renders the reductionistic method of doing science possible. That is precisely what reductionism is, a method, not a metaphysics. It is not a philosophy of reality. When Arthur Eddington, for example, said that solidity is an illusion, that it is not real, because this table is made up of atoms that are mostly empty space, he was substituting ordinary pre-scientific knowledge with a knowledge derived from a method. It was a knowledge issue at the root of his absurd claim. But test that hypothesis on anyone who maintains it; throw a brick at him and watch how quickly he gets out of the way. Why? He knows that brick is solid; solidity is a property that belongs to things, and we know things ordinarily, and that ordinary pre-scientific knowledge is not illusion. If it were, so too is the knowledge derived from a scientific method; for there is only one faculty of knowing, and if it is defective and unreliable on the initial level, it is unreliable on all subsequent levels.

Without the self-consciousness of your own radical unity, you could not know "parts" to be what they are, namely "parts of a whole", and thus you would never come to know a being (a thing). Again, although one cannot lose a sense of this self-consciousness and continue doing science, one can indeed never come to an explicit awareness of the role this self-consciousness plays in rendering an empiriometric and reductionistic method possible and fruitful.

In sum, the word "determinant" is a perfect word to use in this discussion. Note the etymology of the word: *de term* or *de limit*. To determine is to "terminate" or end; something which has a term has an end; it is finite. A motion that terminates is a motion that comes to an end. Now, when treating motion or change, we studied the four causes (agent, formal, material, and final). The final cause is the end or term; a motion comes to its end (for example, a carpenter stops building the table) when the form (formal cause) is achieved, that is, when the motion is perfected (made through). A determinant determines, that is, specifies, or informs. What radiates from the object determines or specifies the sense organ. It informs it. Knowledge, whether it is sense knowledge or intellectual knowledge, is about being "informed", that is, it is about a power (sense or intellect) becoming specified (sensible species or intelligible species).

Chapter 36: A Closer Look at Free-Choice

The activity of choosing freely is a complex process involving the reciprocal activity of intellect and will. Intelligence is the ability to grasp the existence and natures of things. As such, it can grasp the intelligible relationships between beings. Not only do I grasp the intelligible relationships between beings outside of me, I am immediately aware of my relationship to the objects of my knowledge, that is, my relation to beings that exist outside of me. I know that "I" am knowing something that is not me (the object of my knowledge). That is why I can say that I am a subject of knowledge. Hence, subjectivity and objectivity are, to intelligent persons, meaningful terms, for they describe a real intelligible relation.

The things I know in the world are related to one another. A thing can be in front of another thing, beside something else, an animal can be related to another animal as parent to offspring, one human being might be related to another as employer to employed, etc. Some things are related to one another as means to ends. I perceive a knife and fork, and I perceive food on a plate, but it is the intellect that recognizes means *as means* to ends. For example, I not only pick up the fork to eat what is in front of me, I recognize the fork as a means to an end; that is why the human person is capable of designing and making new tools.

Now, I know that I desire happiness as an end, and I know that a good life is not possible outside of the good society (the common good), for I know myself as a person who has a natural inclination to establish relationships. I also know that I can treat a human person as a means to an end; at the same time I know that I can treat another as an end in himself. I recognize the former as morally deficient—for I would not want to be treated as a means to an end—, and I recognize the latter as morally noble and more conducive to genuine community. Furthermore, I recognize that an education in political science, for example, is a means of bettering society, and bettering society is a means of my happiness, since the good of others (their happiness) is my happiness, if I truly love others as another self.

Now, if we did not have the ability to recognize means *as means* to ends, we would be determined to the end by one means only. Freedom involves the choice between alternatives or means whereby the end is to be attained.

The object of the will is the good as such, without qualification, as opposed to merely one kind of good. For example, if the object of the will were one kind of good only, such as the flavor "sweet", then free choice would not be possible. One would be determined to that option which is the sweetest. The intellect knows supra-sensible goods or intelligible goods. In other words, we do not merely desire goods that are the object of sensation, such as a juicy steak. Supra sensibles or intelligibles such as education, the common good of society, justice, integrity of character, marriage, the contemplation of beauty, etc., are also desired by human beings. The will is the intellectual appetite that follows upon the intellectual apprehension of beings and their relations, not a sensible appetite that follows upon sense knowledge.

One of the distinguishing characteristics of intellectual knowledge, as opposed to sense knowledge, is that it can be universal. For example, we understand the concept of man in general, or education in general, or justice in general, etc, and that is why the will can be moved by a universal object. Thus we are able to choose a general course of action, such as always to be kind, always to be just, or always to be humble, etc. We can also choose a general course of action that appears to us as good, but is really deficient morally. For example, we can choose to look out for the self first, generally speaking, or we can choose to hate a class of people, etc. We can make and embrace universal laws. In this way we can transcend the limits of the present and the material world. But we can also will particular acts and objects, for example, to give to this charity at this moment, or to obey this order despite my appetite for rest or food, etc. It is in this way that the object of the will is the good without qualification.

In everything that we will there is some good, and it is by virtue of its goodness that we are drawn to it. I want to jump out of the window of this burning apartment and onto the trampoline at this moment because I see my life as good; I want to pick up the phone and call this person because I apprehend friendship as a good to be had for its own sake; we repent of wrong doing because we apprehend the integration of character and action as a good, etc. Again, it is not the good as pleasant to sensation that is the specific object of the will— the pleasant good is the object of the concupiscible appetite—, but rather the good without qualification. That includes all that the intellect understands as good, including sensible goods. For example, I know sensible goods to be goods, and so I can choose, for example, to keep this money to spend on my sense appetites instead of paying the debt I owe my neighbor, who has forgotten all about it.

Now the reason we deliberate before choosing is that when we apprehend alternatives, we see that each alternative contains some good that is not present in the other alternatives. For example, in our pursuit of education, which is a known intelligible good, we grasp that there is some good in pursuing psychology that is not present in the alternative to pursue philosophy, and vice versa. There is some good in pursuing political science that is not present in the other two alternatives, and vice versa. There is some good in pursuing and achieving a nursing degree that is not present in studying accounting; nursing will do a great deal of good for me and for society, and so too the study of psychology, or accounting, etc. In other words, each alternative is experienced as a finite good. If any alternative contained in itself all the good contained in the others, there would be no choice to make. The will would deliberate no more and would necessarily choose that alternative. But we continue deliberating because the intellect presents to the will known finite goods that do not contain the perfections of all the other alternatives, and so a choice has to be made.

And so the intellect moves the will, that is, presents the will with known goods, but the will in turn moves the intellect, causing it to continue presenting alternatives, that is, to continue deliberating. Decision occurs at the command of the will; for the very word "decide" comes from the Latin: *de secare* (dissect), which means literally "to cut off". At some point the will commands the intellect to "cut off" its deliberation (decide). The will orders the intellect to impress upon the will (itself) a definite known good for the last time. For example, if the person is deliberating over four alternatives (A, B, C, D, representing four local universities), the will, in deciding for alternative A, commands the intellect to present alternative A for the last time. Thus the will, by terminating the intellectual process, is actually determining (de-terminating or defining) the course of action to be followed, that is, which means is to be chosen. In this way the will specifies itself, and in specifying itself, it determines its own character or identity; for the identity or character of a person is described by recounting the kinds of choices that he makes, i.e., he's the kind of person who does not pay his debts, or he lies, or he will give you the shirt off his back, etc. To choose freely means to determine oneself (self-determination).

From the General to the Particular

Before I know the precise nature of any material being in my environment, I first apprehend that what I know is a being. In this way, our knowledge proceeds from the general to the particular. Similarly, the first free choices that we make are the more general choices, and it is in the context of these more general choices that we make more particular free choices, as a novelist conceives the whole novel very generally, and only later begins to fill in the particular parts, chapters, paragraphs, and sentences, that give expression to the original idea. He knows where he is going from the start. In other words, the whole is prior to its parts. Now the more universal the decision, the less motivated it is by sensible goods, and the more free and self-determined it is. But particular decisions motivated by strong passion can mitigate against personal responsibility. For example, if we were to place a Hershey bar and a carrot in front of an overweight and immature boy and ask him to make a choice, we can reasonably expect that he will choose the Hershey bar, because he is immature and has little control over his sense appetites (his will is weak and his sense appetite strong). But the more universal an idea is, the more abstracted it is from matter. So too, the more universal the choice, the more it exceeds the influence of the sense appetites.

Now, at a certain point in our lives, we make a very general choice about ourselves (by no means an irreversible choice). We choose to be a certain kind of person. This choice does not take place in a vacuum, but within an environment containing many different kinds of people. Very early on we choose to be like him, or like her, or not like this person or that person. In freely choosing certain acts, we choose to be a certain way. The actions that we choose constitute that particular way of being. For example, a child might want to be like his mother who is a kind and loving nurse, and he might want to be a person who cares for people, tends to their needs, etc. Or, a child might want to be part of this crowd and want the identity of belonging to it: "I want to be one of these, not one of them."

It is on the basis of this more general decision that other alternatives become more appealing, for they are more in accordance with the kind of character that the person originally chose for himself. Conversely, certain alternatives drop out of consideration—lose their appeal—because they are inconsistent with the kind of character he has chosen for himself. For example, he does not choose, like other kids he knows, to spit at seniors as he rides his bike past the nursing home every day because he does not want to be that kind of person. He loves those people. Why? Because he has chosen to, not for any ulterior motive (although that is a real possibility), but ultimately because that is the kind of person he has determined himself to be, the kind of person who relates to people this way, that is, in a way that loves them for their own sake.

It is possible for a person to choose to always look out for himself first, to make himself the very center around which his life will revolve. For example, a person can decide that feeling comfortable is more important to him than the wishes of others, or even the well-being and rights of others. He might accept that this is the kind of person he has become, that is, one with a less noble identity than that of a person who has made a better, less self-centered, choice. He experiences himself as rather unsightly as a result of that general decision and the choices that ensue, but he accepts that identity, and he will probably do his best to hide from the subtle awareness of his relatively rotten character. He does not intend that unsightly character, but he does intend to make himself the center of his life; it just so happens that this renders him unsightly to others and to himself, so he will attempt to disguise his true character and attempt to appear better, perhaps as a paragon of virtue, in order to procure the affirmation of others.

There are always certain choices that are consistent with the general decision that we make about ourselves, and there are choices that are inconsistent with it. As was said, these latter tend to lose their appeal. For example, if I decide that I always want to be "top dog", and I want others to either love me or barring that, fear me, then things like doing volunteer work or giving generously to charitable causes, tend to lose their appeal, unless they can be a means of maintaining my facade. Watching certain kinds of shows or applying for certain courses of study, etc., will also lose their appeal, while others will acquire a greater appeal. Consider, for example, how appealing education becomes to a person who has made a commitment that requires some years of schooling.

It is not necessarily possible for us to determine exactly when this very general choice was made by a particular person, but some of us remember moments in our own childhood when we became conscious of having made a simple and general decision to be "like this person" or to strive to be "like that person", or to be "a good person", or "a notorious person", etc. There is no need to search for the cause of this decision. The choice is self-determined, or self-caused. The power to choose freely is really the power to "make oneself", and what is made, the character that is established, is more intimately ours than anything else that we might own. We are the kind of person that we are because we willed that identity into existence. Contrary to Schopenhauer, a person indeed can will what he wills as well as do as he wills; for he can know that he knows and know what he wills and will otherwise.

It is true that much of what we carry on the level of the emotions will affect the way we interpret the world around us. This in turn will affect our decision making and possibly limit the degree of freedom underlying it. As an analogy, consider what it would be like having to live with fresh burns on your back and arms. An unintended collision with another would certainly cause great pain and the burn victim might very well experience a surge of intense anger. One's condition has made it much easier to incorrectly interpret the situation, reading into it an intentional affront when it was nothing of the sort. So too, a person may be carrying around deep emotional scars that keep him from correctly assessing the situations in which he finds himself. For example, he might read into another's glance or words intentions and sentiments that have no real basis. Many of his decisions might very well be rooted in his distorted judgments for which he is not entirely responsible. If a course of action was not rooted in a free choice because it was the result of a psychotic episode or some serious mental illness that rendered a person unable to come to a genuine apprehension of the alternatives before him (i.e., he was not in touch with reality), it would not shape that person's character or moral identity. It would seem that it is possible for a person to have killed another without being criminally responsible, and thus who is not a killer, and who otherwise has good moral character.

On the other hand, a person might very well be capable of an accurate assessment of things despite having emotional scars. And even if his judgment is distorted, his decision in the face of what he inaccurately perceives to be the situation at hand is something that he might be responsible for. For example, a person might misinterpret the gestures of another, reading into them racist sentiments that are really not part of the other's mindset at all, and he might not be entirely responsible for this misinterpretation. But his decision to assault or kill him is still made freely and deliberately. Moreover, he might very well be responsible for certain decisions that resulted in emotional wounds that in turn contributed to his distorted perception of reality.

And so it is not always possible to know just how free a person's individual choices are at a given time. But the assertion that a person is entirely a victim of his environment and thus entirely determined is as unfounded and "judgmental" as the assertion that a person is always totally free and entirely responsible for every decision that he has made or will make.

Another reason why it is not possible to accurately judge the degree of freedom involved in a particular decision is that the degree of freedom also depends upon the number of options or alternatives. One cannot reasonably say, for example, that "you could have chosen to go to Princeton, but you chose York University". Princeton was not an option for the vast majority of us. Man is not, contrary to Sartre's contention, absolutely and totally free. But at the very core of our spiritual nature, the will cannot be moved by any other agent. The very notion that the will can be moved by another is self-contradictory. And within the limited context of my environment, I am always confronted with alternatives. That is why Sartre is not entirely off the mark either. He writes:

...man is in an organized situation in which he himself is involved. Through his choice, he involves all mankind, and he can not avoid making a choice: either he will remain chaste, or he will marry without having children, or he will marry and have children; anyhow, whatever he may do, it is impossible for him not to take full responsibility for the way he handles this problem....moral choice is to be compared to the making of a work of art...It is clearly understood that...the artist is engaged in the making of his painting, and that the painting to be made is precisely the painting he will have made...Never let it be said by us that this man -- who, taking affection, individual action, and kind-heartedness toward a specific person as his ethical first principle, chooses to remain with his mother, or who, preferring to make a sacrifice, chooses to go to England -- has made an arbitrary choice. Man makes himself. He isn't ready made at the start (**Sartre**, *Existentialism*, pp. 41-43).

And so it is not that we are determined by our environment. Rather, the environment is in large part determined by us. As Aristotle says, the intellect is in a sense all things. The mind becomes what it knows in an immaterial way. As intellectual creatures, we know our environment; it is within us and in a sense is us immaterially, at least when known. We transcend our environment in knowing it. And that environment that we know or that is within us is the result of the choices of other people; the characters of others are part of my environment. They are within me when known, not simply outside of me causing me to behave a certain way. As within me, I transcend them, I know them, and I know my relationship to those characters as objects of my knowledge, and I can choose for myself a like identity. I establish my own character, my moral identity, by the choices that I make within this environment and in relation to it, an environment that is both within me and outside of me.

Thus in choosing, I contribute to the making of this environment for others. As Sartre puts it: "...to act is to modify the shape of the world; it is to arrange means in view of an end" (*Being and Nothingness*. P. 433). I have no control over others' choices, and so a good part of the environment is out of my control, but I do have control over my own choices, and so as I enter into relation with that environment, I am able to change its character as I will, at least in part. Psychotherapist Rollo May writes:

Freedom and will consist not in the abnegation of determinism but in our relationship to it Man is distinguished by his capacity to know that he is determined and to choose his relationship to what determines him. He can and must, unless he abdicates his consciousness, choose how he will relate to necessity, such as death, old age, limitations of intelligence, and the conditioning inescapable in his own background. Will he accept this necessity, deny it, fight it, affirm it, consent to it? (*Love and Will*, pp. 269-270).

There is no denying, however, that a correlation exists between poverty and crime. The more poverty there is in particular neighborhoods, the greater will be the incidents of crime. Can we conclude that poverty, therefore, causes crime? That would be an unwarranted conclusion. Human persons cause their own criminal acts. But how, then, do we explain that reducing poverty results in a reduction of crime? This is a good and complex question. Firstly, in many cases—certainly not all—, it is deficient character that causes poverty. Some school boards, for example, spend an exorbitant amount of money on programs that provide students with good academic, psychological or behavioral, and financial support, and some students choose, nevertheless, a criminal lifestyle. They are liars and users, and the social benefits that surround them have not changed their character in the slightest, because it cannot. And of course, not everyone who finds him or herself in circumstances of poverty chooses crime as a way of dealing with it. Criminals have brothers and sisters, many of whom have gone on to make something very good of their difficult lives.

But explaining the correlation between crime and poverty is nonetheless not easy. I offer the following as a possible explanation. I may know the personalities of my students, but I cannot say with any certainty that I know their individual character or moral identity. Adverse circumstances test and often reveal a person's character. Out of a classroom of 30 privileged students, it is quite possible that a small percentage will make criminal choices that they are fully responsible for, because their love of self is far greater than their love of justice. In fact, they don't love justice at all. Out of that same group, there might be an equally small percentage of students who would never choose to hurt, rob, or deprive anyone, should they find themselves in extremely difficult circumstances, and who would be willing to live in very poor conditions before they'd compromise their character. These are the ones who love justice more than they love themselves. In between, we find people of varying degrees of self-love. Although some may not be willing to die for another, they are not willing to compromise their principles for a particular living standard (i.e., moderately well off). But, there are some who are very willing to compromise their character to avoid a lower standard of living (relative poverty). That is why although poverty does not cause crime, reducing poverty will increase alternatives and will remove certain environmental conditions to which specific individuals will freely choose to relate in a criminal way.

Chapter 37: Reverence for One's Opponents in Debate

Publisher Frank Sheed wrote: "Bigotry does not mean believing that people who differ from you are wrong, it means assuming that they are either knaves or fools. To think them so is an immediate convenience, since it saves us the trouble of analyzing either their views or our own."

Today, for some reason, we are inclined to see ourselves as more open minded and tolerant of opposing viewpoints than those of any other era; but on closer inspection, we really are a terribly bigoted people. We are blind to it, probably because, as Sheed implies, we're lazy—if we admit it to ourselves, we'd have to allow our opposition to have his word, and then we'd have to engage in the hard and uncomfortable work of thinking about what it is we really hold to be true and why, and that begets uncertainty, and uncertainty is, for many of us, uncomfortable. I'm willing to argue that we inculcate our own bigotries in the context of the classroom—and I am not referring to racism, anti-Semitism, or homophobia, etc. I mean the bigotry that Sheed defines above; for we are no longer a culture of debate—and that's only because political correctness mitigates against a spirit of openness and debate.

On more than a few occasions I've been accused of being "stuck in the Middle Ages" for teaching students to think on the basis of principles, rather than through the lenses of an ideology. The label "Middle Ages" is used primarily to destroy the credibility of those whose views we regard as old and traditional, and it succeeds in doing what it was intended to do, only because most people are ignorant of history; for anyone who has studied intellectual history in particular will know that some of the most brilliant thinkers—who in many ways are still ahead of our time—lived in the medieval period.

What is interesting about the International Baccalaureate Theory of Knowledge course that I now teach is that the rubric for the final essay includes a requirement to give careful consideration to different perspectives, that is, to carefully explore and evaluate the counterclaims of one's opposition. I am not entirely sure of their reasons for this requirement—whether it is simply the result of an aversion to any kind of absolutism and thus a subtle embrace of relativism, or whether it stems from an appreciation of the limits of the human perspective and a genuine love of truth. Regardless, the requirement is an important one. But there is nothing new in this, at least not for a Catholic. The formal structure of the medieval method of writing, at least in the high Middle Ages, is that of a debate, always on a particular question, and the elucidation of the question always begins with a careful consideration of the current and most difficult objections.

For example, consider St. Thomas Aquinas' question in *The Summa Theologica* "Whether God exists?" Before doing anything else, Aquinas argues that God does not exist. He writes: "It seems that God does not exist; because if one of two contraries be infinite, the other would be altogether destroyed. But the word "God" means that He is infinite goodness. If, therefore, God existed, there would be no evil discoverable; but there is evil in the world. Therefore God does not exist."

That's a very interesting argument. I don't know of anyone clever enough to imagine such a difficulty with the very idea of God—certainly no one among the "new atheists" (i.e., Dawkins, Hitchens, Harris, etc.). Moreover, I know very few theists who could adequately respond to it. But that is not the only objection he raises. Consider the second objection: "Further, it is superfluous to suppose that what can be accounted for by a few principles has been produced by many. But it seems that everything we see in the world can be accounted for by other principles, supposing God did not exist. For all natural things can be reduced to one principle which is nature; and all voluntary things can be reduced to one principle which is human reason, or will. Therefore there is no need to suppose God's existence."

This is not an instance of the fallacy of the straw man, and this is a far cry from ridiculing the opposition; for most serious Catholics could not answer this second objection.

Consider an easier question: "Whether happiness consists in pleasure". Before arguing that happiness does not consist in pleasure, Aquinas articulates three counterarguments: "It would seem that man's happiness consists in pleasure. For since happiness is the last end, it is not desired for something else, but other things for it. But this answers to pleasure more than to anything else: "for it is absurd to ask anyone what is his motive in wishing to be pleased". Therefore happiness consists principally in pleasure and delight."

With that argument, I could walk into any philosophy class of mine and convince students that happiness is nothing other than pleasure, and if anyone dares to argue against me, I can raise the second objection in that same article: "Furthermore, 'the first cause goes more deeply into the effect than the second cause'. Now the causality of the end consists in its attracting the appetite. Therefore, seemingly that which moves most the appetite, answers to the notion of the last end. Now this is pleasure: and a sign of this is that delight so far absorbs man's will and reason, that it causes him to despise other goods. Therefore it seems that man's last end, which is happiness, consists principally in pleasure." Aquinas offers a final objection: "...since desire is for good, it seems that what all desire is best. But everyone desires delight; both the wise and the foolish, and even irrational creatures. Therefore delight is the best of all. Therefore happiness, which is the supreme good, consists in pleasure."

No one can accuse Aquinas, a 13th century theologian, philosopher, and Doctor of the Church, of having a closed mind or of failing to revere his opposition. But such reverence is a thing of the past. Recently I was browsing through a local newspaper and found all sorts of articles attacking the Conservative government. And that's fine, but none of those articles, not one, gave serious consideration to a different and more conservative perspective, nor did one article carefully consider counter arguments before setting out to attack government policy. And so we inevitably get the feeling that the country is being governed by a bunch of fools, which gives rise to fear, which in turn gives rise to anger that the majority government could possibly consist of a group of rich and cold hearted knaves. But have I been persuaded of that? Or, have I been manipulated? I am left with nothing that allows me to assess the opposition with any kind of objectivity, so all I can do is trust the newspaper.

The fact of the matter is that our opponents in debate do us a tremendous service. Only those, however, who love and pursue truth can acknowledge that. One way I was able to gain clarity for myself on a number of issues over the years was through the clever and thoughtful objections of my students. Their ability to imagine difficulties—not to mention the courage they showed in voicing them—helped me and future students in ways they hadn't imagined. Nonetheless, it takes a long time for students to begin to trust that I will not deduct marks for argument, for opposing me in class, for questioning, expressing doubt, raising objections, and forcing me to explain myself more thoroughly; for they were brought up in an educational environment that confuses an argument with a quarrel and in a culture that believes education is about power, not truth; which is why questioning, opposing, doubting, imagining difficulties and debate were stifled. The result is that students readily believe everything their teachers tell them. They certainly believe me; they trust me and will not challenge me - initially, and unless of course I push them to challenge me. This is a problem, because soon these students will enter an institution of higher learning, and a professor with more letters after his/her name will stand before them, and it will more likely than not be a professor who will ridicule their moral convictions, if those convictions are at odds with popular culture. What will these students do then? Many will do the same as they have always been encouraged to do, namely, put their faith in the one standing before them, the one with power.

Chapter 38: The Problem with Passionate Views

Interestingly enough, the hardest part of a research essay, for the majority of my students, is not articulating and defending their own position, but coming to understand the position of their opponent, regardless of the claim they are choosing to defend. It is no wonder that the weakest part of their essay is typically this part, namely, the clear and credible defense of their opponent's point of view. They are inclined not to bother with their opposition; it fails to dawn on them that anyone who opposes their own point of view might have some good reasons for doing so and might actually help them to understand their own position more fully and refine it accordingly.

And that's the culture in which they live and breathe; a culture with a reigning orthodoxy, and if anyone chooses to dissent from that reigning cultural ideology, they are ridiculed and dismissed out of hand.

Recently, an educator told me that watching a certain news station would cause her blood pressure to go up, so she stopped watching it. She was referring to my favorite news channel. Her reaction is revealing, not to mention ironic; for an emotional reaction is rooted in a judgment, because emotion is an appetitive reaction that always follows upon cognition of one kind or another. And so in this case, at the very least, her reaction is rooted in a judgment that this person is wrong. If, however, the emotion arising out of that judgment is one of anger, then the judgment is much more than a simple "...this person is mistaken". Anger is a natural response to a perceived injustice; thus, it is a judgment that an injustice has been committed.

Now it is one thing to judge that a person holding certain political and economic views is mistaken and to react quickly for fear of the negative repercussions that the mistaken position will have on society as a whole—and that's just what it is, namely fear. But anger is a response to a moral offense, an injustice. Thus, I have made a judgment, conscious or unconscious, that this person I am watching is, in the very point of view he or she is articulating, a moral fool who is violating another's basic rights.

Granted, some of the hosts are annoying, possibly even obnoxious at times, and all of them certainly controversial, counter cultural, and politically incorrect, but if any of them give rise to anger, I have to wonder what exactly the apparent injustice at the root of that anger is.

I suspect there isn't a genuine injustice at all. People are very passionate about their views, but that is the last thing in the world we should be passionate about. We ought to have, on the contrary, a passion for truth, a passion for learning, but not a passion for our views. To love learning is to be open to learn, but anyone who is genuinely open to learn is comfortable with the sense of his own limitations and his need to be expanded. Those who are passionate about their views, however, lack a healthy sense of their own limitations and are not as open to learning as they might believe themselves to be; for they fear opposition for what it reveals about what they love, which is their view, or what amounts to the same thing, themselves. If my viewpoint is wrong, then I am far more limited than I originally suspected, and if that's an insight to which I am closed, I will resent anyone who forces me to acknowledge the fact.

To get a better sense of the how unwarranted is anger against one's opponents in debate, let us review what we discussed in a previous chapter, namely the levels of abstraction and some of their implications. The mind in search of "science", or the "reasoned facts" for things, always abstracts from the individuating conditions of material things in order to possess necessary and universal conclusions, such as $a^2 + b^2 = c^2$; or the amount of usable energy in a closed system will decrease over time, or what amounts to the same thing, the entropy of the universe always increases in the course of every natural change, etc. Now, there are three different levels of abstraction. The first level is that on which the physical sciences take place. Here the mind abstracts from individual matter, but it does not abstract from common sensible matter. Biology, for example, abstracts from this body, this bone, these nerves, but it does not abstract from "bone, nerves, cells, etc." At this level, we theorize, we posit a hypothesis, i.e., the cause of cancer. Experiment and empirical data are needed to verify the hypothesis, but a verification of a hypothesis is no guarantee that the effect cannot be accounted for through another cause or explanation. The history of science is filled with examples of such revisions and counter theories.

The second level of abstraction is the mathematical. On this level, the mind considers quantity abstracted from material things. Geometry considers shapes and lines that have no sensible matter (i.e., wood or steel) and concerns itself solely with the properties and relationships of continuous and discrete quantities (numbers) considered in themselves.

The highest level of abstraction deals not with any specific mode of being, such as living being, or quantified being, or human being, or chemical entities, etc., but with being insofar as it is being. Since outside of being is non-being, it is impossible to abstract any further.

Now what is particularly noteworthy about the levels of abstraction is that the higher the level of abstraction, the greater the certainty and the less do our conclusions depend on empirical investigation. For example, we can be absolutely certain that "nothing can both be and not be at the same time and in the same respect". To deny it, one has to assume it is true; thus, it is impossible to deny it with any consistency. Moreover, there is no need for any experiment to verify it.

Mathematics also enjoys tremendous certainty; for there are no conflicting schools of mathematics. If anyone is in doubt about the truth of a mathematical problem, one simply takes out a pencil or a piece of chalk and rationally demonstrates how the answer was derived.

Certainty, however, is far more difficult to come by on the first level of abstraction; one must empirically investigate in order to establish one's conclusion with relative certainty, thus one needs more than a pencil and paper; one needs a lab.

But consider how much more labor is required to arrive at any kind of certainty in history, for example, which is not an abstract science, for its object is particular events that are past. To do history well requires a great deal of reading, sifting through archives, deducing and inferencing, etc., but in the end, one is very often far from certain of one's conclusions.

Economics and politics are both sciences, and they are very low on the levels of intellectual abstraction. To know the laws of economics requires a study of particular economies—which are vast and complex—, and economic theory requires empirical evidence that this or that theory actually increases the overall living standard of a state. There are also a myriad of aspects in political life, and individuals only have a very limited area of expertise; thus every political leader needs advisors from a wide variety of backgrounds. Political prudence requires a great deal of experience, for there is a very steep learning curve here, as there is in other smaller administrative positions.

So, unless I am watching a Klu Klux Klan rally or something of the sort, what right do I have to become incensed at another person's political or economic arguments? Curious? Yes. Fearful? Perhaps. But angry? There's only a small area of this universe about which any of us can hope to enjoy a degree of certainty, and although some people may be clearly mistaken, there are often a host of reasons for the mistaken views they hold, and the more we try to get a handle of some of those reasons, the less anger we'll experience and the more we will understand the scope of our own position. We might even discover that they are not mistaken after all.

For the sake of the truth, which is always much larger than ourselves, we ought to pay more attention to our own emotional reactions to others, because they tell us far more about ourselves than they do about the ones we're listening to, or refusing to listen to.

Chapter 39: Politics and Principles

I am always delighted when young people show some degree of interest at election time, but the exhilaration I experience is often dampened upon realizing that so many of them choose their candidate not on the basis of reason, that is, after a careful consideration of the issues, but on irrelevant factors and, most notably, on the media's popular depiction of the one person they don't want to see elected to office—almost always a conservative. In other words, rarely do young people vote on the basis of principle, but almost always on faith in what others tell them about the candidates. The following is an attempt to provide some kind of framework for principled thinking as it relates to politics, and so I would like to begin by laying the groundwork with some basic philosophical principles.

Firstly, government is for the common good. Now the common good is the good of the social whole, which is not the same as my own private good. The common good consists of the entire set of conditions that enables the members of the civil community to attain for themselves their own fullness of being. It is possible for me, however, to pursue my own good (the delectable good) at the expense of the common good, and so in this case I oppose my own private good to the common good.

Justice is the constant will to render what is due to another; and there are three kinds of justice that correspond to the three different kinds of relationship possible for human persons: commutative, legal, and distributive justice. Commutative justice orders relations between individuals (i.e. I willingly pay the money I owe you). I not only have a debt to certain individuals, however, I also have a debt to the civil community as a whole. In fact, that is a debt that I cannot fully repay. Nevertheless, the civil community as a whole has a right to expect a great deal from me, for example, that I remain a law abiding citizen and contribute to the common good. This is legal justice. The criminal has little or no regard for his

debt towards the civil community as a whole, thus he has little
or no regard for legal justice. Finally, the civil community as a
whole has a duty towards the individual, for the common good
is the set of conditions directed towards enabling all human
persons to flourish, not just the few. And so the government
is elected by the people in order to secure the common good
of the civil community, for the sake of individual human
persons. Thus, a republican form of government is
government of the people, by the people, and for the people.

What is unfortunate is that many people vote not so much
for the candidate most qualified to restore and maintain the
common good, but for the one who promises to promote their
own limited interests. Furthermore, there is often a
tremendous amount of bigotry behind our decision for or
against certain candidates, and bigotry blinds the intellect.
Publisher Frank Sheed once wrote: "Bigotry does not mean
believing that people who differ from you are wrong, it means
assuming that they are either knaves or fools." One of the
objects of our collective bigotry is conservatives, who are
almost everywhere regarded as cut-throat, cold hearted and
avaricious knaves who are only concerned about their own
private interests. The left leaning, on the contrary, are almost
always regarded as socially conscious and compassionate, and
who are always willing to put people before profit.

If we want to be critical thinkers, and not the gullible who
do nothing more than follow, all the while believing
themselves to be tomorrow's leaders, then we have to be
willing to test these popular assumptions, investigate their
historical roots, and possibly, in the end, face those bigotries in
ourselves that keep us from an objective and accurate
assessment of the way things really are. The world always
makes sense when perceived through ideological lenses, but
there is a real difference between an argument that makes
sense and an argument that is true. A false conclusion validly
deduced from false premises makes all the sense in the world,
but the conclusion is false nonetheless (i.e., All capitalists favor
exploiting the poor; All those who favor a free market
economy are capitalists; Therefore, all those who favor a free

market economy favor exploiting the poor). Thus, "making sense" is not a criterion for truth.

Truth is a relation; it is the conformity between what is in the mind and the real. Those who see the world through ideological lenses—whether those are the lenses of a feminist ideology that interprets all conflict in the world in terms of male dominance, or the lenses of socialist ideology that interprets history in terms of the conflict between the working class and the bourgeoisie class—are indeed able to evaluate critically and make sense out of the world we live in, which is why ideologies are so attractive. The problem is that the ideology does not include the tools necessary to critically evaluate the ideology itself, thus enabling us to determine whether the world as it appears through these lenses really is pink as it appears to be, or yellow, etc. Thinking via an ideology is not the same as thinking on the basis of first principles. And you can always tell the difference between a principled thinker and an ideologue: the principled thinker is not threatened by debate because his chief end is the possession of truth; the ideologue is closed to debate, is threatened by it, may even become angry and shut it down, for he protects the ideology at all costs, because without it, the world is absurd and unintelligible, and an unintelligible world is frightening.

It is wonderful to see more and more people watching presidential debates, but one has to wonder about the use of it all when so few are able to evaluate a debate on the basis of truth and the issues, when most people today score a debate as they would a boxing match (i.e., which one was more aggressive, who threw the most zingers, who was more condescending, etc.). Indeed, we do not live in a culture that fosters a spirit of genuine debate, because debate is no longer about truth, but power. And that is itself a symptom of the postmodern culture in which we live and breathe; a culture that denies any kind of objectivity to what is said to be true and good.

Some Political Implications of Individualism

Politics is a branch of ethics, and ethics is founded upon the philosophy of human nature. Behind different political parties and their different visions of the ideal state is a different ethics, which in turn is founded upon a different philosophy of human nature. It is very important to get a handle on the ethics and philosophy of human nature that underpins and governs the various political platforms if we want to understand and critically evaluate them.

The western world has been very much influenced by the philosophy of Individualism—and by Individualism I do **not** mean the capitalist notion of individual initiative and the entrepreneurial spirit. I am referring to the Individualism rooted in the Existentialism of French philosopher and playwright, Jean Paul Sartre, who in 1964 won the Nobel Prize for Literature. Sartre distinguishes between **etre en-soi** (being in itself) and **etre pour-soi** (being for itself). Being **in itself** is the unconscious material being that is the object of the sciences (trees, minerals, crystals, etc.). Being **for-itself** refers to conscious being (i.e. you and me). The human individual is a "for itself" (pour-soi).

In order to know being, which is unconscious, I must somehow stand outside of being, or transcend it. But outside of being is non-being, or nothing. Hence, it is only by way of nothingness that one can come to know being. Nothingness lies at the heart of the pour-soi. The pour-soi is a blend of en-soi and non-being (nothingness). Non-being is a hole in the heart of being, which gives rise to consciousness.

For Sartre, existence precedes essence. What this means is that at the beginning, a pour-soi is a pure existent without an intelligible nature or essence. He is a nothing and a something, a composite of en-soi and nothing. Because existence precedes essence, man is totally free to determine "what is he", that is, his essence. He determines his essence by the free choices that he makes. And so, in contradistinction to classical thought, there is no initial nature or essence that man must live in accordance with. Whereas traditionally, a morally good act is one that promotes the fullness of our nature, in a Sartrean framework we have no nature; we determine our nature by our choices, and so there is no universal moral law, that is, no natural moral law, and thus no universal right and wrong. One may do as one pleases—but one must be willing to deal with the consequences of one's freely chosen acts.

This is **Individualism**. And this individualism becomes more radical as we consider that all relationships between human beings are, according to Sartre, characterized by conflict. As one pour-soi gazes at another pour-soi, he objectifies him, thus reducing him to an en-soi by his very gaze. The other resists this reduction of himself to an en-soi by gazing back at the other, reducing him in turn to an en-soi.

Thus, genuine love is not possible. In fact, Sartre declares that hell is "the other". The pour-soi struggles to maintain himself, but doing so is destined to fail. I am most fully myself the more I escape the influence of others, but as I choose to be the individual I will to be, the more I fill up my nothingness and become an en-soi. Yet I cannot help but choose. The pour-soi is destined to become an en-soi. To successfully resist this movement towards the nausea of being is to cease to be. Thus, there is no such thing as an absolute pour-soi (God), because an absolute pour-soi with no admixture of en-soi, would be absolute nothingness. In other words, it is not that there is no evidence for God's existence; rather, it is impossible for God to exist. And yet this is precisely what every pour-soi desires to be, namely one who has successfully resisted the reduction of himself to an en-soi and to be an absolute pour-soi, which is God (i.e., pure nothingness).

It follows that no one may tell me that I ought to choose this or that course of action, or that I have a duty to choose such and such, i.e., to go to battle to defend the country, remain faithful to my spouse, etc. What "ought" to be done has meaning only within the framework of an already established "essence". But the choices I make define me, thus I choose my own essence, and the duties that belong to the essence of another may not belong to that which I have determined for myself. So I have no intrinsic or natural obligations, because there are no universal obligations or precepts rooted in a universal human nature; for there is no universal human nature, only the essence that I determine for myself. I simply have the right to make myself into the person I choose to be.

We see the influence of this radical Individualism in the "meism" or "me generation" of the 60s. What is noteworthy, however, is the radically new way of conceiving human freedom. According to a classical philosophical mindset, freedom means **not** doing what you want to do, but knowing what you **ought** to do and possessing the virtues that alone enable you to do it. But within the Individualist frame of mind, I am only free when I am free from anything that "ties me down", such as responsibilities towards others, commitments, the burdens of working and raising a family, etc.

It was precisely this notion of freedom that was behind the Sexual Revolution of the 1960s (to the 1980s). With the invention of the birth control pill, it was now possible to engage in sexual intercourse without having to worry about the responsibility and burden of taking care of a child, or the responsibility to love and commit to the person with whom one is having sex. The pill became a symbol of freedom.

And then the peace movement: "Make love, not war". Why not make war? Because war is bad—but not because human life is intrinsically good; for the American Law Institute, in 1959, proposed a model penal code for state abortion laws, advocating for the legalization of abortion for a variety of reasons, one of which was evidence of a handicapped child in the womb. This was one more stage in the gradual construction of the anti-life culture in which we now live and breathe. Rather, the reason war is so repugnant is that it implies a universal precept, namely the duty to serve the "common good", to willingly put oneself in harm's way for the sake of a larger good. Such notions belong to the "old morality". Fundamentally, there is no duty to go to war to defend the freedoms that countless others who have gone before us fought and died for.

The Individualist sees only his rights, not his obligations; for these latter are burdens that deprive me of my freedom.

Note that the *Canadian Charter of Rights and Freedoms* makes no mention of "duties" or "obligations", that is, there is nothing in the entire Charter about what the civil community as a whole has a right to expect from individual citizens.

It should come as no surprise that we've seen a steady decline in marriage since the late 1960s; this was the result of the rebellion against conventional western principles rooted in a Judeo-Christian ethics. This period of rebellion was a very comfortable atmosphere for relativists, hedonists, as well as socialists (devotees of Marxism).

A brief summary of Marxism

Karl Marx (1818-1883) was moved by what he perceived to be the injustices of the Industrial Revolution and he certainly had as his goal an economic system that would help rectify these inequalities. The basic premise of Marxist socialism is that private property is evil and that the state must own all means of production (capital) in order to insure a fair and equitable distribution of wealth.

Man, according to Marx, develops himself through labour, but certain economic structures and labour relations impede his development and alienate him from his product. This alienating system, according to Marx, is capitalism, for within this wage labour system, the product of a man's labour does not belong to him, but to the one who owns the means of production.

In response, the working class seeks to recover itself, to overcome this alienation, and according to Marx it can do so only through a social revolution through which it abolishes private property and brings about the transition to communism.

It is important to keep in mind that in Marxism, the basic historical reality is not the individual person, who, for the Western Judeo-Christian tradition, exists in the image and likeness of God, and who is endowed with a spiritual and immortal soul. Rather, the basic historical reality is, for Marx, **social man** in his economic activity in nature. The individual *is merely a part of social man.* He wrote: "In its reality it [the essence of man] is the ensemble of social relations." And so Marxism concerns itself primarily with social acts, not acts that lack an immediate and obvious social significance (i.e., reading pornography in the privacy of one's bedroom, having sex with someone else's spouse, having an abortion, etc.).

Furthermore, it is the labour of social man, his specific method of production and the economic relations it generates that determine the form of political life, the content of law, and the prevailing morality of the period, not vice versa. It is not that the individual person is able to apprehend the nature of things, such as human nature, or the nature of the state, or the natural moral law, thus allowing him to accurately determine what constitutes just civil law, etc. Rather ideas, including religious ideas, are determined by the specific economic relations and conditions that prevail in a society. In other words, man is essentially an ensemble of social relations, and economics determines everything. Moreover, history is in process, and so too, therefore, are human ideas. Thus, for Marx, there are no "eternal verities" or absolute truths.

In a capitalist society, according to Marx, law, social structures, morality, current ideas, etc., are all shaped by the dominant class (exploiters/oppressors) for the sake of maintaining power. But such morality, for Marx, has no more objectivity than a fable. Communist morality, on the other hand, is characterized by the revolutionary imperative. In 1920, Lenin wrote: "...for the communist, morality lies entirely in this compact, united discipline and conscious mass struggle against the exploiters. We do not believe in an eternal morality, ...we say: morality is what serves to destroy the old exploiting society and to unite all the toilers around the proletariat, which is creating a new communist society...Morality serves the purpose of helping human society to rise to a higher level and to get rid of the exploitation of labour."

Marxist ethics is an ethics of results. Contrary to classical natural law morality, there is no such thing as an act being intrinsically evil or having intrinsic goodness. The goodness and evil of acts are measured by the degree to which they further the cause of the self-emancipation of the oppressed class (the working class). So, intentionally killing another human being is not "intrinsically" evil, for one may hang capitalists "from the nearest lampposts", said Marx; doing so only furthers the historical movement towards final emancipation. In short, one may do "evil" that good may come of it; for doing so is not, in the end, evil.

Combine this with the fact that for Marx, the basic historical reality is social man, it is obvious why the fundamental virtues of a Marxist worldview are class solidarity, hatred of all oppression—which means hatred of the rich, who are the oppressors—, discipline, and devotion to the construction of a classless and communist world.

Personalism and its political implications

It shouldn't be too difficult to see why the radical Individualist and the Socialist get along well and found one another in the rebellious atmosphere of the 60s. In socialism, morality is no longer a personal matter, but a matter for social man, or the communist party; in other words, all moral responsibility is shifted to the party. This is attractive to the Individualist, because in his mind he does not have any fundamental obligations, only rights, and he is entitled to those rights; the government alone has the duty to distribute benefits and wealth equally, without making any burdensome demands on him. And so the radical Individualist of the 1960s naturally favored the more left leaning or Socialist political parties who proposed to increase the size of government, raise taxes, increase spending and intensify government regulations, to provide not simply for those who cannot take care of themselves, but for all individuals. And that has been the attitude of a great many young people in North America since that time, an attitude of entitlement, and an attitude that naturally regards all social problems as the responsibility of government, not individuals.

Introduction to Philosophy for Young People

But where, we have to ask, will government get the money it needs to expand and spend? The answer is, of course, the individual tax payer, not to mention private corporations that provide employment. But the more a corporation is taxed, the less it pays to produce, so production naturally decreases, growth slows down, and unemployment rises. As Individualism spreads throughout a culture, as it had begun to do in the mid 60s, marriage declines—why impose unnecessary restrictions on myself by getting married? And where marriage does endure, families become smaller, because it has become more difficult to support a large family, not to mention that Individualism does not foster generosity, self-sacrifice, and fidelity—these values belong to an older morality. Smaller families means less demand, and less demand means less need for things that any family would require (diapers, clothes, food, larger house, etc.), and less demand means higher prices. Thus, it becomes much more difficult for families to make ends meet and for young people to find work.

But man is not a pour-soi (a for-itself); rather, he is a "for another". The word "person" is from the Latin *persona* (through sound). A person is a communicator, that is, one who becomes fully the person he is meant to be in community. It is not true that I am free when freed from burdens and responsibilities; that is an illusion of freedom, a confusion between the freedom proper to a brute animal and a genuinely human freedom. The human person has a rational nature, and the more knowledge we possess, the more free we are, that is, the more able we are to determine ourselves towards what is truly good. And the greater our freedom, the greater our responsibility—we do not hold animals responsible for the things they do, for they are governed not by reason, but by their instincts. Genuine human freedom means knowing what I ought to do, that is, knowing what promotes the fullness of my nature, and it means possessing the virtues necessary to carry out what I ought to do. This means, of course, that I can turn out to be my own worst enemy. Hell is not the other; rather, hell is the result of never having loved others for their own sake, that is, anyone other than myself. Hell is an eternal

270

boredom, because boredom "is the self being stuffed with itself" (Walker Percy).

The human person only discovers himself by forgetting himself, especially in the pursuit of the common good of the civil community. That is, we discover ourselves when we live for a good larger than ourselves. Moreover, "rights" are not primary; rather, they are the flip side of the fundamental responsibilities that inhere in the nature of each human person; for existence does not precede essence, rather, both are simultaneous, for each human person possesses the same nature, namely, a human nature. In other words, obligations are primary; you have rights only because I have obligations. For example, your right to your reputation is nothing other than my obligation not to destroy it, and my right not to be lied to is nothing other than your obligation to be truthful, etc. If I have no obligations, then you have no rights.

The civil community as a whole has a right to expect from me, the citizen, a wide variety of things, for I have a number of duties towards the civil community, for I and everyone else are the beneficiaries of the labour and sacrifices of countless men and women who have gone before us, having worked to establish the conditions that now enable us to attain for ourselves our own well-being. In fact, the debt we have to the civil community as a whole—which includes those who have died—is a debt we cannot fully remit. But I am obligated to remit it to the fullest extent possible, and I do that by cultivating the virtue of patriotism and legal justice, among other virtues, that is, by loving and serving the country as a whole, and venerating those who hold public office, working to maintain the common good, etc.

That duty to serve the common good might very well include a duty to serve militarily. At the root of the peace movement in the 1960s was, I would argue, a misunderstanding of the meaning of *pax* (peace). Most of us regard peace as an absence of conflict. Its original and more direct meaning, however, is 'unity'. A virus is a threat to an organism's unity or physical integrity, which is why a very complex biochemical army goes to work to eradicate the virus.

Our immune system is a peacemaker, for it preserves the integrity, the unity or *pax* of the organism. The state of peace as absence of conflict is *the result of* the work of the immune system, which is a work of conflict, a battle. Without that biochemical army, there is no peace, whether that is taken to mean integrity (unity), or whether it is taken as a state characterized by an absence of conflict.

Similarly, every nation and city has its own immune system, which is its military and police force respectively. Without them, there is no "pax", no peace. A country is not a collection of individuals, each one possessing their own unique essence which was determined by the choices that they have made; that is more akin to a corpse, which does not have an immune system, because it lacks unity. A country is a unity of human persons, each one having the same nature and set of natural obligations.

The government does not exist to take care of me as a parent takes care of the child. The role of government is to maintain the entire network of conditions that enables all citizens to attain for themselves their own fullness of being, and excessive government impedes that attainment by doing for citizens and smaller communities what these latter can and should be doing for themselves; for there is no human flourishing without personal initiative, activity, and a certain degree of independence.

We need to keep in mind that politics is a branch of ethics, and the human person is a moral agent. A political party whose moral vision is permissive, i.e., allowing recreational marijuana, abortion, low age of sexual consent, pornography, etc., is one whose moral sphere does not include individual persons, but is limited to the level of "social man". This is a party that leans to the left (towards socialism). The more it leans in this direction, the less does personal morality become an issue, and whatever social problems develop in a society, they become the responsibility of the party to fix, that is, they become a matter of social policy. In other words, individuals are more or less free to do what they wish morally, just not economically.

Within a Personalist frame of mind, this is backwards. Government is "by the people". *The Declaration of Independence* outlines some of these fundamental principles: "We hold these truths to be self-evident, that all men are created equal, that they are endowed by their Creator with certain unalienable rights, that among these are Life, Liberty and the pursuit of Happiness. — That to secure these rights, Governments are instituted among Men, deriving their just powers from the consent of the governed, — That whenever any Form of Government becomes destructive of these ends, it is the Right of the People to alter or to abolish it, and to institute new Government, laying its foundation on such principles and organizing its powers in such form, as to them shall seem most likely to effect their Safety and Happiness."

In other words, existence does not precede essence, because all men are created equal, for they are of the same nature. Moreover, all men are created, and thus there is something higher than the state, namely the Creator, which means that the state is not the only source of our rights; there are inalienable rights that we received not from the state, but from God, the author of our nature. Among these rights is the right to life. Thus, the individual human person is not a mere part of the state as the cog is a part of the wheel, as Totalitarian forms of government conceive of the individual (Nazism, Fascism, and Communism). Your right to life is nothing other than my and everyone else's obligation not to kill you for whatever ends we might have in mind. And we have the right to liberty and the pursuit of happiness, which implies that I and everyone else have an obligation not to impede your liberty and the pursuit of your own integrity and well-being, which implies that you, as an individual person, are a primary moral agent, not "social man" or the state. You have a duty to pursue your own happiness, and happiness is not pleasure, but the fulfillment of one's nature (it is "activity in accordance with perfect virtue"). The people have a right to abolish the government that is destructive of these ends. That implies, of course, that the people have a duty to establish a government that serves not merely their own private interests, but a government that serves these larger ends. Thus, citizens old enough to vote have a duty to become informed, to think critically and in view of the common good, to listen carefully to the issues and be wary of their own bigotries and propensity to irresponsibility.

Just as it is not necessarily the case that all those who are poor are lazy, or all Jews are stingy, or all those who favor more social legislation are communists, so too it is not necessarily the case that the wealthy are exploiters. Behind this prejudice is the zero-sum fallacy, which in economics is based on the mathematical representation of a zero–sum game: a participant's gain is exactly balanced by the losses of the other participant(s). When we add up the entire gains of the participants and the total losses are then subtracted, the sum will be zero. A tug of war is a zero sum game, but the learning process that takes place within an educational institution, for example, is not a zero sum process. The gain of one participant (i.e., student) does not automatically result in a proportionate loss of another participant. All may gain at the same time, and if one loses, one does so not by virtue of another's gain, but by virtue of a number of other possible factors (i.e., the decision not to study, not to listen, to skip class, or lack of ability, a teacher's lack of clarity, lack of sufficient resources, etc.).

When applied to economics, the zero sum fallacy is the **presupposition** that the increase of economic prosperity in one party is exactly balanced by the economic loss of another party. Thus, the rich are regarded the principal causes of poverty. Or, the reasoning might run something like the following: the political, social, and economic conditions that permit certain others to become economically prosperous (i.e., the free market) are the same conditions in which the economic hardships of the poor arose. Thus, the cause of poverty is precisely these economic and political conditions which allow a person to become economically prosperous. In other words, capitalism (the free market) is the cause of poverty.

But the prosperity of some is not necessarily at all the cause of the misery of others. Those individuals with a healthy entrepreneurial spirit do a great service to the common good by providing employment, creating community and a certain degree of interdependency, among other things. Indeed, some people cannot work as a result of some debilitating condition (mental or physical illness) that they are not responsible for, and government has the responsibility of ensuring the conditions that will enable these people who cannot take care of themselves to receive the care they need—how best to achieve this is not for philosophy to determine; it is a scientific question (the science of economics). But some people make choices that land them in the difficult situations in which they find themselves; some people would rather the government take care of them so that they can remain, psychologically and emotionally, children without responsibilities, entirely dependent upon someone else, as a child depends on his parents—for we all remember how wonderful it was to be a child, free to live in the world of the imagination where everything is exactly as we want it to be, without fear, risk, and distress.

But reality is much harder, it does not so readily conform to the way we want things to be; it is often cold and bitter, but we are called to rise up and in a spirit of magnanimity, generosity, and gratitude to God, country, and parents, to direct our lives towards the common good of the civil community, which includes the conditions for the well-being of future generations. Government intervention and regulation is meant to ensure the conditions for human flourishing, conditions that permit persons to work creatively, with initiative, to fulfill the obligations that are theirs as human persons; but government is not there to usurp what can be done by individual persons, families, and smaller communities. History has shown that heavy government regulation makes it much more difficult for these smaller communities and businesses to operate, thus increasing unemployment and dependency upon the state. The complex details of the laws of economics exceed the scope of this book, but young people need to study the basic principles of economics in order to understand better why it is that socialist governments have always managed to suffocate the nations, states, or provinces they have intended to help, and why right leaning governments that lower taxes and shrink the size of government and deintensify regulation always manage to improve a nation's standard of living.

It is true that a capitalist society is a society of inequalities, but contrary to a socialist frame of mind, inequality is not the same as injustice. All injustice is an inequality, but it does not follow that all inequality is an injustice. Human beings are essentially equal, but not "accidentally" so. Many people are vastly superior to me in a variety of ways (athletic, intellectual, musical, have a more astute mind for business, are superior artistically, etc.). By virtue of this accidental inequality, it follows that we are not all going to get rich at the same rate, just as we do not all learn at the same rate. But if government creates and maintains the conditions for a healthy free market economy, we are all nevertheless going to get richer.

Answers to Exercises on the Categorical Syllogism

1.
All C is P.
J is P.
Ergo, J is C.
Valid [ ] Invalid [x]
Reason for Invalidity: Undistributed middle term.

2.
Some Kobo readers are philosophers.
Sean is a philosopher.
Ergo, Sean is a Kobo reader.
Valid [ ] Invalid [x]
Reason: Undistributed middle term.

3.
No man is perfect
Some men are presidents.
Ergo, some presidents are not perfect.
Valid [x] Invalid [ ]
Reason:

4.
All matter obeys probability equations
All waves obey probability equations
Ergo, all matter is waves.
Valid [ ] Invalid [x]
Reason: Undistributed middle term.

5.
All human action is conditioned by circumstances.
All human action involves morality.
Ergo, all that involves morality is conditioned by
circumstances (moral relativism).
Valid [ ] Invalid [x]

Reason: Any term distributed in the conclusion must be distributed in the premises. The minor term "all that involves morality" is distributed in the conclusion, but undistributed in the minor premise.

6.
All that is good is pleasant.
All eating is pleasant.
Ergo, all eating is good.
Valid [ ] Invalid [x]
Reason: Undistributed middle term.

7.
All patriots are voters.
Some citizens are not voters.
Ergo, some citizens are not patriots.
Valid [x] Invalid [ ]
Reason:

8.
All those who cause poverty exploit the poor.
All those who exploit the poor are rich.
Therefore, the rich are (or being rich is) the causes of poverty.
Valid [ ] Invalid [x]
Reason: Any term distributed in the conclusion must be distributed in the premises. The minor term "the rich" is distributed in the conclusion, but undistributed in the minor premise.

9.
All A are B
Some C are not B.
Ergo, some C are not A.
Valid [x] Invalid [ ]
Reason:

10.

All a priori categories are conditions for the possibility of knowing anything.

Some a posteriori imperatives of an a-cosmic ethics are not conditions for the possibility of knowing anything.

Ergo, some a posteriori imperatives of an a-cosmic ethics are not a priori categories.

Valid [x] Invalid [ ]

Reason: The syllogism is valid, but the premises are completely meaningless. The argument does not have to be meaningful in order to be logically valid.

11.

All socialists favor higher taxes.

Some Liberals favor higher taxes.

Ergo, some Liberals are Socialists.

Valid [ ] Invalid [x]

Reason: Undistributed middle term.

12.

All educated people have worked hard.

Some students are not educated.

Ergo, some students have not worked hard.

Valid [ ] Invalid [x]

Reason: Any term distributed in the conclusion must be distributed in the premises. The major term "worked hard" is distributed, but it is undistributed in the major premise.

13.

Mathematicians know what mathematics is.

No philosopher is a mathematician.

Ergo, no philosopher knows what mathematics is.

Valid [ ] Invalid [x]

Reason: Any term distributed in the conclusion must be distributed in the premises.

14.

All scientific knowledge is a work of reason.

All scientific knowledge is true.

Ergo, all that is true is a work of reason.
Valid [ ] Invalid [x]
Reason: Any term distributed in the conclusion must be distributed in the premises.

15.
All married people know about marriage problems.
No priests are married people.
Ergo, no priests know about marriage problems.
Valid [ ] Invalid [x]
Reason: Any term distributed in the conclusion must be distributed in the premises.

16.
All C are B
All T are B
Ergo, all T are C
Valid [ ] Invalid [x]
Reason: Undistributed middle term.

17.
Nothing easy is worthwhile.
Nothing good is easy.
Ergo, nothing good is worthwhile.
Valid [ ] Invalid [x]
Reason: No conclusion can be drawn from two negative premises.

18.
All contraceptives acts are for avoiding pregnancy.
All use of NFP is for avoiding pregnancy.
Ergo, All use of NFP is contraceptive.
Valid [ ] Invalid [x]
Reason: Undistributed middle term.

19.
All Germans despise Judaism.
All of the people reading this text are German.

Ergo, all of the people reading this text despise Judaism.
Valid [x] Invalid [ ]
Reason: The logic is valid, although the premises and conclusion are false.

20.
All parts of a living organism are inside the body.
The fetus is inside the (mother's) body.
Therefore, the fetus is a part of the living organism (mother's body)
Valid [ ] Invalid [x]
Reason: Undistributed middle term.

Answers to Exercises on the Conditional Syllogism

1.

If one chooses vice over virtue, one will suffer in life.
One is suffering in life.
Ergo, one has chosen vice over virtue.
Valid [ ] Invalid [x]
Reason: Affirming the Consequent.

2.

If government is for the common good, it is not for the good of only the few.
Government is for the common good.
Ergo, government is not for the good of only the few.
Valid [x] Invalid [ ]
Reason: Affirming the Antecedent.

3.

If life exists on Mars, then there is water on Mars.
There is water on Mars.
Ergo, life exists on Mars.
Valid [ ] Invalid [x]
Reason: Affirming the Consequent.

4.

If life involves quantity, it is physical.
Life does not involve quantity.
Ergo, life is not physical.
Valid [ ] Invalid [x]
Reason: Denying the Antecedent.

5.

If atoms are ultimate particles, they are indivisible.
Atoms are not indivisible.
Ergo, they are not ultimate.
Valid [x] Invalid [ ]
Reason: Denying the Consequent.

6.

If the premises of this argument are true, then the conclusion of this argument is true (i.e., the argument is valid).

The conclusion of this argument is true.

Ergo, the premises of this argument are true.

Valid [ ] Invalid [x]

Reason: Affirming the Consequent.

7.

If the premises of this argument are true, then the conclusion of this argument is true (i.e., the argument is valid).

The premises of this argument are not true.

Ergo, the conclusion of this argument is not true.

Valid [ ] Invalid [x]

Reason: Denying the Antecedent.

8.

If you learn to type fast when you are young, you will be grateful later on.

You are learning to type fast when you are young.

Ergo, you will be grateful later on.

[x] Valid [ ] Invalid

Reason: Affirming the Antecedent.

9.

If you breath in mold or mildew, you will get a cold.

You have a cold.

Ergo, you breathed in mold or mildew.

[ ] Valid [x] Invalid

Reason: Affirming the Consequent.

10.

If you pray, God will draw close to you.

God did not draw close to you.

Ergo, you did not pray.

[x] Valid [ ] Invalid

Reason: Denying the Consequent.

11.

If you eat right, you will be healthy.
I don't eat right
Ergo, you are not healthy.
[ ] Valid [x] Invalid
Reason: Denying the Antecedent.

12.

If you learn to think, life will be much easier for you.
Life is not much easier for me.
Ergo, you didn't learn to think.
[x] Valid [ ] Invalid
Reason: Denying the Consequent.

13.

Eat lots of vegetables and fruit, and you reduce your risk
of cancer.
I eat lots of veggies and fruit.
Ergo, I have reduced my risk of cancer.
[x] Valid [ ] Invalid
Reason: Affirming the Antecedent.

14.

If Robert has moral scruples against drinking, then Robert
never drinks.
Robert never drinks.
Ergo, Robert has moral scruples against drinking.
Valid [ ] Invalid [x]
Reason: Affirming the Consequent.

15.

If the defendant is willing to testify, then he is innocent.
The defendant is not willing to testify.
Ergo, the defendant is not innocent.
Valid [ ] Invalid [x]
Reason: Denying the Antecedent.

Answers to Exercises on the Logic of Induction

1.

85% of polled grade 9s thinks that Rohan should be elected
President of the Student Council.
Therefore, 85% of the students at McGivney think that Rohan
should be elected President of the Student Council.

Valid Inductive Argument.   *Invalid Inductive Argument.*

[The sample is unrepresentative]

2.

80% of the citizens of this country think abortion is wrong.
Since Billy is a citizen of this country, Billy thinks abortion is
wrong.

There is an 80% probability that this statement is true.
There is a 20% chance that this statement is true.

[Over 50%; this is a good statistical argument]

3.

35% of the remarks made by Steve are insulting. The next
remark made will be insulting because Steve will make the
remark.

It is improbable that this statement is true.
It is highly probable that this statement is true.

[Under 50%; this is an invalid statistical argument]

4.

600 of the tickets in the drum were purchased by grade 12s, 90
of the tickets were purchased by grade 11s, 60 tickets were
purchased by grade 10s, and 50 of the tickets were purchased
by the grade 9s. The winning ticket will be drawn from the

drum. Hence, the winning ticket was purchased by a grade 12 student.

The conclusion is probably true.
The conclusion is probably false.
No probable conclusion can be drawn.

[75% of the tickets were purchased by grade 12s; this is a good statistical argument]

5.
75% of polled students at McGivney think that we need to change the uniform.
Therefore, 75% of all the students at McGivney think that we need to change the uniform.

The students polled were the IB students in grade 9 (pre-IB), 10 (pre-IB), 11 and 12 IB.

Valid Inductive Argument.
Invalid Inductive Argument.

[This is a modified induction by enumeration; it is invalid because the sample is unrepresentative. IB students represent a minority of the school population]

6.
75% of polled parents think that we need to change the uniform.
Therefore, 75% of all the parents think that we need to change the uniform.

The parents polled were selected from 50 grade 9 students (randomly chosen), 50 grade 10 students (randomly chosen), 50 grade 11 students (randomly chosen), and 50 grade 12 students (randomly chosen)

Valid Inductive Argument.
Invalid Inductive Argument.

[The sample is large enough and representative]

7.
87% of polled Catholics from Holland are in favor of IVF.
Mr. McManaman is a Catholic.
Therefore, Mr. McManaman is in favor of IVF.

This is a good statistical syllogism.
This is an invalid modified induction by enumeration.
It is a good statistical syllogism in that it has a high probability of being
true, even though it is actually false that he favors IVF.

**[The sample "Catholics from Holland" is not representative.
One will have to sample from other countries]**

8. "I spent my last two weeks of August last year in Rome, and
although Italians drive fast, I didn't see one accident. I am now
convinced that because people drive so fast in Italy, they are
naturally more aware, more alert, more on the watch for
pedestrians. In Canada, people drive more slowly, so they are
not as aware, hence the reason I've witnessed many accidents
within the past 5 years."

What kind of argument is the above?

Deductive (categorical syllogism).
Statistical argument.
Hypothetical argument.
Induction by enumeration.

**[It is also invalid; for my experience was a sample of Italy. It
was limited to one city, and it was limited by a period of only
two weeks, and most Romans are on vacation in August]**

9. "I've been dating this guy for 3 months now, he's really
charming, he's nice to me, and whenever we get together, we
have a great time. Only two or three times did I have my

doubts about his character. All the other times were great. That's why I've consented to marrying him—all future times with him will be great as well. The wedding is next week."

The conclusion in the above is a form of:

Deduction
A statistical argument
Induction by enumeration
Modified Induction by enumeration

[One could make the case that it is also invalid; thus an imprudent decision. 3 months of dating is a small sample, and for that reason it may be unrepresentative. Furthermore, she ought to pay attention to those 3 red flags]

10. "Betty, Jason, and Carole had the highest overall average, in the nation, upon graduation from high school. They all went to St. Mary's High School. Therefore, St. Mary's High School is the best high school in the nation."

This is necessarily true.
This is an invalid induction by enumeration.
Given the evidence, it is highly probable.
This is a good statistical argument.

Suggested Reading

Adler, M. J. *Ten Philosophical Mistakes.* N. Y.: Macmillan, 1987.

_____. *The Four Dimensions of Philosophy.* N. Y.: Macmillan, 1993.

_____. *How to Think about The Great Ideas.* Ed. Max Weismann. Chicago, IL.: Open Court, 2000.

Adler, M. J. "Questions Science Cannot Answer." *The Logic of Science.* Ed. Vincent Edward Smith. N. Y.: St. John's University Press, 1963, 1-16.

Aquinas, Thomas. *Basic Writings of Saint Thomas Aquinas.* 2 vols. Ed. A. C. Pegis. N. Y.: Random House, 1945.

_____. *On Being and Essence.* Trans. A. Maurer. Toronto: Pontifical Institute of Mediaeval Studies, 1949.

Aristotle. *The Basic Works of Aristotle.* Ed. R. McKeon. N.Y.: Random House, 1941.

Azar, L. *Man: Computer, Ape, or Angel?* Hanover, Mass.: Christopher, 1988.

Centore, F. F. *Persons: A Comparative Account of the Six Possible Theories.* Westport, Conn.: Greenwood, 1979.

_____. *Being and Becoming: A Critique of Post-Modernism.* Westport, Conn.: Greenwood, 1991.

_____. *Two Views of Virtue: Absolute Relativism and Relative Absolutism.* Westport, Conn.: Greenwood, 2000.

_____. *Theism or Atheism: The Eternal Debate.* Burlington, VT.: Ashgate, 2004.

DiBlasi, F. *God and the Natural Law: A Rereading of Thomas Aquinas.* South Bend, IN.: St. Augustine's Press, 2006.

Feser, E. *Aquinas: A Beginner's Guide.* Oxford, England: Oneworld, 2009.

Gilson, E. *God and Philosophy.* New Haven, Conn.: Yale University Press, 1941.

_____. *The Unity of Philosophical Experience.* N. Y.: Scribner's, 1947.

_____. *Being and Some Philosophers.* 2d ed. Toronto: Pontifical Institute of Mediaeval Studies, 1952.

_____. *From Aristotle to Darwin and Back Again.* Trans. C. Gilson. N.Y.: Random House, 1962.

_____. *The Christian Philosophy of St. Thomas Aquinas.* Trans. L. K. Shook. N. Y.: Random House, 1956.

_____. *The Elements of Christian Philosophy.* N. Y.: The New American Library, 1960.

Grisez, Germain. *Beyond the New Morality: The Responsibilities of Freedom.* Nortre Dame, IN: Notre Dame University Press, 1980.

Hayek, F. A. *New Studies in Philosophy, Politics, Economics and the History of Ideas.* Chicago: University of Chicago Press, 1978.

Hittinger, Russell. *A Critique of the New Natural Law Theory.* Notre Dame, IN: Notre Dame University Press, 1987.

Lewis, C. S. *The Four Loves.* Glasgow: Collins, 1977.

_____. *Mere Christianity*. N. Y.: Macmillan, 1986.

Maritain, J. *Existence and the Existent*. Trans. L. Galantiere and G. B. Phelan. N.Y.: Pantheon, 1948.

_____. *Approaches to God*. Trans. P. O'Reilly. N. Y.: Macmillan, 1954.

_____. *An Introduction to Philosophy*. Trans. E. I. Watkin. N. Y.: Sheed and Ward, 1962.

_____. *Moral Philosophy: An Historical and Critical Survey of the Great Systems*. N. Y.: Scribner's, 1964.

_____. *The Person and the Common Good*. Trans. J. J. Fitzgerald. Notre Dame, IN: Notre Dame University Press, 1966.

May, R. *Love and Will*. N. Y.: Norton, 1969.

Owens, J. *A History of Ancient Western Philosophy*. N. Y.: Appleton-Century-Crofts, 1959.

_____. *An Elementary Christian Metaphysics*. Milwaukee: Bruce, 1963.

_____. *St. Thomas Aquinas on the Existence of God: Collected Papers of Joseph Owens*. Ed. J. R. Catan. Albany: State University of New York Press, 1980.

_____. *Human Destiny*. Washington, D. C.: Catholic University of America Press, 1985.

Pieper, J. *Happiness and Contemplation*. South Bend: Indiana, St. Augustine's Press. 1998.

Sartre, J.-P. *Existentialism and Human Emotions*. N. Y.: Philosophical Library, 1957.

_____. *Being and Nothingness.* Trans. H. E. Barnes. N.Y.: Washington Square Press, 1966.

Smith, V. E. *The Elements of Logic.* Milwaukee: Bruce, 1957.

_____. *Science and Philosophy.* Milwaukee: Bruce, 1965.

_____. *Idea-Men of Today.* Milwaukee: Bruce, 1950.

Sowell, T. *Basic Economics: A Common Sense Guide to the Economy.* N. Y.: Basic Books, 2011.

_____. *A Conflict of Visions: The Ideological Origins of Political Struggles.* N.Y.: Basic Books, 2007.

Index

Made in the USA
Las Vegas, NV
04 April 2021

20824059R00174